D1611542

YALE HISTORICAL PUBLICATIONS,
MISCELLANY, 128

KANAZAWA
A SEVENTEENTH-CENTURY
JAPANESE CASTLE TOWN

JAMES L. McCLAIN

Yale University Press
New Haven and London

Published under the direction of the Department of History of Yale University with assistance from the income of the Frederick John Kingsbury Memorial Fund.

Designed by Nancy Ovedovitz
and set in VIP Garamond type.
Printed in the United States of America by
The Murray Printing Co., Westford, Mass.

Library of Congress Cataloging in Publication Data

McClain, James L., 1944–
    Kanazawa : a seventeenth-century Japanese castle town.

    (Yale historical publications. Miscellany ; 128)
    Bibliography: p.
    Includes index.
    1. Kanazawa-shi (Japan)—History. 2. Kaga-han
(Japan)—Politics and government. I. Title. II. Series.
DS897.K3253M35   952'.15   82-40166
ISBN 0-300-02736-2   AACR2

10   9   8   7   6   5   4   3   2   1

To Jung-Kang

CONTENTS

LIST OF MAPS

ACKNOWLEDGMENTS

In the course of researching and writing this book, I have incurred a large number of debts. The greatest of these is to John W. Hall, A. Whitney Griswold Professor of Far Eastern History at Yale University. As my adviser and thesis director, he helped me to gain a sense of the historiographic issues central to the study of Japanese history, kept my research on track with his probing comments and questions, and was patient enough to read several drafts of this manuscript. His own writings have inspired more than a generation of scholars, and I count myself fortunate to have received his assistance and counsel. I also wish to acknowledge a special debt to Professor John B. Merriman of Yale University for sharing with me his own enthusiasm for historical research and for taking the time to read several versions of this manuscript. I have benefited greatly from his insights and criticisms. William B. Hauser of the University of Rochester deserves special thanks as well for his encouragement over the years.

In Japan, Professors Abe Yoshio and Kanai Madoka of the Historiographic Institute of the University of Tokyo introduced me to the use of local documents, while Shimemoto Naoya, also of the University of Tokyo, met with me once a week for two years to coach me in the intricacies of the language used in those documents. Professor Wakita Osamu of the University of Osaka generously commented on the early chapters of this book, and the long hours we spent arguing interpretations helped me to expand both my "problem consciousness" and my knowledge of the facts of seventeenth-century Japanese history. Professor Tanaka Yoshio of Kanazawa Economics University guided my efforts at exploring the document collection at the Kanazawa City Library and discussed with me the problems involved in studying Japanese castle towns. The librarians and archivists of the Kanazawa City Library and the Ishikawa Prefectural Library cooperated by providing me with access to documents and maps. Mr. and Mrs. Yamamura Katsuro were kind enough to host me in Kanazawa and to treat me to a succession of memorable dinners and conversations. I also recall with fond appreciation a winter's afternoon spent with the late Professor Toyoda Takeshi at the Faculty Club of the University of Tokyo. I continue to be grateful for his gentle encouragement and for his advice to have the courage to pursue my own ideas about the nature of Japanese urban development.

My written work has benefited from the criticisms of many scholars in the United States. Professors Jonathan D. Spence and James B. Crowley of Yale University read the entire manuscript in draft form. Professor George Elison of Indiana University took a fine-toothed comb to it on two separate occasions, thereby saving me from several errors of fact. Professor Henry D. Smith II of the University of California, Santa Barbara, provided many valuable ideas that I have incorporated into chapter 2, while Professors Jerome B. Grieder, Howard P. Chudacoff, and Philip Benedict of Brown University contributed useful suggestions. Sally Serafim of Yale University Press edited the manuscript with a careful eye to both detail and style.

This study would not have been possible without substantial financial assistance. I am indebted to the Japan Foundation, the Social Science Research Council and the American Council of Learned Societies, and the Fulbright-Hays Commission for underwriting two years of study in Japan and to Yale University for graduate scholarships and a Sumitomo Prize Fellowship. Brown University provided funds to prepare the maps included in the text. A portion of the introduction and chapter 2 previously appeared in condensed form as "Castle Towns and Daimyo Authority: Kanazawa in the Years 1538–1630," published in the *Journal of Japanese Studies* 6:2 (Summer 1980), and I am grateful to the publishers for permission to use the material here. I wish to express my appreciation to all of the above persons and organizations for their kindness and assistance and, at the same time, to absolve them from responsibility for any errors of fact or interpretation that remain in this text.

My deepest thanks of all go to my wife, Jung-Kang, for sharing together the good times and the hard, and to our daughter Anne, for bringing her own brand of energy and joy into our lives.

EARLY MAEDA DAIMYO

Toshiie	?1538–1599	ruled 1583–1599
Toshinaga	1562–1614	1599–1605
Toshitsune	1593–1658	1605–1639
Mitsutaka	1615–1645	1639–1645
Tsunanori	1643–1724	1645–1723

INTRODUCTION

Japanese urban growth between the years 1580 and 1700 constituted one of the most extraordinary periods of urbanization in world history. During this century and a quarter, the population of Japan nearly doubled, reaching approximately 30,000,000. Concurrently, the percentage of persons living in urban settlements of more than 10,000 residents probably multiplied more than tenfold, coming to account for over ten percent of the country's total population. This made Japan one of the most urban countries in the world. In the year 1700, slightly over two percent of Europe's population lived in communities with populations of 100,000 or more. In Japan, five to seven percent of the population lived in such cities, a figure matched only by the Netherlands and England-Wales. Only fourteen cities in all of Europe had reached the 100,000 mark; in Japan alone, five had done so. Edo (present-day Tokyo) had become the world's largest city, and the populations of Osaka and Kyoto approached those of London and Paris, the two largest cities in the West.

This remarkable urban growth was intimately associated with Japan's passage from a medieval to an early modern society. This transition from a fragmented to a centralized polity was made possible by the military reunification of the country during the late sixteenth century, and it was capped by the creation in 1603 of the Tokugawa shogunate, the government of the family that ruled Japan until 1868. The basis of Tokugawa hegemony was the personal control by the Tokugawa house over approximately one-fourth of the land in Japan as well as all of the nation's major ports and mining settlements. Beyond this, the Tokugawa rulers claimed powers that were national in scope and represented the greatest concentration of centralized political authority yet assembled in Japan. The shogunate, for instance, imposed controls over the emperor and imperial court in Kyoto, reduced the secular power of major religious institutions, and assumed the prerogatives of maintaining the nation's defenses and conducting foreign policy. Subordinate to the shogunate were the great regional lords, or daimyo, approximately 250 in number, who ruled over large, self-administered domains, referred to by historians as *han*. While these daimyo acknowledged the suzerainty of the Tokugawa shogunate, they also enjoyed a considerable degree of autonomy, for within their

1

individual jurisdictions they asserted proprietary rights, levied taxes, established judicial procedures, and issued laws and decrees.

As these daimyo took up residence in their domains during the late sixteenth and early seventeenth centuries, they constructed castle towns, or *jōkamachi*. Very quickly, more than 200 new communities—one in nearly every domain—dotted the Japanese countryside. The daimyo summoned their warrior retainers, or samurai, and invited important merchants, such as armorers, to live in the settlements, which were dominated by huge castles, defensive citadels that also housed the daimyo's service and administrative personnel. Some of these castle towns eventually grew to astonishing proportions. By the 1700s, the shogun's castle town of Edo, a mere village a century earlier, boasted a population well in excess of 1,000,000. Kanazawa and Nagoya, two castle towns in western Japan, could be counted among the twenty largest cities in both Europe and Japan. With populations of more than 100,000 each, they rivaled in size such cities as Rome, Amsterdam, Madrid, and Milan.

Unfortunately, Japanese historians have not yet turned their awesome research energies to the study of castle towns during the period of their early growth and development, from roughly 1580 to the late seventeenth century. What studies do exist have tended to be either very general surveys or short articles limited to a single aspect of urbanization, typically urban planning or commercial development. The conclusions that they draw about the nature of castle town growth and the relationship between government and urban society, however, are surprisingly uniform. In general, Japanese historians argue that the early castle towns were chiefly the result of autocratic, daimyo-centered planning. Moreover, many of them couple to that theme a conception of coercive, and at times even repressive and despotic, daimyo government.

Perhaps the historians' favorite example of daimyo intervention in the urbanization process concerns the use of urban space. In his classic 1950s study, Harada Tomohiko defined the basic spatial patterns of early castle towns and attempted to illustrate how daimyo unilaterally decided the locations of the castles, warrior residences, and religious institutions in order to provide military security for their cities.[1] For convenience of political administration and tax collection, the daimyo of communities such as Sendai and Utsunomiya divided the city's artisans into groups according to occupational specialty, assigned each group to a specific residential area, and tried to restrict intraurban mobility. Such instances of what would appear to be all-encompassing planning from the top led Murai Masuo to write that "castle towns, which constituted the overwhelming majority of cities during the Edo period, did not evolve naturally. Rather, the daimyo created those cities in a planned, systematic, and political fashion."[2]

Another common conception shared by many Japanese historians is that daimyo-initiated policies shaped the pace and direction of urban economic development.[3] In response to the constant threat of warfare that accompanied national reunification during the late sixteenth and early seventeenth centuries, daimyo throughout Japan attempted to create economically self-sufficient domains. One cornerstone of that policy was to make the castle town the focus of an integrated domain economy. Thus, the daimyo closely regulated many aspects of urban commercial activity, often down to the most minute detail, by means of ordinances that, for example, compelled rural tradesmen to move to the castle town, or banned the export of certain items of military importance, or decreed special tax exemptions for merchants who supplied essential goods.

Toyoda Takeshi, a pioneer of urban studies, is among the many historians who portray the daimyo as the political architects of castle towns.[4] They argue that daimyo possessed virtually unrestricted powers of governance since they issued laws, set taxes, and controlled the police and judicial apparatus. Although some of these historians admit that certain administrative functions, such as the settlement of neighborhood quarrels, were delegated to representatives of the townspeople, they claim that such functions were relatively insignificant and did not impinge on daimyo authority. Researchers also point out that the daimyo ordinances occasionally attempted to regulate even minor facets of daily life, such as the clothing townspeople were allowed to wear or the foods they were permitted on festival days. This daimyo monopolization of the decision-making process, as well as the apparently heavy burden of daimyo rule, has prompted some to label government as oppressive and tyrannical. Typical is the judgment of Tanaka Yoshio, a specialist on Kanazawa, who claims that castle towns "were the product of the despotic exercise of power by the daimyo."[5]

As in Japan, the sixteenth and seventeenth centuries in Europe also saw the final decline of the medieval political order and the emergence of new forms of political authority that characterized the early modern nation-state. Across the face of the continent, political leaders laid ideological claim to a new, nationwide basis of authority and attempted to exert tighter control over the people and institutions of their countries. The particular structure that government assumed varied according to the historical circumstances of the individual countries. In England and Holland, for example, the upper classes gained political predominance over their monarchs and asserted control over the organs of state. More common, however, was royal absolutism. From Louis XIV in France to Peter the Great in Russia, autocrats symbolized the new concentration of statist powers: they possessed large standing armies, the power to levy taxes, the undisputed right to issue laws and to judge, and the privilege to declare war.

New philosophical rationales provided support for this unprecedented aggrandizement of princely power. In France, justification for absolutism came from a group known as the *Politiques,* whose most influential member, Jean Bodin, argued that a true state could exist only when it had a sovereign who was the sole legislator and who exercised "supreme power over citizens and subjects, unrestrained by law."[6] Peter the Great was described in equally succinct terms: "His Majesty is [an] absolute monarch who need not answer for his acts to anyone in the world, but has power and authority as a Christian sovereign to govern his states and lands according to his will and his benevolent understanding."[7]

Supported by such notions of kingship, many of Europe's seventeenth-century monarchs, in collaboration with the ruling classes, attempted to create urban centers that would given expression to their absolutism. The result was a new style of urbanism and urban environment: the genesis of what historians have come to refer to as the baroque city. The outstanding characteristic of the baroque city was its physical design, which was intended to serve the needs of the absolute monarchs and privileged upper classes.[8] To this end, new palaces were erected in many of Europe's capitals during the seventeenth century, usually in the center of an existing city, but sometimes outside the capital, as was the case with Maria Theresa's Schönbrunn. Built in a grand style, these new palaces were intended to glorify the king and impress upon the masses the superiority of governmental authority. Louis XIV's chief minister, Colbert, said it well: "Nothing marks the greatness of mind of princes better than the buildings that compel the people to look on them with awe, and all posterity judges them by the superb palaces they have built during their lifetime."[9] But palaces also served the more practical purpose of accommodating the bureaucrats and administrators necessary to the exercise of centralized authority. Schönbrunn was the home of the Austrian government; the Catholic church ran its affairs from the Vatican palace; and the ministries of the Swedish government were clustered around the royal palace in Stockholm. Indeed, the notion of a governmental center within a capital city first took shape during the early modern period.

The urban elite added other elements of grandeur to the baroque cities. In Paris, the aristocracy demanded town houses with inner courts and grand gardens, while in London the upper classes of the seventeenth century lived in terrace houses, often built around squares. Pope Sixtus V (1585–90) obliterated the old medieval and Renaissance design of Rome by raising the dome of Saint Peter's and by constructing long, broad avenues that linked together the monumental points of the city—the entrance gate designed by Michelangelo with the papal palace of the Quirinale, the basilica of Santa Maria Maggiore with Santa Trinita dei Monti. In London, Christopher Wren completed the vast dome of Saint

Paul's Cathedral and then turned to building suburban mansions for the well-to-do. In these cities we glimpse some of the architectural ideals of urban baroque: the extravagant shapes and emotional exuberance of the south, as expressed in Rome's fountains and piazzas; the north's greater emphasis on openness, clarity, and the regulation of space, as evident in Wren's more orderly vistas and facades.

The complex links between absolutist rulers and urbanism can be seen clearly in Louis XIV's relations with Paris, a city whose population reached perhaps one-half million by the end of the seventeenth century.[10] When Louis was just thirteen, a Parisian mob—part of the uprising known as the Fronde (1648–52)—forced him to flee from the palace through his bedroom window. So great was the Sun King's subsequent distrust of Parisians that he built a new residence at Versailles, a palace designed as a baroque town, and a long trek for any mob setting out from Paris. As much as Louis might detest Paris and its residents, however, the city remained his official capital, and Louis's enormous pride and over-whelming sense of *noblesse oblige* demanded that he make it a monument to his reign.

Louis XIV's attempts to remodel Paris included the construction of several of those roadways that remain as the *grands boulevards* of modern Paris. In 1670, confident that his armies could protect the capital against foreign assault, Louis ordered the old medieval fortifications destroyed and the ancient ramparts turned into thoroughfares. In place of the moats, Louis proposed to encircle the city with a tree-lined boulevard. Work began on the north side, but it took until the end of the century to complete the promenade, or Cours as it was called, on the Right Bank. Beyond this, the city's medieval gates were also razed, the more famous to be replaced by *arcs de triomphe*. Porte Saint-Denis, Porte Saint-Martin, and Porte Saint-Antoine, completed in the early 1690s, were all ornately baroque, heavy with statuary and medallions glorifying the Sun King's triumphs.

Louis XIV also attempted to reform the administrative machinery of Paris, which was traditionally a welter of competing jurisdictions. The two principal organs of administration were the Châtelet, which was the seat of justice for the king's representative in the city, and the Hôtel de Ville, which was the Parisian municipality proper, and each claimed authority over such matters as sanitation and the regulation of commerce. Complicating administrative matters even further was the existence of a complex web of overlapping seignorial bailiwicks, a legacy of medieval times. Even as late as the 1640s more than half of Paris was under the jurisdiction of the *seigneurs,* most of whom were ecclesiastical officials: the abbot of Saint-Germain-des-Prés, for example, was the *seigneur* of an entire faubourg and thirty additional streets in Paris, while the Archbishop claimed rights over 164 streets, the abbot of Sainte-Geneviève, 54.

Louis XIV set out to rationalize city administration and bring all Parisians more directly under his own authority. In March 1667, he issued an edict that created the post of Lieutenant of Police, and delegated to him powers that roughly approximated those of a modern mayor. Among other things, the Lieutenant of Police was charged with the supervision of street cleaning, fire fighting, and flood control; regulation of retail prices; investigation of illicit assemblies; supervision of guilds; and enforcement of ordinances against carrying weapons. The autonomy of the *seigneurs* was further curtailed when the prerogatives of the Lieutenant of Police were extended over certain other broad areas; an edict of April 1667, for instance, gave him jurisdiction over all goods necessary for provisioning the capital. Finally, in February 1674, Louis XIV abolished all remaining judicial and administrative prerogatives of the *seigneurs,* some of which dated back a millennium. Administratively as well as physically, Paris was becoming a royal city.

Louis XIV intervened as well in the economic life of his capital. In the belief that economic prosperity would add to his prestige as a ruler, he reduced internal barriers to trade, constructed new roads and canals, and encouraged certain new industries such as silk and glassmaking. But since he was also anxious to bring the economic classes under his direct purview, he attempted to extend his control over the corporate guilds of the city. Even earlier, Henry III in 1581 and Henry IV in 1597 had aimed at subordinating these medieval autonomies to the state by ordering all French trades and professions to have their statues confirmed by the king. In 1673 Louis XIV continued to expand state control by ordering every French urban worker to become a member of a guild. While it was impossible to assure universal compliance with the edict, vigorous enforcement did bring about a higher level of guild membership, and the number of guilds increased from 60 in 1672 to 129 by 1691.

Finally, Louis XIV attempted to shape the style and texure of the cultural life of Paris. The Sun King patronized sculptors, painters, architects, and musicians, but his most lasting contribution came in helping to found both the Opera and the Comédie Française. Interested since childhood in dance and music, in 1669 he granted a certain Abbé Perrin royal permission to establish a "musical opera." When Perrin's promotional activities failed, Louis in 1673 gave the same opportunity to Jean Baptiste Lully (Florentine Giovanni Battista Lulli), who, armed with this monopoly on musical presentations in the capital, made the Opera an enormous success. Several years later, in 1680, the Comédie Française came into being when Louis issued an ordinance combining two acting troupes. The king maintained a close interest in this new acting group. He personally selected or approved of the troupe's some thirty actors and actresses, patronized the theater's playwrights, and, near the end of the century, granted the Comédie Française a monopoly on the spoken theater to match the Opera's musical monopoly.

If Paris represents a city remodeled by an absolute monarch, Saint Petersburg is the quintessential example of one that was planned from the beginning. In many ways an artificial creation, Saint Petersburg was the product of the iron will of a man who named the city in honor of his patron saint.[11] Peter the Great (reigned 1689–1725) initiated the Great Northern War against Sweden in the autumn of 1700 in order to reclaim territory he considered to be Russian and to acquire an adequate seaport for the proposed expansion of Russian trade. Three years later, in 1703, Russian troops captured the mouth of the Neva River, where it empties into the Gulf of Finland. Here, on a swampy bog—Neva derives from a Finnish word that means mud—Peter decided to build a city. He wanted a city that would serve chiefly as a fortress to guard against Swedish counterattacks and as a port to help open Russia to the West. But he also sought a monument to his present and future accomplishments.

The physical layout and architecture of the new city were keyed to these needs. The first permanent structure to be erected was the Peter and Paul Fortress, whose foundations were laid on May 27, 1703. Peter himself chose the site, an island in the main channel of the Neva, and oversaw the construction of the fortress's six great bastions. For additional security Peter began construction in 1704 of a shipyard. known as the Admiralty, on the left bank of the Neva just downstream from the Peter and Paul Fortress. Protected by stone ramparts and deep moats, the Admiralty became a second stronghold almost as impregnable as the Fortress. This area soon became the government section and housed the tsar's administration. The State Chancellery and the Government Printing Office were situated just to the east of the Fortress, while other government offices and the tsar's first Winter Palace were clustered along the south bank of the river.

As the settlement grew, Peter imported famous architects to give the city a more elegant design. First came the Italian, Domenico Trezzini, who arrived in 1703 and for nine years supervised all official construction. Later, in 1716, the French architect Alexandre Jean Baptiste LeBlond, a pupil of Le Notre, who designed the gardens at Versailles, became the tsar's adviser. He created a French-style formal garden at the tsar's small Summer Palace and built three summer pavilions. Although the architectural style of Saint Petersburg would not become fully identified as baroque until the reign of Elizabeth, even in Peter's lifetime the city began to take on a feeling similar to that of western European capitals: Trezzini drew upon northern baroque inspiration for his Peter and Paul Cathedral, with its soaring four-hundred-foot golden spire; LeBlond drove the city's great main boulevard, the Nevsky Prospect, straight through two and a half miles of meadows and forests from the Alexander Nevsky Monastery to the Admiralty and opened up the kinds of vistas so prized in western European capitals; the gigantic squares and gardens sprinkled throughout the city echoed the feeling of the southern baroque.

Constructing this city in the drizzle of the Baltic coast, on the same latitude as the upper shores of the Hudson Bay, was not an easy task. Marshes had to be filled, forests cleared, hills leveled, buildings erected: the labor requirements were enormous, and compulsion necessary. Year after year, Peter issued edicts summoning carpenters, stonecutters, and even unskilled laborers. The conscripts received a travel allowance and six months' subsistence, after which they were permitted to return home, although many never did—ten thousand workers are thought to have died from scurvy, dysentery, malaria, and the other diseases that swept through the labor camps.

Peter's heavy hand fell also on the Russian professional and commercial classes. When the tsar settled in the new city, much of the old Moscow bureaucratic class had little choice but to migrate to what Peter increasingly referred to as "my Paradise." Few others came voluntarily, however, and in March 1708, the Russian autocrat had to order his sister, two half-sisters, two tsarevnas, and two dowager tsaritsas, as well as hundreds of Muscovite noblemen, high officials, and wealthy merchants to join him in the new capital, where they were obliged to construct new residences. Peter chose the locations: noble families were instructed to build on the left bank of the Neva, the merchants and tradesmen on the opposite side. For all, house size was to be proportional to the dimensions of the abandoned residences in Moscow. And, to add to the grandeur of the city and to ensure the proper vistas, Peter instructed his architects to provide free house plans of suitable design. He specifically ordered the nobles on the left bank to use beams and plaster, "in the English style."

The tsar struggled to turn his new capital into a great port and commercial center as well. To encourage merchants and traders, he set up a central marketplace, near the Peter and Paul Fortress, and persuaded commercial vessels to call at the city by granting permanent exemptions from Russian tolls and customs duties to many of the first ships to arrive. By the 1720s the new capital had become the leading port on Russian soil, with nearly a thousand Western ships arriving in 1725.

Peter the Great was determined that the residents of his new capital should enjoy some of the same social activities that he had discovered during his Great Embassy to western Europe in 1697–98. Thus in 1718 he instructed Saint Petersburg's nobles and high officials to hold evening parties during the winter season where, in a novel idea for early modern Russia, men and women might mingle together, as the tsar's decree so carefully explained, either for diversion or to discuss their daily affairs, to confer on business, and to inquire after domestic and foreign news. In addition he endowed the city with museums, an art gallery, a library, and even a zoo—a menagerie of apes, monkeys, lions, and even an Indian elephant, although that hapless creature died after exposure to just a few northern winters.

Not only have these studies on Japan's castle towns and Europe's baroque cities provided a wealth of valuable information about early modern urban centers, they have also made it possible to ask new questions about the urbanization experience. Perhaps the most intriguing of these concerns the role of urban commoners. In Japan, especially, scholars have amply described the ways in which the decisions of the daimyo affected the physical and economic growth of the early castle towns, but they have not yet fully explored the possible influence of non-elites upon the urbanization process during the seventeenth century. This seems somewhat curious, in light of our knowledge of other periods of Japanese history. We know that commoners possessed significant political powers in many sixteenth-century communities.[12] In cities like Sakai, Tennōji, Hiranogō, and Tondabayashi, the merchant communities formed corporate groups and claimed the right to exercise several judicial and police functions, including the investigation and prosecution of crimes. They also directed self-defense programs, such as constructing moats. Moreover, many historians who have studied Osaka and Edo during the final century and a half of the Tokugawa period, from roughly 1700 to the 1860s, have shown that a great deal of cultural and economic change resulted from the initiative of urban commoners.[13] The rise of great merchant houses, such as the Mitsui and the Sumitomo, for instance, is viewed as a product of merchant enterprise and ingenuity. Likewise, the flowering of an urban, popular culture during the Genroku period (1688–1704) can be seen as an illustration of commoner social and economic independence. These observations point out the need to reassess Japan's dramatic period of urban growth between the years 1580 and 1700. Surely the period was no anomaly—a time when the strength of the political elites was so overwhelming that they were able to dominate the other segments of the population. If commoners played an important political role in the sixteenth century, and a significant economic and cultural role during the eighteenth century, it becomes difficult to accept the contention that they were so lacking in influence during the intervening period, the seventeenth-century era of castle town construction.

A similar point arises when we examine the literature on European cities. While most recent studies have stressed the relationship between absolutism and city-building, they have also included information which serves to illustrate ways in which urban commoners might have played a role in structuring a distinctive urban culture and in shaping the character of a city's economic and social life. In Paris, for instance, we learn that the old guilds, although licensed anew, managed to retain a degree of self-administration; in Saint Petersburg commoners enjoyed a street culture that centered around visiting troupes of jugglers, acrobats, and animal trainers; and, in many cities, districts of "Turkish" and "Russian baths," in fact houses of assignation, flourished despite self-righteous attempts by urban governments to eliminate them. Extensive neighborhood development took place in Paris outside of Louis XIV's purview. Syndicates of professional financiers backed the construction of *places royals,* such as the Place Louis-le-Grand (the modern Place Vendôme), while other land speculators bought up tracts of land on the outskirts of the city, subdivided them, and sold the plots after providing streets and water supplies. Leaving aside any direct comparisons, this kind of evidence does suggest that it is necessary to search out the limits of early modern princely power, in both Europe and Japan.

In sum, the rapid urbanization of seventeenth-century Japan may well have been a more complex phenomenon then previous research has suggested. The fundamental concern of this study will be to re-open the question of how and why castle towns emerged in Japan during the seventeenth century. The central purpose will be to evaluate the extent and significance of daimyo intervention in the city-building process and to suggest the motives that may have inspired that intervention. But this will be balanced by an attempt to analyze the ways in which the townspeople themselves may have acted as significant historical agents and contributed to the growth of cities and urban institutions.

This kind of detailed inquiry into the growth process of the castle towns is most illuminating when confined to a single urban unit. Kanazawa, the administrative headquarters of Kaga *han,* the largest daimyo domain in Japan, seems ideally suited for that kind of analysis. The decentralized nature of the Tokugawa political system meant, of course, that there was no single "typical" castle town, mirroring in perfect image the growth and development of all the others. But Kanazawa recommends itself for numerous reasons. First is the nature of the city's history. In many ways, Kanazawa passed through the various phases of urban growth at a pace which duplicated the experience of other castle towns. Kanazawa's initial growth began in the late sixteenth century, and its population peaked about one hundred years later. Similarly, the institutions of political governance did not mature until the middle of the seventeenth century, following years of experimentation—a pattern seen in most other castle towns.

The location of the city is an important consideration as well. The few studies of urban life in Tokugawa Japan tend to deal chiefly with the major cities along the Pacific seaboard, especially the three great metropolises of Edo, Osaka, and Kyoto. As a consequence, relatively little is known still about the economic and cultural life of the regional castle towns. One scholar has recently conceptualized Japan's castle town urbanization in terms of hierarchy, with Edo at the top and distant regional castle towns forming the base. One implication of this notion is that the development of any particular castle town depended to some degree upon the intensity of its relationship with Edo.[14] Kanazawa, located on the coast of the Sea of Japan and separated from Edo by three mountain ranges, provides an excellent opportunity to study urban life in a regional setting and in relative isolation from the influence of the shogun's city.

The size of Kanazawa also favors its choice. Edo and Osaka were simply too large to be used for an initial inquiry into the castle town phenomenon. With a maximum population of about 120,000, Kanazawa offers a more manageable unit of study. At the same time, its size makes it a city of significance and ensures that the major components of the urbanization process can be readily observed.

Documentation provides another reason for Kanazawa's selection. The city has been favored with a succession of distinguished local scholars, who have collected and published over sixty volumes of documents. Although most of these works bring together source materials concerning domain government and life in the agricultural villages, there are also numerous documents which bear witness to life in the castle town. Additional unpublished sources are available at the Kanazawa City Library and Ishikawa Prefectural Library in the form of domain ordinances, maps, accounts of criminal cases, family histories compiled by merchants and artisans, and contemporary descriptions of urban social life. Fortunately, a great deal of this documentation covers the history of the city in the late sixteenth and early seventeenth centuries. This is rare for Japan, where fires, earthquakes, and the World War II bombings have taken a heavy toll of such early records in most places. Despite some gaps in the material, the documentary base is sufficiently broad to permit a multifaceted investigation of Kanazawa's urban growth going back to the origins of the city as a castle town.

Given our present lack of knowledge about Japanese cities, an initial study of the castle town phenomenon should be placed in as broad a context as possible. Thus the format chosen for this study is a holistic analysis; that is, an analysis in which urban growth is viewed in relationship to the political, social, and economic transformations which were sweeping society in general. As Charles Tilly has so aptly pointed out, a holistic approach illuminates two important principles about urban communities. First, in many ways cities sum up the civilizations which give birth to them. Second, much of the special character of urban centers derives from their relationship to the rest of society.[15] This holistic approach, then, seems particularly appropriate for an initial study of castle towns, since attempts by daimyo to secure greater control over the land, people, and resources of their realms had profound implications for urban growth. At the same time, it permits a thorough investigation of the respective contributions of daimyo and commoner to the city-building process.

A holistic study offers several other advantages. Such an approach, for instance, examines the entire round of activities—social and economic as well as political—which take place within an urban setting. Specifically, this study of Kanazawa will investigate the nature and determinants of class composition and will also examine urban social and cultural activity, including the development of new urban tastes in the performing arts, the recreational pursuits of the various status groups, and the ways in which the dominant cultural motifs changed over the course of the seventeenth century. Moreover, it will deal with urban economic development, the organization of merchant and artisan groups, and the initiative that these groups showed in creating new businesses in response to shifting consumption demands. It will also discuss the organization and nature of urban government, the impact of political decisions upon urban life, the interplay between officialdom and the commoner population, and the degree to which government policy dovetailed or conflicted with the needs and desires of the city's inhabitants.

Finally, a holistic study encourages reflection on the nature of society itself and produces insights into issues of general historical concern. This study of Kanazawa will comment on the character of political rule during the seventeenth century, the emergence of bureaucratic forms of authority, the structure of political rights, the character and pace of cultural and institutional innovation, and the development of a new Confucian philosophy of government. It will also confront the issue of whether the "system" was coercive and restrictive, and thereby limited change, or whether it was flexible enough to permit, and, at times, even encourage it.

Three broad secondary objectives underlie this study and bring into sharper focus the questions and analytical techniques discussed above. The first is to add to our meager fund of knowledge in English about Japanese urban communities by writing a history of a single city over the first century of its development. John W. Hall's essay "The Castle Town and Japan's Modern Urbanization" remains the most significant work on castle town development, but it was written in the 1950s and deals with the urbanization experience at a highly general level. E. Sidney Crawcour has contributed numerous articles on Tokugawa merchants, and Gilbert Rozman and William B. Hauser have written on the economic importance of Edo and Osaka.[16] These too are important works, but they focus on certain partial aspects of urbanization only. One purpose of this essay, then, is to flesh out the above studies and to provide a more complete sketch of life in a type of community which has not been treated in depth in English.

A second objective is to introduce the phenomenon of castle town urbanization to as wide an audience as possible and to do so by asking the same kinds of questions about Japanese castle towns that other historians have posed about European cities. Unfortunately, it is still too early to attempt an in-depth comparison of Japanese castle towns and the cities of early modern Europe. Such a study is highly desirable, of course, but it involves a great deal of synthesis that will become possible only after many more studies of individual cities have been completed. Yet one can begin to make some tentative gropings in this direction by asking, in the study of Japanese cities, the universalistic questions put forth by the historians of Europe: What is the relationship of the individual to the state? How does the city produce its wealth, and how does it spend it? What are the goals of intellectual and cultural activity? How do the achievements of the city in architecture, art, and literature reflect the citizens' conception of themselves and their universe?[17]

A final purpose is to offer a new organizational approach to the study of Japan's premodern local history. Within the last decade scholars concerned with America and Europe have come forth with a new genre of historical literature, the community study. So popular has this type of study become that one reviewer has termed it a "virtual cottage industry for academics."[18] The basic purpose of these studies has been to promote a more holistic view of the society under study and of the changes occurring within that society. To do so, scholars have developed a rich conceptual vocabulary for urban analysis and have set forth a wide variety of new approaches and questions of the sort posed earlier. As yet no such community study of any premodern Japanese city has appeared, in either Japanese or English. Kanazawa seems an ideal place to begin.

ONE
NATIONAL REUNIFICATION AND MAEDA TOSHIIE'S ENTRY INTO KANAZAWA

The sweep of nearly one hundred years from the Ōnin War (1467–77) to the middle of the sixteenth century is known evocatively as the *Sengoku jidai*—the era of warring states, a century when Japan was racked by widespread warfare among local military elites. During this period of domestic strife, the traditional centers of national political authority were on the decline. The emperor and his military delegate, the Ashikaga shogun, retained their formal offices in Kyoto, but in actuality neither possessed sufficient military power to influence events decisively outside the immediate environs of that ancient capital. In the absence of any effective integrating power on the national level, Japan splintered into hundreds, perhaps thousands, of small territorial holdings ruled over by local military figures who controlled only as much land as they could protect by force of arms.

This political fragmentation reached its most extreme degree about midway through the sixteenth century. After that, a few of the local commanders who were stronger and more skilled than their rivals began to consolidate their authority over larger and larger domains. By the late 1550s some three hundred of these lords, who by now had become known as daimyo, had extended their control over approximately two-thirds of the land base of Japan. These larger daimyo domains provided the building blocks for the political reunification of the country. Gradually, over the closing decades of the sixteenth century, three men—Oda Nobunaga (1534–82), Toyotomi Hideyoshi (1536–98), and Tokugawa Ieyasu (1543–1616)—imposed their military hegemony over the daimyo. Concurrently these national unifiers, and the daimyo on the local level, created new forms of political authority that made early modern Japan more centralized and more comprehensively governed than at any time in the past.

The first of the great national figures, Oda Nobunaga, began his rise to power from a relatively small holding in one corner of the ancient province of Owari in central Japan. During the decade of the 1550s Nobunaga was victorious in a series of campaigns against other contenders for local power—including his own younger brother—and by 1559 had secured his hold over the province. Nobunaga fought his way to national prominence during the decade of the 1560s. His stunning victory over the vastly more numerous forces of Imagawa Yoshimoto in the Battle of Okehazama in 1560 allowed Nobunaga to expand his sphere of influence into portions of the strategically located provinces of Suruga, Tōtōmi, and Mikawa. His next major breakthrough came in 1568 when Ashikaga Yoshiaki, a claimant to the position of shogun, requested Nobunaga's help in advancing his cause. Nobunaga responded by leading a force of some thirty thousand men into Kyoto and installing Yoshiaki as shogun, but only after Yoshiaki had agreed to follow Nobunaga's advice in making all political decisions. By 1573 Nobunaga had concluded that he could dispense with Yoshiaki altogether and drove the last Ashikaga shogun out of the city of Kyoto. Possession of the traditional capital provided Nobunaga with a strong central base for campaigns against his rivals, and during the late 1570s Nobunaga's forces, led by his generals Toyotomi Hideyoshi and Akechi Mitsuhide, swept into western Japan, into the provinces of Tamba and Tango, Inaba and Harima.

Oda Nobunaga also brought his power to bear against those religious institutions which over the centuries had acquired massive land holdings and become important secular powers. His single most dramatic attack against the Buddhist establishment occurred in the autumn of 1571, when he unleashed his armies against the soldier-monks at Enryakuji monastery on Mount Hiei. By the time the fighting ended, some three thousand buildings had been destroyed by fire and several thousand monks killed.

Nobunaga's most tenacious religious opponent was the Ikkō sect, and the clash of arms between his armies and this sect would have an influence on the later development of the castle town of Kanazawa. Originally founded in the thirteenth century, the Ikkō sect had steadily expanded its following and, during the Sengoku period, had also greatly increased the amount of land under its control. As warfare in central Japan worsened during the sixteenth century, the sect in 1532 constructed in Osaka an elaborate monastery-fortress known as Ishiyama Honganji. To defend itself, the sect recruited groups of "fighting monks" and, by the middle of the sixteenth century, the Ikkō sect rivaled many of the great daimyo in terms of wealth and military strength.

Moreover, the Ikkō sect headquarters also concluded military alliances with groups of Ikkō adherents in other parts of Japan. The most famous of these was with believers in the province of Kaga on the coast of the Sea of Japan.[1] The religious teachings of the Ikkō sect first became popular in this region when Rennyo, the eighth head priest of the sect, traveled through the area in the late fifteenth century and helped to organize groups of worshipers (*kō*) in each village as well as a province-wide network of temples. In time this religious organization became the basis of a political and military federation known as the Kaga *Ikkō-ikki*. As the centralized political order collapsed in the late fifteenth century, a number of aspiring military hegemons competed for power in this area. Local elites—wealthy peasants and persons who might most aptly be described as part-time farmers, part-time warriors—sought a way to resist these military commanders and, concurrently, to maintain their own positions of authority within the rural villages. Most of these local elites were Ikkō adherents as well, and they used their control over the local *kō* groups and temples to forge horizontal alliances among villages and to recruit military units to resist those warrior groups who might try to impose their authority over the area from the outside.

By the 1480s the local elites in the Kaga area had built an effective fighting machine, and in 1488 they were able to defeat the forces of Togashi Masachika, whose family had claimed political authority over the Kaga area for more than a century in their capacity as military governors (*shugo*) appointed by the central government in Kyoto. The victory by the Ikkō federation of believers gave the federation superior political and military rights in the area. In particular, it was now able to organize the area's defenses, exercise administrative and judicial rights in rural villages, and determine the tax rates that villagers had to pay to support the federation.

At first, these rights were exercised by officials of local Ikkō temples and by the local elites that had helped to organize the federation. Because of the continued unrest of the times, however, these men felt the need to establish a closer relationship with the sect headquarters in Osaka in order to buttress their own claims to authority within Kaga and also to act as a deterrent to any military commander who might contemplate an attack against the federation. Consequently, they invited officials of Ishiyama Honganji to dispatch representatives to Kaga both to symbolize the new relationship and to help with administrative duties.

This influx of outsiders necessitated the construction of new temples and office buildings. Since the early medieval period a small trading community had existed in the Kaga area, sitting astride the main trading route that ran from the capital area of Kyoto to northwestern Japan. In 1546, Ishiyama Honganji priests chose this small community, nestled between the Sai and Asano rivers, to be the site of its local headquarters. The community became known as Oyama Gobō, and its population numbered at least 3,000 and perhaps as many as 5,000 persons.[2] It was from this headquarters that the Ikkō federation, in concert with Ishiyama

Honganji officials, ruled the surrounding area through a combination of techniques that were nearly identical with those employed by the emerging daimyo. And it was this small settlement of Oyama Gobō that eventually became the castle town of Kanazawa.

The Ishiyama Honganji, with its massive fortified headquarters in Osaka and its alliance with the federation in the Kaga area, represented a serious obstacle to Oda Nobunaga's quest for national hegemony. Throughout the early 1570s Nobunaga probed for weaknesses along the perimeter of outer castles that the Ikkō sect had constructed around their Osaka stronghold. In the late 1570s, he intensified the attacks with armies sometimes numbering more than sixty thousand men. Finally in 1580 his forces surrounded the Ishiyama stronghold and accepted the surrender of the Honganji monks.

The campaign against the Ikkō federation in Kaga was also long and costly. As early as 1573, forces commanded by Nobunaga's generals Akechi Mitsuhide and Hashiba Hideyoshi had driven through Echizen and into the southern portion of Kaga. When a sharp counterattack by federation troops brought this attack to a halt in 1574, Nobunaga himself took over command of the main armies. The next year Nobunaga moved out from his base at Tsuruga and swept through Echizen, recapturing that province from federation forces. The Akechi and Hashiba armies continued the offensive into Kaga, taking in rapid succession the castles at Daishōji, Hinoya, and Sakumi. By the end of 1575, the southern half of Kaga was firmly under Nobunaga's control and the Ikkō federation was beginning to come apart.

In 1575, Nobunaga assigned the province of Echizen to one of his most trusted supporters, Shibata Katsuie, who continued to apply military pressure to the Ikkō federation. In 1576, for instance, elements of Shibata's armies, commanded by his nephew Sakuma Morimasa, advanced deeper into Kaga and secured a defensive position at Miyukizuka (later renamed Komatsu). At the same time, the Ikkō federation was experiencing internal tensions as Honganji officials dispatched from Osaka and local elites argued over tactics and the division of administrative responsibilities. In 1580 Shibata took advantage of the dispute to launch an attack into northern Kaga. In the fourth month of that year, just as Nobunaga's attacks upon the Ishiyama Honganji fortress in Osaka were reaching their bloody climax, Shibata forces, spearheaded by Sakuma, captured the town of Oyama Gobō, and the religious federation that had ruled Kaga for nearly a century came to an end.

With his flank in Hokuriku secure, Nobunaga was now prepared to make an all-out attack against his rivals in western Japan, and in the spring of 1582 he announced that he would personally assume command of the entire expedition. But while he was passing through Kyoto on his way to the front he was assassinated by Akechi Mitsuhide, who aspired to Nobunaga's position. Although Nobunaga was killed before he could achieve his goal of national conquest, he had during his lifetime brought some twenty provinces, nearly one-third of the total, under his command. This area included the richest and most centrally located portions of the country, and it would provide the basis for the national reunification that was to follow.

It was not just in military terms that Nobunaga's achievements constituted an important legacy for Japan's future, for he also initiated several

Map 1: Kaga Domain, 1600–1630

institutional innovations that would, when carried to completion by his successors, transform society and provide a completely new basis for the national polity. In 1571, for example, he undertook a cadastral survey (*kenchi*) in the province of Yamashiro. This inspection of agricultural land and measurement of its productive capacity anticipated the more complete surveys of the final decades of the century that ultimately resulted in new forms of village organization and tax collection. Five years later, in 1576, Nobunaga also started to disarm the peasants within his domains, an action that foreshadowed the more complete separation of the peasant and warrior status groups that would eventually constitute the cornerstone of political authority in early modern Japan.

Oda Nobunaga's sudden death in 1582 touched off a rivalry among his chief lieutenants for control over his territory and his band of warrior retainers. Within months two principal contenders had emerged: Toyotomi Hideyoshi, who had begun his career as a lowly Foot Soldier (*ashigaru*) and gone on to become a brilliant general, and Shibata Katsuie, who commanded a large army composed of his own samurai and contingents supplied by allied daimyo in the Hokuriku area, including Sakuma Morimasa, who had taken up residence in Oyama Gobō. In 1583, Shibata marched his regiments through the early spring snows of Echizen and into Ōmi where they joined combat with Hideyoshi's armies at Shizugatake, near the northern shore of Lake Biwa. The outcome was quickly settled. Hideyoshi assumed personal command of his forces and pushed Shibata back into Echizen. Shibata took refuge at his castle at Kita-no-shō (modern-day Fukui), but committed suicide when the castle fell after a three-day siege.

His victory over Shibata in 1583 made Hideyoshi one of the strongest generals in the country. Soon, other major daimyo began to submit pledges of allegiance, and with the support of these new allies, Hideyoshi was ready to push on with the completion of the military reunification of Japan. His enemies fell quickly. All of the major daimyo of Shikoku capitulated in 1585; by the early summer of 1587 all of the important Kyushu daimyo had acknowledged Hideyoshi's overlordship; and organized resistance ended with the surrender of the Hōjō family of the Kantō region in 1590. Hideyoshi had brought all of Japan under his military dominion.

Having unified the country militarily, Hideyoshi also sought to create a basis of political legitimacy that would justify his claims to national authority. In 1585, for instance, he assumed the ancient court position of *kanpaku* (Imperial Regent) and six years later, when he retired, he became the *taikō* (Retired Regent). These posts put him close to the emperor and permitted him to claim that he ruled through a delegation of authority from the imperial sovereign. Hideyoshi also secured a greater measure of control over the country's daimyo by demanding that they submit specific oaths of allegiance to him, and he even made some send their wives and children to his Osaka castle to serve as hostages.

Perhaps Hideyoshi's most significant reform measure was to carry further what Oda Nobunaga had started by implementing a series of cadastral surveys known as the *taikō kenchi*. Beginning with the province of Ōmi in 1583, Hideyoshi ordered that all territory under his overlordship be surveyed, on a province-by-province basis, and by his death in 1598 all provinces in Japan had been surveyed, though not each one in its entirety. The surveys had a number of important social consequences, for they created a status division between the peasantry (*hyakushō*) and the warriors (*bushi*). The persons who were listed on survey registers as cultivators, along with their families and attached personnel, were now legally defined as peasants, while those persons carried on domain registers as fief holders constituted the samurai, or *bushi,* class of warriors. This process of separation by status was given further impetus by the "sword hunts" (*katanagari*) ordered by several daimyo during the 1580s and on a nationwide scale by Hideyoshi in 1588. These hunts effectively disarmed the rural populace and restricted the bearing of arms to members of the samurai class. The surveys and sword hunts in tandem laid the basis for the more complete separation of society into status groups that would take place during the seventeenth century.

The cadastral surveys also provided a new method for assigning daimyo domains. Survey teams measured the productive capacity of rice fields in terms of a new unit called the *koku,* theoretically the amount of rice needed to feed one person for one year (approximately five bushels of unhulled rice). The new unit of land measurement permitted Hideyoshi to use *koku* as the basis for assigning domains to daimyo. Now, by definition a daimyo was a territorial lord who received from the national hegemon a grant of land assessed at ten thousand *koku* or more.

Hideyoshi's death in 1598 brought to center stage the third of Japan's unifers, Tokugawa Ieyasu. Castellans at Okazaki in the province of Mikawa, the Tokugawa family had won control of about one-half of that province by the middle of the sixteenth century. For a time the Tokugawa family acknowledged the overlordship of Imagawa Yoshimoto, but when he fell to Oda Nobunaga in 1560, Ieyasu, who by then had become head of his house, quickly switched his allegiance to Nobunaga. Under Nobunaga's aegis, Ieyasu was gradually able to expand his authority. Following Nobunaga's death in 1582, Ieyasu briefly flirted with the idea of challenging Toyotomi Hideyoshi but after a few inconclusive military engagements decided to accept Hideyoshi's overlordship. During the balance of the 1580s Ieyasu continued to add gradually to his holdings, and, when he made a significant contribution to the campaign against the Hōjō in 1590, Hideyoshi rewarded him with a major grant carved out of the former Hōjō lands in the Kantō region. This increase made Ieyasu the largest daimyo in Japan, with a domain whose productive capacity exceeded two and a half million *koku*. To administer these territories he built a new castle on the site of a small fishing village named Edo.

With this expanded power base Ieyasu became one of the leading contenders for Hideyoshi's mantle in 1598. Ieyasu, of course, had sworn allegiance to Hideyoshi and had also pledged his loyalty to Hideyoshi's infant son and heir, Hideyori, who was in residence at the Toyotomi castle in Osaka. But the pull of ambition and the dream of national overlordship could not be ignored. Ieyasu soon began to move troops into Osaka and to accept oaths of allegiance from other daimyo. Such moves did not go unchallenged: by 1600 Ishida Mitsunari, another powerful ally of Hideyoshi and an old protagonist of Ieyasu, had put together an opposition coalition of daimyo, mostly from western Japan. In the 9th month of 1600 the armies of these two contending alliances met in the famous Battle of Sekigahara. The Tokugawa victory, aided by the prearranged defection of one of the members of the western alliance, provided Japan with a new ruling family. Over the course of the next several decades, as we shall see later, the Tokugawa family went on to establish a new shogunate and create the most centralized and powerful government that Japan had yet experienced.

It is against this background that the Maeda family became one of the most powerful daimyo houses in Japan and ruled over extensive territorial holdings from its headquarters in the castle town of Kanazawa.[3] The man recognized as the founder of the Maeda line of daimyo, Maeda Toshiie, was the fourth son of the castle master at Arako (within the city limits of modern-day Nagoya), born sometime in the late 1530s, probably in 1538. In 1551, while still in his early teens, Toshiie became a Page (*koshō*) in the service of Oda Nobunaga and was granted an annual stipend of fifty *kan*, equivalent to approximately 125 *koku* of rice. During his early years of service to Nobunaga, Toshiie's record was exemplary, and in 1556 his stipend was tripled after he suffered a wound in the right eye during an attack on Nobunaga's younger brother Nobuyuki.

However, in 1559 Toshiie became involved in a quarrel with another of Oda's retainers and killed the man. As punishment, Nobunaga dismissed Toshiie from his service. Nevertheless, Toshiie felt that his own future was still tied to Nobunaga's and so for the next two years Toshiie, on his own initiative and without official authorization, joined Nobunaga's armies in several battles in the hope of achieving a record of outstanding battlefield exploits so that he would be forgiven by Nobunaga and reinstated to official position. This tactic was common among young warriors who were seeking a pardon for an indiscretion, and it worked for Toshiie.

In 1560 Toshiie participated in the Battle of Okehazama against the forces of Imagawa Yoshimoto and presented Nobunaga with two heads taken in the encounter; later the same year he again demonstrated his bravery in the campaigns in western Mino province against Saitō Tatsuoki; and in 1561 he took the head of Nobunaga's rival Adachi Rokuhyōe. Impressed by Toshii's loyalty and zeal, Nobunaga reinstated him and later raised his stipend to 450 *kan* (1125 *koku*). With a string of battlefield successes behind him, Toshiie in 1569, at the age of thirty-two, bypassed his three elder brothers to assume the Maeda family headship. Concurrently he was appointed castle master at Arako. It was from this position that Maeda Toshiie was able to thrust himself into the ranks of the major daimyo. Toshiie and his men were thus among the forces that fought their way into Echizen in the 1570s under Nobunaga's banners. At the same time that Nogunaga assigned Echizen to Shibata Katsuie, who took up residence at Kita-no-shō, he also appointed Toshiie and two other men as Overseers (*metsuke;* also known as the *sanninshū*) to report on Shibata's conduct and assigned them to two districts (*gun*) in Echizen. In effect, this gave Toshiie a 33,000-*koku* fief and a status equivalent to that of a daimyo. To carry out his new duties, Toshiie moved to Echizen Fuchū (the present-day city of Takefu in Fukui Prefecture). For the next several years Toshiie supported Shibata Katsuie in suppressing the Ikkō federation in Kaga and in defending Echizen against the armies of the hostile Uesugi family to

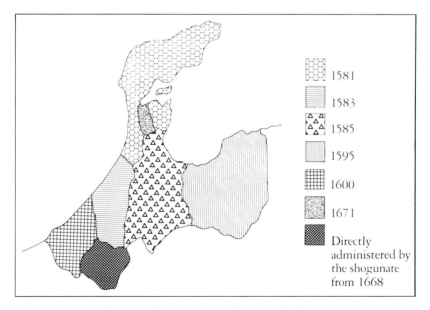

Map 2: The Expansion of Maeda Holdings

the north. As a reward, Toshiie was named in the autumn of 1581 as the daimyo of the entire province of Noto, later assessed at over 200,000 *koku*, and he built a small castle and established a military garrison at the town of Nanao.

When Oda Nobunaga was cut down in 1582, Toshiie had to decide whether to cast his lot with Toyotomi Hideyoshi or Shibata Katsuie. Toshiie knew both Hideyoshi and Katsuie well. All three men hailed from Owari; all had served Nobunaga for more than twenty years; and all had risen through the ranks to become powerful lords. But since Toshiie shared a border with the stronger Shibata, he perhaps had little choice but to contribute troops to his neighbor's campaign against Hideyoshi. After Hideyoshi repulsed Shibata's attack at Shizugatake in 1583, however, Toshiie very quickly reassessed the situation and declared that he would accede to Hideyoshi's overlordship. Hideyoshi, himself aware that the Maeda family could be a powerful ally, accepted Toshiie's pledges of loyalty. Consequently Maeda forces were in the vanguard of Hideyoshi's armies as they swept into Echizen and defeated Shibata at his fortress in Kita-no-shō. Toshiie himself led the subsequent attack against the remnants of Shibata's troops at Oyama Gobō. He trapped the bulk of the opposition forces outside of the fortress and was able to make a bloodless entry into the city on the 27th day of the 4th month. The next day Toyotomi Hideyoshi triumphantly paraded into the city and immediately reconfirmed Toshiie's holdings in Noto and granted him two additional districts in Kaga, which nearly doubled the size of Maeda's domain. Hideyoshi also instructed Toshiie to move his headquarters to Oyama

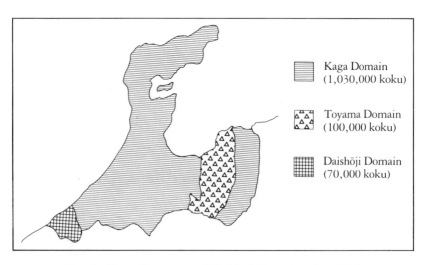

Map 3: Kaga, Toyama, and Daishōji Domains after 1639

Gobō, which was generally referred to thereafter as Kanazawa (and was also pronounced Kanezawa at that time). It was from this castle town headquarters that the Maeda family ruled its territories for nearly three centuries until the domain system was abolished following the Meiji Restoration of 1868.

The transfer to Kanazawa in 1583 did not mark the end of Toshiie's military campaigns, however. The very next year his immediate neighbors to the north, the Sassa, sent an army of eight thousand horsemen against Maeda warriors. Toshiie repulsed this attack, but fighting continued along the Kaga-Etchū-Noto borders until 1585, when Hideyoshi sent reinforcements to aid Toshiie. This joint army made short work of the Sassa forces, and Hideyoshi assigned the Sassa holdings to Toshiie, a grant that again doubled the size of the Maeda territories and made the Maeda house one of the most powerful families in all of Japan. Two years later, in 1587, Maeda forces participated in Hideyoshi's Kyushu campaigns. At that time Toshiie commanded forces that guarded Kyoto, while Toshinaga, his eldest son, led three thousand Kaga troops onto the battlefield.

In the tumultuous years following Hideyoshi's death in 1598, the Maeda family had to decide whether or not to support Tokugawa Ieyasu. Although the Maeda would ultimately accept Tokugawa overlordship and achieve their greatest successes within the context of the Tokugawa shogunal system, tension and distrust characterized relations between the two great families in the period immediately after Hideyoshi's death. In 1597 the gravely ill Hideyoshi created the Board of Regents (gotairō). This Board consisted of five of the largest daimyo in the land, who were sworn to support Hideyoshi's infant son, Hideyori, and were supposed to administer Toyotomi affairs until Hideyori could assume power in his own right. Hideyoshi appointed both Tokugawa Ieyasu and Maeda Toshiie to this board. But Hideyoshi seems to have placed his greatest confidence in Toshiie, for his will actually instructed Toshiie to provide troops to garrison Osaka castle, the residence of the young Hideyori.

Few daimyo, however, believed that the hastily created Board of Regents structure could contain the powerful ambitions of the great lords who would be tempted to succeed Hideyoshi by pushing his son aside. Indeed, the short-lived balance of power among board members began to come apart as soon as Maeda Toshiie died in the spring of 1599, and Japan became rife with rumors of intrigues both real and imagined. Not long after Toshiie's death, Tokugawa Ieyasu received a report that Maeda Toshinaga, who had succeeded his father, was deeply committed to an anti-Tokugawa plot being formulated by Ishida Mitsunari. Ieyasu immediately began to draw up plans to attack the Maeda castle headquarters in Kanazawa. To this day, historians are not certain of the extent to which Toshinaga was involved with Ishida. Certainly he must have been pulled by conflicting emotions. His father's will had enjoined him to support the Toyotomi heir. At the same time, Toshinaga realized that he commanded the second largest fighting force in the country and, with the reunification drama entering its final, culminating act, the notion of a contest with the Tokugawa for national hegemony must have been a strong temptation. But Toshinaga was also well aware that his father had become a great daimyo by supporting others who thirsted for national leadership, and, in the end, he decided that he could best advance his family's interests by adopting the same tactic. Consequently, Toshinaga declined to become an ally of Ishida, and, when he learned of the report to Ieyasu, Toshinaga dispatched his most trusted retainer, Yokoyama Nagachika (Yamashiro no Kami) to visit Ieyasu. Yokoyama explained the Maeda house was not party to any intrigue, roundly condemned the plot, and suggested that Ishida had spread rumors of Toshinaga's involvement in hopes of driving a wedge between the Maeda and Tokugawa families. To further demonstrate the sincerity of his intentions, Toshinaga sent his mother, Hōshun'in, to Edo to serve as a hostage and also arranged the engagement of his younger brother, who would eventually succeed him as daimyo, to a daughter of Ieyasu's son Hidetada, who himself would become the second Tokugawa shogun.[4]

When Ishida was finally successful in 1600 in mobilizing a coalition of western daimyo to contend with Ieyasu for national hegemony, the Maeda family threw its support behind Ieyasu. Although Toshinaga did not take part in the decisive battle at Sekigahara in the fall of 1600, his armies were active throughout the summer of that year in campaigns against Ishida supporters along the coast of the Sea of Japan.[5] For this the Maeda were rewarded with the remaining districts of southern Kaga. This gave the Maeda family control over the three provinces of Kaga, Noto, and Etchū. This domain was usually referred to as Kaga *han,* and it had a productive capacity close to one and a quarter million *koku* of rice.[6] In size and power, the Maeda family now stood second only to the Tokugawa house itself.

The creation of a new national hegemony by Japan's three unifiers during the second half of the sixteenth century was in large part, of course, the product of military conquest. But having achieved military hegemony, each of the unifiers also implemented reforms designed to enhance and perpetuate the institutional basis of their authority. This same process was evident on the domain level.[7] Men like Maeda Toshiie became daimyo because of their military skills and prowess. Yet they were also aware of the need to develop new mechanisms of control. Consequently, after Maeda Toshiie settled in Kanazawa in 1583, he and his successors put into effect a set of institutional innovations that expanded their authority over the human and material resources of Kaga domain. In broad outline, Maeda policies followed the same general pattern evident in other daimyo domains in Japan. And, as elsewhere, the decades of daimyo rule at the end of the sixteenth and beginning of the seventeenth centuries can be characterized as tentative and experimental. It is important to note here some of the details of the major policy initiatives, for they had a direct impact on the pace and direction of urbanization in Kanazawa in the years from 1583 to 1630.

One problem confronting all daimyo during the turbulent sixteenth century was to secure firm control over the members of their vassal warrior bands (*kashindan*). This problem was particularly acute in the case of the Maeda house because the number of retainers expanded so dramatically during the late sixteenth and early seventeenth centuries as the Maeda family acquired new territories. In the 1570s, when Toshiie first obtained daimyo status at Echizen Fuchū, he had just thirty-one warrior followers to whom he assigned fiefs with productive capacities of 100 *koku* or more. By the early 1610s, there were 590 such retainers. Within the next decade this nearly doubled, to 1,040 fief holders. This figure does not include lower-ranking *bushi* who did not hold direct fiefs, and when they are added in, the total number of warrior households probably numbered more than 10,000 by the 1620s.[8]

In order to extend its authority over the warriors and to ensure effective mobilization of the fighting forces in periods of warfare, the Maeda house early on divided the corps of retainers into status-based subgroups and exercised control through group command.[9] Except for retainers of the top status, all warriors were grouped into personnel units captained by superior officers. There were a handful of Senior Advisers (*hakka*) who supervised dozens of Commanders (*hitomochi*) who, in turn, directed numerous Unit Leaders (*kumigashira*). Although this system was designed chiefly for military purposes, it provided the daimyo with a structure through which he could exercise administrative and civil authority as well. When the second Maeda daimyo, Toshinaga, issued legal codes in 1601, for instance, he made the Advisers, Commanders, and Unit Leaders responsible for ensuring that samurai under their supervision obeyed the laws.

The daimyo's ability to limit the authority that retainers exercised over their fiefs provides another index of the daimyo's increased governing powers over both the warriors and the peasantry. Throughout late sixteenth-century Japan, the direct fief system—in which a daimyo assigned a fief to a vassal retainer who administered that fief personally and received tax dues from its inhabitants—was common practice. But the daimyo were aware of the dangers inherent in that kind of system. In the middle of the sixteenth century, many retainers had turned their fiefs into independent power bases from which they defied daimyo orders, or even rose in revolt against their masters. Consequently, in the late sixteenth century, daimyo began to curtail vassal power by imposing their own supervisory authority between the retainers and the residents of the retainers' fiefs. To accomplish this, the daimyo created status distinctions between peasants and rural warriors (the well-known *hei-nō-bunri* decrees), required the samurai to move off the land and into the castle town, and appointed daimyo representatives to oversee some aspects of village administration and tax collection.

The Maeda joined other daimyo throughout Japan in implementing these kinds of policies. When Toshiie first received the Noto-Kaga area in the early 1580s, he employed a direct fief system.[10] A scarcity of documents leaves unclear the exact reasons why Toshiie granted fiefs to his retainers, but enfeoffment was undoubtedly essential to his ability to hold his territory. Many of the rural elites in Kaga had supported the Ikkō federation and resisted the outside authority of military lords. Shibata and Maeda had to win Kaga by conquest, and surely the easiest way for Toshiie to impose some form of control over local, outlying areas was to station his own retainers in them.

Quickly, however, the Maeda daimyo acted to prevent the enfeoffed retainers from putting down permanent roots in the countryside. The opening move was a set of cadastral surveys.[11] Toshiie ordered surveys of some districts during the 1580s and 1590s, and the entire domain was surveyed in 1616 and again in 1620. As elsewhere, the cadastral surveys in Kaga domain represented the daimyo's claim to ultimate proprietary authority within the domain and demonstrated his right to intervene in the affairs of his vassal's fiefs. Beyond this, the surveys also created status distinctions between the peasants, who were listed on the survey documents, and the *bushi,* who were carried on the Maeda's roster of fief holders and stipendiaries—a distinction that was reinforced by the sword hunts of the 1580s and 1590s.

Once the concept of status distinctions had been initially formulated, the Maeda daimyo further separated samurai from peasants, this time in a physical sense, by compelling the warriors to move out of rural areas and to establish residences around the castle in the town of Kanazawa. The initial movement of *bushi* into the castle town took place in the late sixteenth and early seventeenth centuries and nearly all warriors had assumed residence in Kanazawa by 1614.

The Maeda house extended its authority over the realm in additional ways. As they withdrew the samurai from the countryside, the Maeda daimyo also began to structure a new system of rural administration in order to gain better control over the peasantry.[12] The Rural Magistrates (*kōri-bugyō*), who received their instructions from the daimyo through the

Office of the Comptroller (*san'yoba*), constituted the top level of the new administrative pyramid.[13] Gradually, the daimyo attempted to shift authority away from the samurai fief holders and into the hands of these new appointees. A 1591 ordinance, for example, urged peasants to report directly to the Rural Magistrates all complaints about samurai fief holders, and a later ordinance gave the Rural Magistrates the power to intervene in many aspects of rural administration on private fiefs.[14]

The Rural Magistrates also supervised the activities of the Senior Village Headmen (*tomura*), the next level in the new administrative structure.[15] These men were appointed from rural elites and received a salary from the domain. Each had jurisdiction over thirty to forty villages, and they helped to settle intervillage disagreements about water rights and village boundaries, transmitted peasant complaints to the Rural Magistrates, and worked with the Village Headmen (*kimoiri*), the next lower administrative post.[16] These Village Headmen, usually one in each village, ensured that members of their villages obeyed domain laws. They also negotiated tax rates with fief holders and helped to settle any quarrels or disputes which threatened village tranquillity. Within the villages, all households were organized into Household Groups (*goningumi*) whose members were supposed to report any unlawful activities of their neighbors, help each other in times of economic distress, and patch up neighborhood disputes before they became a problem to higher officialdom.[17]

Yet another central concern of the Maeda daimyo was to create a domain that was economically self-sufficient so as to be prepared for any contingencies which might arise during these decades of military uncertainty. One essential component of this policy was to invite to Kanazawa merchants and artisans who could supply military and other essential goods and services to the daimyo and his warrior followers. A simple invitation to a merchant or artisan would not ensure his coming to Kanazawa, however, since daimyo throughout Japan were competing for the services of those persons. Consequently, Maeda policies took on the appearance of a recruitment program, and various incentives were offered to merchants and artisans in order to entice them to migrate to the emerging castle town in northwestern Japan. The inducements included free residential land, tax exemptions, and assurances of orders from the domain for their goods and services. This guarantee of domain business has supplied the generic name for this group of privileged commoners, who became known as *goyō shōnin* and *goyō shokunin*, merchants and artisans honored as purveyors to the daimyo. They included merchants who could supply arms, rice, and gunpowder, and artisans such as carpenters, roof thatchers, and swordsmiths. Certain other policies, such as restricting the horse traders' market and other key markets to sites within the castle town and constructing new roadways to encourage the movement of goods into the city, underscored the depth of the Maeda commitment to the ideal of self-sufficiency.

The implementation of these policies, particularly the reform of the fief system and the enforced residence of the samurai class in the castle town, profoundly affected the pattern of urban growth in Kanazawa. No reliable population statistics exist prior to the 1660s, and even after this date census counts tallied only the commoner population. Still, by 1614 almost all of Kaga's samurai families had established residences in the city, and a conservative estimate would put the city's warrior population, including all household members and servants, in the neighborhood of 30,000 to 40,000 persons, although it may have been as high as 50,000. The samurai population of Kanazawa peaked at approximately 67,000 in 1721, and then leveled off to the 60,000 range for the remainder of the Tokugawa period. [18]

A second migration, this one among rural people who became the city's commoners (chōnin), accompanied the movement of samurai into Kanazawa. The construction of the castle and samurai residences entailed a tremendous outlay of capital expenditures, and thousands of rural men poured into the city to take up jobs in the booming construction trades. As the samurai set up urban households, they employed servants—even a modest warrior family would usually employ an attendant, a valet, and a couple of women servants—thus creating additional employment opportunities for rural immigrants. Urban bushi households also generated enormous consumption demands. Restricted by daimyo fiat to military and bureaucratic careers, the samurai relied upon commoners to provide them with both military equipment and a variety of everyday goods and services, and this situation also attracted would-be merchants and artisans to the city. A few hundred of these came because they were invited to purvey goods and services to the daimyo, while thousands of others arrived on their own, hoping to take advantage of the new commercial opportunities by setting up shops to provide everyday goods—umbrellas, footwear, pots and pans.

By the early decades of the seventeenth century, perhaps as many as 30,000 to 40,000 commoners lived in Kanazawa. [19] The city continued to grow throughout that century. An official domain census taken in 1667 enumerated 59,101 chōnin, [20] and the city's population totaled more than 100,000 persons. Forty years later, in 1710, the chōnin population had swelled to 64,987, [21] and the city's aggregate population, including samurai, priests, and outcasts, stood in the neighborhood of 120,000 persons. The population then stabilized and hovered around that mark until the 1860s. [22]

In many ways, castle towns can be seen as the by-products of the implementation of those daimyo policies whose purpose was to establish daimyo authority firmly over the people and revenue base of the domain. But city-building per se was also important to the Maeda daimyo. They sought to create a garrison city which was large and militarily secure, and they used their castle town as a base to dominate the coastal plain, which contained the major rice producing villages, and also to control the lines of transportation and communication radiating into the countryside. The attempt to encourage and center economic activity within Kanazawa was fundamental to the broader objective of creating a powerful and self-supporting domain economy so that the Maeda house need not fear attack from outside. Thus, some of the policies discussed above, such as the requirement that samurai reside in the castle town and the issuance of invitations to selected merchants and artisans, should also be viewed as attempts to gather human and material resources in the city. As such, the city-building program meshes neatly, if somewhat complexly, with other policies that shaped the emerging power structure in early modern Japan, such as restructuring rural administration and reforming the fief-holding system.

TWO
THE FORMATIVE YEARS,
1583–1630

THE EARLY USE OF URBAN SPACE

Little is known before 1583 of the settlement that became Kanazawa.
When the town served as the Honganji headquarters it was composed of a
set of concentric circles, with the main Honganji temples and administrative offices at the center of the community, on a rise of land between the
Sai and Asano rivers. Lesser office buildings and lodgings for the priest-
administrators surrounded the core area, and an outer ring of merchant
shops and residences completed the community. Following the defeat of
the Ikkō federation, Sakuma Morimasa took up residence in the town. He
utilized the former temples and office buildings in the heart of the settlement as his own headquarters, built a few short earthen walls, and dug a
new moat along the eastern side of the complex. It is also possible that one
or two new merchant sections came into existence at this time. But
beyond this, the settlement witnessed few changes during Sakuma's brief
tenure.[1]

When Maeda Toshiie settled in Kanazawa in 1583, fresh from the
campaigns against Shibata and Sakuma but with his own position in the
Toyotomi power structure still uncertain, his principal concern was to lay
out a castle town which would be secure against outside attack. At the
center of the emerging city was, of course, the new castle itself. When
Toshiie arrived in 1583 he decided to locate his castle on the site of the
former Honganji headquarters, which had occupied the highest ground
between the Sai and Asano rivers.[2] Like Peter the Great, Toshiie was
concerned with security, and he immediately began to construct elaborate
stone fortifications around the central citadel and to dig the intricate set of
interconnecting moats and canals which eventually extended throughout
the castle town.

Construction of the castle walls began in 1592. At that time Toshiie
was in Kyoto, assisting with preparations for Hideyoshi's proposed invasion of Korea, and in the 2nd month of that year he sent a message to

Toshinaga at Kanazawa instructing him to proceed with construction. This was no minor undertaking. Walls were built around the entire circumference of the fortress, which then measured approximately 675 meters east to west and 670 meters north to south. Other walls were erected internally in order to divide the castle into enclosures (*maru*). At some points, the walls towered more than sixty meters higher than the nearby riverbanks. Construction teams quarried the rocks—many of them more than two meters on a side—at Mount Tomuro, nearly eighty kilometers to the east, and dragged them to a staging area to the southeast of the castle where they were cut to shape before being lifted and fitted into place. The undertaking was hazardous. Twice during construction, portions of the walls collapsed, killing dozens of laborers. Toshiie finally employed two men with extensive experience in castle construction, Shinohara Dewa no Kami and Gotō Mokubei, and dispatched them to Kanazawa to supervise the completion of the project. Under their engineering direction, the castle became a work of beauty as well as strength. The long sweep of the walls gave the castle a sense of permanence, while the white stucco watchtowers dramatically set off the massive turrets and gates. Awed, some contemporary observers boasted that Kanazawa castle was equal in magnificence to the Toyotomi fortress in Osaka.[3] Had he but known, Louis XIV's minister Colbert would certainly have approved the way that the Maeda gained both security and prestige from their castle-building efforts.

The Maeda also constructed a complex system of interconnecting moats and canals to encircle the newly walled castle. Honganji administrators had dug a few short moats prior to 1583 to protect the temple's administrative headquarters. But from the 1590s the Maeda began to expand the system. When the stone fortifications were being put up in 1592, Toshinaga dug a moat on the southeast side of the castle. In 1599, when warfare with the Tokugawa Ieyasu threatened and the Maeda were suspected of anti-Tokugawa plotting, Toshinaga constructed an inner moat system (*uchisōgamaebori*). Reportedly dug in just twenty-seven days, the inner moats flowed in two branches parallel to, but a short distance from, the eastern and western walls of the castle before emptying into the Asano River. The area bounded by the inner moats defined the "castle complex," the strategic heart of the city, and the Maeda daimyo were particularly concerned with its military integrity.[4]

Between the Battle of Sekigahara in 1600 and the campaigns at Osaka castle in 1614–15, the Maeda daimyo completed an additional system of outer moats (*sotosōgamaebori*). Like the inner moats, the system began upstream on the Sai River and then snaked through the castle town in a manner which provided protection for the castle as well as for the residences of major samurai retainers. Constructed under the direction of

Shinohara Dewa no Kami, the outer moat system measured well over four kilometers in length and defined a secondary defense perimeter.[5]

Tied into the moat systems were numerous canals built in the 1583–1630 period. One purpose of these canals was to provide drinking water for the city's expanding population, but they also twisted through samurai sections of the city and connected into the moat systems, thereby helping to buttress the castle's defenses. In all, the system wove its way through the castle town for nearly fifteen kilometers, a tribute to the capacity of the Maeda daimyo to mobilize men and resources.[6]

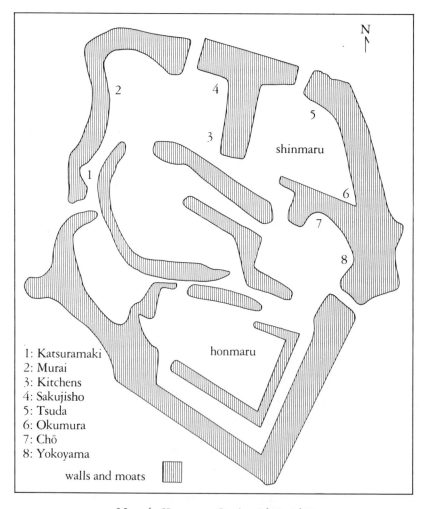

1: Katsuramaki
2: Murai
3: Kitchens
4: Sakujisho
5: Tsuda
6: Okumura
7: Chō
8: Yokoyama

walls and moats

Map 4: Kanazawa Castle, 1600–1615

The castle itself was home to the daimyo and his most important retainers. Stone walls and gates divided the castle into nine easily defendable enclosures. In those early years of uncertainty, the Maeda family lived in the main enclosure (*honmaru*), the best protected of the units. They constructed a new enclosure (*shinmaru*) during the crisis of 1599 in order to provide additional military protection. There the daimyo assigned residences to important samurai such as Okumura Inaba no Kami and Tsuda Genba. Certain other high-level retainers were located at tactically important points within the castle. These included Chō Hisatsura, Murai Dewa no Kami, Yokoyama Yamashiro no Kami, and Katsuramaki Hayato. Also given shelter within the walls were service offices, such as the kitchens; warehouses for weapons and military provisions; and important bureaucratic offices such as the Construction Office (*sakujisho*), which was in charge of domain building projects.[7]

Soon the Maeda began to move the retainers who lived inside the castle to sites outside the fortress. Although some retainers continued to live within the castle for several more decades, the Chō and many other families departed the protection of the castle walls during the 1610s. The fundamental motivation at this time was military, for the new placements were designed to create a better overall defense posture. The new Chō residence, for example, was located to the west of the castle and adjacent to the outer moat. There, it blocked any potential attack from the plain that stretched off to the northwest.[8] To the southeast, on the high plain which ran between the two rivers, stood the residences of Yokoyama Yamashiro no Kami, Okumura Inaba no Kami, and Honda Awa no Kami. Honda, the second son of Honda Masanobu, who was a direct retainer of Tokugawa Ieyasu and an adviser to the second shogun, became the largest Maeda vassal, with fief holdings assessed at 50,000 *koku*. Some contemporaries felt that the sprawling Honda residence with its elaborate gates and stone walls "was like the castle of a small domain."[9]

In the early 1600s, the Maeda announced the formal assignment of residential land (*yashiki*) to retainers who held fiefs assessed at 150 *koku* and above.[10] Shortly thereafter, samurai with fief assessments of 3,000 *koku* and above received additional grants of supplementary residential land (*shimoyashiki*) so that they could provide housing for their own rear vassals and service personnel.[11] Residential lot size was pegged to assessment so that, for example, a retainer with holdings assessed at 8,000 *koku* received a lot roughly sixty-three by seventy-three meters, while a samurai of 4,000-*koku* status received a plot measuring approximately fifty-five by fifty-five meters. The domain, through its newly appointed Residential Land Magistrates (*yashiki-bugyō*), made the actual allotments, and made them with military considerations in mind. For instance, Matsudaira Genba and Maeda Mannosuke, two retainers with fief assessments of over

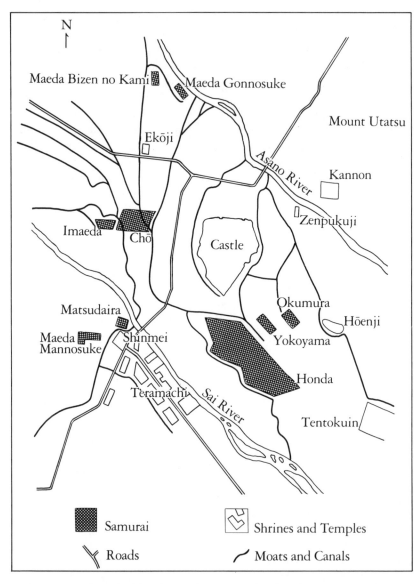

Map 5: Domain Planning and the Use of Urban Space, 1538–1630

3,000 *koku* each, received land close to the only bridge spanning the Sai River. The supplementary residential land of Imaeda Minbu helped to guard the western approaches to the castle, while Maeda Gonnosuke and Maeda Bizen no Kami protected the northwest.[12]

Military defense considerations also shaped domain policy toward shrines and temples. Both Toshiie and Toshinaga took steps to extend their control over the rural temples which had been closely associated with the Honganji alliance. They accomplished this by transporting the temples to new sites in Kanazawa, usually within a kilometer or so of the castle. Thus, the temples were brought under the closer scrutiny of domain officials, and the daimyo was provided with a series of buildings located at strategic points which could be garrisoned if some outside invader threatened the city. In all, the Maeda moved more than twenty temples into the city, most in the years 1583 to 1620. Two examples are noted on map 5: Zenpukuji, which was relocated in 1601, and Ekōji, which was moved in 1626.[13]

A second category of shrines and temples consisted of those which enjoyed a special relationship with the Maeda family. Toshiie physically transported some of these to Kanazawa when he came in 1583, while others were built after that date on land granted by the domain. In addition to land grants and occasional funds for building construction, the domain provided the special religious institutions with operating funds by allowing them to collect the tax revenues from specified villages. In exchange, the shrines and temples conducted official ceremonies and worship services for the daimyo.[14]

The Maeda maintained an especially close relationship with five shrines. The largest, popularly known as Kannon or Utatsuyama Hachiman, was actually a collection of shrine and temple buildings erected during the Keichō period (1596–1615) on a vast tract of land made available by the domain. Toshinaga and Tentokuin, wife of the third daimyo, Toshitsune, provided funds for some of the buildings within its extensive precincts. Toshinaga often prayed there before battle, and it became customary for male offspring of the Maeda family to be taken there for their first shrine visit (*miyamairi*).[15] Significantly, the shrine was located on a rise of land overlooking the plain on the northern side of the Asano River, a position which blocked any threat to the castle from that direction. Shinmei was another special shrine which received generous land grants during the early seventeenth century. Situated next to the residences of Maeda Mannosuke and Matsudaira Genba, it provided additional defensive protection for the strategically important bridge which spanned the Sai River.[16]

The three principal temples with which the Maeda family maintained special relations were Hōenji, Nyoraiji, and Tentokuin. Toshiie had con-

structed a temple known as Hōenji in Nanao when he was daimyo of the
Noto area. When he moved to Kanazawa in 1583, Toshiie brought with
him the head priest of that temple, as well as several objects of worship,
and constructed a new Hōenji close to the castle walls. In the early
seventeenth century the government moved the temple to its present site,
nearly a kilometer away and on the flank of the plain which sweeps out to
the southeast from the castle.[17]

The Maeda also carted Nyoraiji with them to Kanazawa. They rebuilt it
on the northern side of the Asano River, not far from Kannon, and in
1616 dedicated it to the memory of Tokugawa Ieyasu. Later, in 1656, it
was reconsecrated to the wife of the fourth Maeda daimyo.[18] The third
daimyo, Toshitsune, constructed Tentokuin temple in the early 1620s.
His wife, who was a daughter of the second shogun, Hidetada, had been
betrothed to Toshitsune following the crisis of 1599 as part of the effort to
establish harmonious relations between the Maeda and Tokugawa families. When she died in 1622 of complications following childbirth,
Toshitsune had this temple built in her honor and named it after her.[19]
But Toshitsune clearly had more than religious or romantic proprieties in
mind, for he located the temple near Hōenji, where it provided an additional defensive anchor to the southeast of the castle.

In 1616, the domain government carried out a major urban reorganization when it compelled dozens of temples to move across the banks of the
Asano and Sai rivers, exempting only the temples with which the Maeda
family maintained special relations and most of the temples, such as
Zenpukuji, which had been moved in from rural areas. With those exceptions, all the temples situated to the southwest of the castle were transferred across the Sai River to form a new urban area, appropriately named
Teramachi (Temple Ward), and the other temples in the city were moved
across the Asano, to the base of Mount Utatsu.[20] Two concerns motivated
this scheme. One was military—to link the temples with the samurai
residences granted a few years earlier in order to create a more secure outer
defense perimeter. A second purpose was to provide additional living
space for the expanding commoner population, for much of the vacated
land was made available for merchant housing.

This Sai River project illustrates some of the differences between the
urbanization process in Kanazawa and Saint Petersburg. In both cities the
rulers faced the problem of getting merchants and artisans to live in their
new urban centers. Peter the Great used a great deal of compulsion,
conscripting carpenters and stonecutters and forcibly requiring some Muscovite merchants to migrate to his city on the Baltic. The Maeda family,
on the other hand, had to compete with fellow daimyo for the services of
merchants and artisans, and thus tended to appeal to the self-interests of
the commercial classes by providing them with incentives to migrate to

their castle town headquarters on the coast of the Sea of Japan. The Maeda were successful, and by the opening decades of the seventeenth century, the growing city of Kanazawa was becoming the home not just of samurai, but also of thousands of commoners. An examination of their residential patterns shows that the independent actions of these merchants and artisans, who were referred to jointly in domain documents as *chōnin,* had a major impact upon the physical shape of the expanding castle town.

The elite of this newly emerging *chōnin* society consisted of the privileged merchants and artisans who received charters guaranteeing that they could purvey goods and services to the daimyo. The Maeda daimyo personally invited many of these merchants and artisans to Kanazawa, and to ensure acceptance of the invitations they often included gifts of land for shops and residences. It is not exactly clear in all cases how the sites for the land grants were decided, but given the daimyo need for these important merchants, it is likely that the commoners themselves chose the plots or negotiated with the daimyo for favorable locations. Certainly the location of the grants, usually near the castle but sometimes even within the moat system itself, illustrates Maeda sensitivity toward fulfilling the expectations of these men.

The histories of the Echizen'ya and Hiranoya families provide convenient examples. Echizen'ya Magobei started life as a *bushi* in the Osaka area. In the late 1570s, he moved to the area around modern-day Fukui, where he was befriended by Maeda Toshiie who employed him as a procurement agent, probably for military supplies. At that time Magobei abandoned samurai status and took the name Echizen'ya. Not long after Maeda moved to Kanazawa, Magobei, whose descendants and relatives became sake brewers, pawn shop owners, and innkeepers, received an invitation to move to the city. A grant of land within the inner moats accompanied the invitation.[21] Later, Echizen'ya received additional grants outside the castle complex and eventually held the astonishing sum of more than four thousand square meters of land, about what a samurai with a fief of 6,000 *koku* would receive for his urban residence.[22]

Like Echizen'ya, Hiranoya Hansuke originally lived in the Osaka area. He also was raised as a *bushi* but later became a merchant and supplied goods to Toshiie on a contract basis. When Toshiie transferred to Kanazawa, he invited Hansuke to the city and offered him residential land near Echizen'ya.[23]

In one documented instance, the daimyo government gave the Echizen'ya and Hiranoya families land of their own choosing within the *chōnin* sections of the castle town. After two devastating fires in 1631 and 1635, the government carried out a general reorganization of the city, part of which involved resettling the merchants and many of the samurai who lived within the castle complex. Interestingly enough, although the bureaucracy unilaterally decided where the samurai were to be relocated, they conferred with individual merchants in order to seek out their opinions. The family histories record with some measure of pride that the official in charge of planning the relocations, Takada Keian, showed Echizen'ya and Hiranoya a confidentially prepared map and allowed them to select the lots they wanted for their individual residences. The Echizen'ya family moved to a merchant ward to the west of the castle, while Hiranoya chose a site along the network of roads between the castle and the Asano River.[24]

The artisans who were invited to Kanazawa by the daimyo typically received land grants clustered according to occupation. Carpenters, coopers, and swordsmiths, whose importance to castle town construction and military preparedness is obvious, are cases in point. In 1584 and again in 1594, Toshiie utilized land grants as a means of attracting groups of carpenters to Kanazawa. Individual plots measured some seven by eighteen meters and were situated near the castle complex. Not far distant were Okemachi (Coopers' Ward) and Kajimachi (Smiths' Ward), the areas granted to the coopers and swordsmiths who arrived about the same time.

The domain was less generous in its approach toward the artisan groups, however, than toward the privileged merchants. The artisan land grants were considerably smaller than those given to the chartered merchants, and it seems that the domain government, not the artisans themselves, decided the location of the grants. The grouping together of persons engaged in the same craft was common in other castle towns as well, and Japanese historians have consistently cited such examples as evidence that daimyo arbitrarily determined all residential land use patterns in order to extend their administrative control more fully over the urban dwellers. But other reasons help to explain why the artisans themselves favored such an arrangement. Since even the privileged merchants sold their goods to samurai and commoners as well as to the daimyo, almost all merchants found it advantageous to live in scattered locations around the city in order to be close to their customers. Some artisans were frequently employed on a group basis, however. They often found it more convenient to live together in the same ward, so that their representatives could more easily inform them of employment opportunities and coordinate work schedules. Moreover, whereas merchants came to Kanazawa as individuals, many of the artisans, such as the carpenters, had organized themselves into groups before their migration to the city and may have wished to stay together upon their arrival. It is interesting to note that after the 1630s, when much of the business from the government dried up, some swordsmiths turned to making household utensils, such as pots and pans. At that time, they moved to scattered locations in the city, where they would be closer to customers and able to do a larger volume of business. That the domain government did not attempt to restrict this intraurban migration suggests an element of voluntarism in the earlier clustering of residences by occupation.[25]

In addition to the few hundred privileged merchants and artisans invited by the daimyo, thousands of ordinary persons who would eventually constitute a rather large commoner middle class, middle class at least in terms of economic prosperity, flocked into Kanazawa in the late sixteenth and opening decades of the seventeenth century to take advantage of new commercial opportunities. Many of the early arrivals moved into the area between the two rivers and built homes on either side of the numerous roads which ran through the city. Examples of this pattern of settlement were the new urban wards (*machi*), perhaps a dozen in all, which sprang up before 1600 along the roads to the north of the castle. Four—Yasuechō, Fukuromachi, Imamachi, and Jukkenmachi—are noted on map 6. There are no extant documents which would indicate that these wards were created by government direction. Rather, it would seem that more natural economic conditions accounted for their emergence, since these wards grew up near major population concentrations and along heavily traveled streets, locations where the new merchants were assured a large volume of potential customers. Indeed, documents from a later period indicate that some of the merchants who settled here became rather prosperous.[26]

As the area between the rivers and close to the castle began to fill up, merchants and artisans built shops and homes along the major roadways which led out of the city and on rural land on the fringes of the expanding castle town, giving the city what Japanese scholars call a "starfish" appearance. Merchants moved into the area about half a kilometer or so to the south of the castle, for example. Some years later the domain government responded to this action by officially incorporating the area, known as Saigawa-aramachi, into the city and placing its residents under the jurisdiction of Kanazawa's City Magistrates (*machi-bugyō*).[27]

More to the northeast, but still between the two rivers, merchant and artisan housing sprang up along the road which ran off toward the southeast. Originally this had been agricultural land, containing hundreds of farming households, but after the merchants and artisans moved in, the domain also shifted this area to the jurisdiction of the City Magistrates. An early document gives some of the flavor of the area's growth:

> The heart of this area was a village . . . which produced a thousand *koku* of rice. . . . There were extensive fields here and they grew fodder for horses and cattle, of which there were many. . . . After Toshiie's arrival, some retainers were settled here, and merchants and artisans also moved in. Daily the population grew larger. . . . There were numerous businesses, such as sake shops and stalls selling foodstuffs and snacks. . . . Vegetables too were sold. All of the farmers who lived in the higher, mountainous areas would use the road which passed through here and many would purchase here their daily necessities, such as salt and miso. . . . It really was a part of the city of Kanefu [Kanazawa].[28]

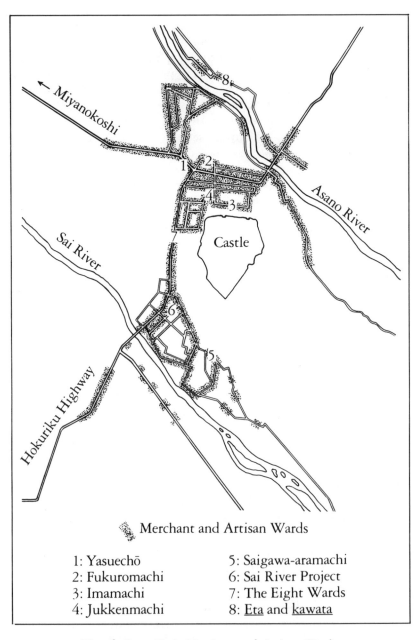

Merchant and Artisan Wards

1: Yasuechō   5: Saigawa-aramachi
2: Fukuromachi   6: Sai River Project
3: Imamachi   7: The Eight Wards
4: Jukkenmachi   8: Eta and kawata

Map 6: Some Early Merchant and Artisan Wards

A similar phenomenon occurred on the opposite side of the town, where merchants and artisans established shops along the highway to the port of Miyanokoshi.[29]

Chōnin housing also sprawled across the Sai and Asano rivers, extending the city in a north-south direction. Even before the temples were moved there in 1616, merchants and artisans lived on the southern bank of the Sai River, and all during the Tokugawa period commoner housing remained sprinkled throughout the Teramachi area. Merchant shops, many offering goods to travelers, lined the nearby Hokuriku highway. Similarly, merchant shops sprang up across the Asano, on the northern extension of the road. Some of these specialized in *ame,* a rice-jelly candy, which they sold both to travelers and to those making visits to the nearby Kannon shrine and temple complex.[30]

The emergence of these middle class areas of merchant and artisan housing constituted spontaneous, "wildcat" growth. Government officials did not, during the early period, attempt to restrict urban expansion. On the contrary, the Maeda were willing to interfere with agricultural production—the primary source of daimyo tax revenues—and to invest considerable capital expenditures in order to provide an environment which would attract merchants and artisans to their castle town. The government, for instance, relocated entire agricultural villages in order to accommodate merchant and artisan housing. As early as 1596, the government moved the villages of Yasujima and Shimeno, which had been situated along the northern bank of the Sai River opposite what later became Teramachi, to sites upriver. Between the years 1583 and 1630, the Maeda resettled the residents of more than a dozen villages on the fringes of the growing city in order to encourage *chōnin* settlement. Several of these villages are shown on map 7.[31]

The Sai River project of the 1610s provides a further example of how the Maeda encouraged urban growth. Until that time, the Sai River flowed in two branches, the present-day main stream and a tributary which swept past the southwest corner of the castle. Thus, the area between the castle and the Sai River bridge had been largely unfit for residential use until Toshitsune undertook a large-scale construction project to divert the secondary branch into the main stream. The old riverbed was then filled in and four new wards opened up to commoner settlement. During the Genna period (1615–24) some influential chartered merchants, such as the Kōrinbō family (medicines), Ikedaya Chōemon (rice warehousing), and Dōjiriya Saburōemon (*mochi* rice cakes), lived there. But the bulk of the new residents were men and women who became part of the city's emerging commoner middle class.[32]

The case of the Eight Wards (*hachi-machi*), the commoner wards which had come into existence before Maeda Toshiie's arrival, illustrates another

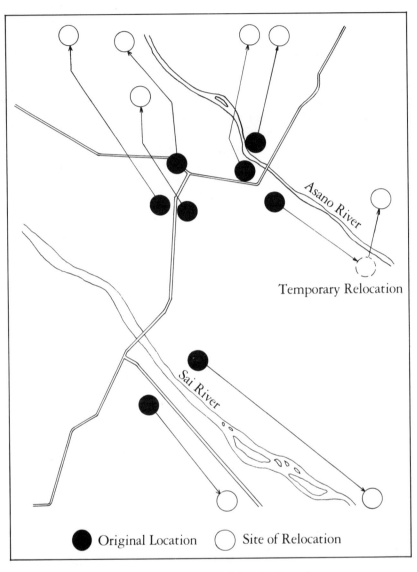

Temporary Relocation

Asano River

Sai River

Original Location   Site of Relocation

Map 7: Villages Relocated by the Domain

facet of daimyo-merchant relations and its impact upon castle town mor-
phology. Before 1583, the Eight Wards had grown up alongside the
fortifications and administrative headquarters of the Honganji sect. When
the Maeda arrived, they left those areas essentially untouched, despite
what would seem to have been a need for additional land for castle
expansion. The reason seems clear. Those wards, adjacent to the castle and
at the heart of the emerging castle town, represented some of the most
desirable merchant land in the city.[33] Even before 1583, important
tradesmen such as Yamazaki Shinshirō and Hirooka Yozō, who dealt in a
malted rice used to manufacture sake and soy sauce, had shops in the area.
Later, many middle-class merchants moved into those wards, and a number of the chartered merchants received grants of land there, including
Kanaya Hikoshirō (lighting supplies) and Noguchi Kurōbe (tatami floor
matting).[34]

Kanazawa also came to contain its share of poorer merchants and artisans whose places of residence reflected their impoverished circumstances. This strata of *chōnin* often settled at the base of Mount Utatsu, far
from the commercial heart of the city, or along the Asano River, on land
subject to periodic flooding. Many of these people had first migrated to
Kanazawa to work as contract servants for samurai or wealthy merchant
families, and when their contracts expired, they decided to stay in the
city. Some became day-laborers. Others, with little or no training in the
more skilled crafts, supported themselves by engaging in simpler trades,
such as making ramie-fiber hats and raincoats for sale to the urban
market.[35]

Small subcommunities of outcasts (*senmin*) resided in and around Kanazawa and can be considered as part of the city's "lower classes." Before
1583 one group of outcasts—a group usually referred to as *eta*—had lived
in one of the Eight Wards next to what would become the northwestern
walls of the Maeda castle, although it was actually the edge of the
pre-1583 town. Soon after his arrival, Toshiie moved this group of *eta*,
who stripped hides from animal carcasses and tanned them into leather, to
the far side of the Asano River.[36]

A second group of outcasts was often called *kawata*, although sometimes they were lumped together with the tanners under the more general
name of *eta*. The *kawata* used the tanned leather from the *eta* to make tools
and equipment for samurai, such as saddles, harnesses, and bindings for
armor. Toshinaga had actually invited two of these men, and possibly
more, to Kanazawa in 1609. Upon their arrival he guaranteed government orders for their products and granted them residential land.[37] Given
the rather heavy demand for military products made from leather during
the late sixteenth and early seventeenth centuries, it is not suprising that
the leather workers received favorable economic treatment from the
Maeda. However, the location of their residences indicates that these men

were victims of various discriminatory pressures, even at this time when
their services were most in demand. The land grants were situated along
the northern bank of the Asano, well away from residences of samurai and
the more well-to-do townspeople. In fact, the *kawata* were actually placed
under the administrative jurisdiction of the Rural Magistrates, and thus
were not even officially part of the city, although their residences adjoined
urban wards and their principal economic and social contacts were with
residents of Kanazawa.

There is no denying that government directives exerted a profound
influence upon the use of space in the emerging castle town, as seen in the
location of the castle, religious institutions, and samurai residences. On
the other hand, the Maeda daimyo clearly had no master blueprint which
dictated all aspects of the urban layout. Rather, the majority of the
commoner residential wards developed unfettered by government restrictions, and in direct response to the overall social and economic
growth of the city. Thus, large areas underwent what was essentially
organic growth, in that the arriving townspeople also lacked any precon-
ceived plan concerning the overall use of urban space. Over time, the
domain government was compelled to react to the enormous influx of
merchants and artisans, and one of their responses was to designate as
urban wards those previously vacant areas, such as Saigawa-aramachi,
where the newcomers had already settled. A second method was to move
farming villages from places where merchant and artisan residences had
become proportionately high, thus officially recognizing the development
of these new wards and at the same time making additional land available
to townspeople. Because the merchants and artisans who arrived uninvited
generally settled where they pleased, that is, wherever it made economic
and social sense for them to do so, they did much to determine the
eventual size and physical arrangement of the emerging castle town.

ECONOMIC DEVELOPMENT AND
THE COMMERCIAL CLASSES

The various Maeda daimyo shared with Louis XIV and Peter the Great the
belief that an economically vital capital city would enhance their security
and their prestige as rulers. Consequently, between 1583 and 1630, the
Maeda government put into effect a set of policies that encouraged commercial activity and contributed to the economic development of the
castle town of Kanazawa. Perhaps the most obvious example concerned
the building projects of the 1610s, with their enormous requirements of
manpower and material. The cash outlays associated with the expansion of
the castle, the construction and transfer of religious institutions, and
undertakings such as the Sai River project generated a great deal of urban

economic growth. In addition, the government's requirement that samurai establish residences in Kanazawa also had important consequences for the building trades. Since many samurai residences had separate outbuildings and dormitories to house rear vassals, it is likely that several thousand structures were put up during this single decade alone. It is impossible to measure with exact certainty the economic impact of this building boom, but the example of the reconstruction of Osaka castle following the sieges of 1614–15 may suggest its possible magnitude.[38] At Osaka, total project expenses may have amounted to an annual equivalent of 260,000 *koku* of rice, enough to support a population base of over 100,000 people. In Kanazawa, the situation differed somewhat. The amount of construction activity, for instance, was undoubtedly less and was spread out over a long period of time. Also, in Kanazawa a portion of the labor requirements came in the form of corvée levies. Still, a tremendous amount of wealth was pumped into the castle town's economy during the 1610s, and the construction workers' wages alone would have stimulated, in turn, other sorts of commercial activity.

The domain government took additional direct measures to promote commercial activity. One factor hindering trade in late medieval Japan had been that traders and manufacturers in various regions of the country used different systems of weights and measures. The size of the standard bolt of silk cloth produced in Kaga, for instance, was somewhat smaller than that of the Kyoto-Osaka region, and the lack of uniformity complicated efforts to sell the Kaga product in that large consumption center. The Maeda were determined to encourage sufficient production of silk cloth both to satisfy needs within their own domain and to earn, through taxes on exports, case revenues which could be used to purchase products not available locally. Consequently, in 1598 the domain decreed that bolts of silk cloth conform to the standard size in Kyoto and Osaka. Similar ordinances brought the *masu,* a measurement of volume, into line with that used in the imperial capital.[39]

Similar confusion existed concerning coins, and from an early date the Maeda daimyo began to mint their own and to decree which coins could circulate in the Kanazawa area.[40] In addition, the domain established the Office of Currency Control (*ginza*) in 1591.[41] The first men to head this office were Yada Kazue and Gotō Shōzaburō, both samurai who had been invited from Kyoto. The office oversaw the domain's minting activities and inspected coins coming into the Kaga area in order to establish their value and to ferret out any counterfeit items.

Like the tsar in Saint Petersburg, the Maeda daimyo in Kanazawa encouraged the development of certain types of marketing activities within their castle town. The horse-traders' market, for instance, was an important periodic market, and domain ordinances established the date

and place of its operation.[42] Of more consequence to the general population were the fish and vegetable markets; in fact, the townspeople petitioned the government to have these established. One set of these markets
was located just north of the castle, near the bridge across the Asano River
(it was later moved to Ōmichō, slightly to the west); a second set, near the
Sai River bridge, was later amalgamated with the markets of Ōmichō.[43]

Another set of policies pursued by both Louis XIV and the Maeda
daimyo aimed at improving transportation facilities in order to promote
the flow of goods into urban markets. In the 1610s, the domain straight-
ened and repaired a twisting roadway which ran from the port of Miyanokoshi to the northwestern entrance of the castle town, thus speeding
deliveries of fresh fish and other foodstuffs to the city.[44] A few years later,
the government dug a canal between the Asano River and the ward named
Shimoyasuechō, to the northwest of the castle, in order to provide additional docking and warehouse facilities for barges coming upriver from the
port of Miyanokoshi.[45] Throughout the domain, the daimyo's government built new post roads or upgraded existing ones, such as the roads
connecting Kanazawa with both sides of the Noto peninsula.[46]

On the other hand, the domain occasionally pursued policies which
might have had a negative effect on certain commercial endeavors. These
included prohibitions against the cultivation of tobacco and periodic restrictions—usually issued during years of poor harvests—on sake brewing.[47] The reasons for this are understandable. Rice, in addition to being
the basic taxable revenue source, was still a crucial military provision, and
the domain feared that lands might be taken out of rice production and
given over to tobacco, or that too much of the rice crop might be diverted
into sake production. In these instances, the government had to decide
between competing priorities, and usually came down on the side of
restrictions, although it is unlikely that these hampered economic development to any significant degree.

On the whole, then, daimyo policies created a favorable economic
environment for the thousands of commoners migrating to Kanazawa.
Once in the city, the migrants opened shops and businesses that influenced the pace and direction of the city's economic development. Their
economic experiences also illustrate how daimyo policies interacted with
chōnin-initiated patterns of development to shape such aspects of economic
life as the nature of merchant-government relations and the internal structure of the merchant and artisan classes.

The elite among the townspeople, of course, were the chartered merchants and artisans mentioned earlier who received economic, social, and
political privileges from the government. In later years, their descendants
often wrote family histories, and the biographies of privileged merchants
and artisans contained therein offer many insights into the economic life
of Kanazawa in the years 1583 to 1630.

Musashiya Shōbei was a fairly typical chartered merchant, and many of his experiences paralleled those of Echizen'ya and Hiranoya.[48] In his youth Shōbei, a low-ranking *bushi* with the surname Ishiguro, lived in the Fushimi area. At some unknown time he abandoned his samurai status, took the name Musashiya, and began to supply goods to various daimyo on a contract basis. His first contact with Maeda Toshiie came in the 1570s, when Toshiie hired him to procure armor for Maeda troops. Toshiie was apparently satisfied with Shōbei's services, for when Toshiie became daimyo of Noto, he contracted with Musashiya to purchase rice in western Japan and ship it to Noto. Then, when Toshiie transferred to Kanazawa, he invited the Musashiya family to move to the castle town and sweetened the offer with guarantees of business and a grant of land. Further, the Musashiya family received permission to use as their family temple Hōenji, the family temple of the Maeda family itself. Interestingly enough, a later Maeda daimyo conferred samurai status on Shōbei's grandchild, Shōtarō, who reverted to using the family's previous surname, Ishiguro. The movement from merchant to samurai status was rather uncommon in Kanazawa, compared to other castle towns. What is more typical is Shōbei's earlier abandonment of the uncertainties of life as a *bushi* in favor of the more appealing economic opportunities available to a merchant. This shift is repeated in the life histories of almost all the chartered merchants and illustrates how status divisions, at least when it came to downward mobility, were still not rigid or unyielding in the early seventeenth century.

The experience of Kanaya family illustrates the way in which important merchant families were able to translate their new economic influence into political and social privileges. Nomura Hachirōzaemon was a low-ranking samurai in the service of Maeda Toshiie and sometime after 1583 ordered his son to become a merchant. This son, who took the name Kanaya Hikoshirō (he was also known as Rōsokuya), obtained a charter to supply lighting oil and gunpowder to the daimyo and received a plot of residential land near the inner moats. In 1604, Toshinaga excused him from paying city taxes and granted him a permanent exemption on all port taxes for the ten ships which he used in his business, privileges which were passed on to Kanaya's descendants. In 1620, a Kanaya became one of the first townspeople appointed to serve as head of the important Office of Currency Control. From its inception in 1591, this office was staffed by samurai appointees, but following some irregularities and allegations of corruption in the late 1610s the domain government decided to appoint to it merchants who were knowledgeable about coinage evaluations and currency transactions. Kanaya family members were also frequently named to the post of City Elder (*machidoshiyori*), the commoner assistant to the City Magistrates (*machi-bugyō*). The family became part of the city's merchant social elite, and, in 1627, Hikoshirō received permission to wear a sword and to use the surname Misu. The Kanaya family head often exchanged gifts of tea and fish with the daimyo, and he journeyed up to the castle each New Year's for an audience with the domain's ruler. A high point in the family's early history came when Gyokusen'in, the wife of Toshinaga, arranged for the daughter of one of her maids to marry the heir to the Kanaya family headship.[49]

The story of the Hiranoya family, who were offered the opportunity to choose their own residential site in the 1630s, played on the same themes. In addition to that residence, the family received business orders from the daimyo and tax exemptions. Members of the family also served in the Office of Currency Control and as City Elders, and enjoyed a close relationship with the Maeda daimyo. The Hiranoya experience shows how one could capitalize on an initial relationship to acquire further business opportunities. After Hiranoya Hansuke give up *bushi* status and moved to Kanazawa as a merchant, he was employed by the domain as a contractor for some work on the castle and in 1601 actually supervised the *bushi* foremen who directed the construction workers. His son, also named Hansuke, received support from Toshitsune when he opened an inn which catered to persons on official government business. This second-generation Hansuke, along with Echizen'ya Magobei and Echizen'ya Jirōbei, was appointed as trustee of a fund established by the domain for Hōenji temple. In 1618, the domain decided to provide for the construction and perpetual maintenance of a special worship hall at Hōenji in honor of Kaga samurai who had died in the attacks on Osaka castle in 1614 and 1615. The government entrusted the sum of one hundred *koku* of rice to the three merchants and instructed them to lend it out to other merchants at an annual interest rate of forty percent. Three-quarters of the interest payments (thirty *koku*) were to be turned over to Hōenji, while the merchants were to keep the remaining ten *koku* to cover their costs and profit margin. If we accept the historian's general rule-of-thumb that 1.8 *koku* of rice were sufficient to cover all the living costs of one person for one year, a profit of nearly three *koku* each was handsome indeed, especially when the government guaranteed its help in collecting any bad debts.[50]

The interesting story of Tōfuya Taemon shows how the daimyo government would occasionally enforce monopoly rights for some of the privileged merchants. This man had originally been of samurai status and was a member of the invasion force sent to Korea in the early 1590s. There he learned to make tofu, the solidified bean curd that even today serves as a major source of protein in the Japanese diet. After he returned to Kanazawa, Taemon abandoned samurai status and opened a shop making and selling tofu. Although tofu apparently has a long history in Japan, Tōfuya family documents claim that Taemon was the first to produce it in the Kaga area. His tofu quickly won popularity with the city's residents and the Maeda considered it an important military provision. The daimyo designated Tōfuya as a *goyō shonin*, a purveyor to the daimyo, and extended to him a grant of residential land. In 1605 and again in 1607, the government erected signboards throughout the city stating that while innkeepers could make small amounts of tofu to sell to their customers, private persons were prohibited from selling bean curd.[51]

There were other chartered merchants who dealt in nonmilitary supplies and resided in Kanazawa even before receiving their charters. The warrior Kōrinbō, for instance, wandered the Hokuriku area for eight years as a masterless samurai (*rōnin*) following his lord's death in 1572. By 1580 he had finally decided that the warrior's lot was not for him, and took up life as a merchant in Oyama Gobō. The family lived in obscurity until Kōrinbō concocted a new eye medicine and presented some to Toshiie, who still suffered from the wound he had recieved in 1556. This potion cured the daimyo's troubles, and he immediately named Kōrinbō as a chartered merchant and provided him with a yearly stipend, although he did not include a grant of residential land. The Kōrinbō family possessed considerable political skills, however, and family headmen frequently served as City Elders and in the Office of Currency Control throughout the Tokugawa period.[52]

The Kashiya family of confectioners illustrates how deep the service ties between chartered merchants and the Maeda family could become. Long-time residents of the city, the Kashiya family became chartered merchants in the early 1600s after Toshitsune's wife, Tentokuin, sampled some of their candies and cakes. Although he apparently received neither a stipend nor tax exemptions, Kashiya was accorded a grant of new residential land. After searching throughout the castle town, Kashiya discovered a site in Bakurōmachi (Horse-Traders' Ward) on the northern side of the castle where he felt the water was especially suited for his baking needs. What is most remarkable about the Kashiya family is their commitment of service to the Maeda family. After Tentokuin died in 1622, the family showed its respect and devotion by sending cakes to the grave site monthly for thirty-six years. They sent cakes to Toshinaga when he retired in 1605, to Toshitsune's grave monthly for seven years after his death in 1658 and to yearly memorial services thereafter, and to every daimyo when he left on journeys to Edo and again when he returned. And so it went throughout the Tokugawa period. There was hardly an auspicious occasion or solemn memorial service that was not graced by a Kashiya confection. The second-generation family head even turned the Kanazawa shop over to his brother and lived at the Maeda residence in Edo for eight years in the 1640s so that the Maeda family might not lack for his tasty creations.[53]

The Kamiya family, however, most clearly exemplified the warm, personal nature of relations between daimyo and chartered merchants

during the 1583 to 1630 period. To read the family history is to become
weighted down by a liturgy of gift-giving. Toshiie presented the Kamiya
family with small pine trees for their garden, and told Kamiya exactly
where he should plant them. When Toshiie had his court rank raised in
1597, a Kamiya traveled all the way to Kyoto to pay his respects and to
offer gifts. A Kamiya served as a quartermaster when Toshinaga prepared
for the Sekigahara campaign, and after the final battles Toshinaga invited
him to the castle for a noh performance and gave him elegant silk garments. The Kamiya family sent a flood of gifts—at New Year's, when the
castle was repaired, for memorial services, when the daimyo traveled to
Edo, and when he returned. But the Maeda reciprocated with presents,
and business opportunities, and those special, envy-creating invitations to
the castle. When Toshinaga's mother Hōshun'in returned from Edo,
where she had been serving as a hostage, Kamiya was invited for a welcoming dinner.[54]

Artisans invited to Kanazawa by the Maeda received somewhat similar
treatment. The history of the carpenters is illustrative.[55] When these fifty
families arrived in the late sixteenth century, Toshiie provided them with
residences close to the castle and exempted them from paying taxes on
that property. These carpenters received more business opportunities from
the domain than perhaps any other artisan group. They did most of the
construction work on Kanazawa castle in the 1590s and early 1600s, a
contingent traveled to Kyushu at the time of the Korean invasion, and
some journeyed to Osaka to assist in the engineering projects associated
with the siege of Osaka castle in 1614–15. The conflagrations that periodically swept through Kanazawa and destroyed parts of the castle and the
office buildings, as well as the fires at the Maeda family mansion in Edo,
kept them in constant employment all through the Tokugawa period.

In the early 1590s, Toshiie appointed one of the carpenters, a man
named Rokusuke, to the post of Carpenter Liaison Agent (*daiku-kimoiri*).
In this capacity, Rokusuke's principal responsibility was to pass on carpenter wishes or complaints to the government and to relay domain
directives to his fellow tradesmen. Such appointments were common
among artisan groups in Kanazawa and other castle towns. Japanese historians usually argue that the creation of such offices represented an attempt
by the daimyo to more fully extend their governing authority over artisan
groups since Liaison Agents were charged with ensuring that their fellow
craftsmen complied with government proclamations concerning working
conditions. Such proclamations in Kanazawa, for example, specified
working hours (carpenters had to appear on the job site by sunrise),
established wage scales, and set the amount of sick-pay due to workers
who fell ill while working on domain construction projects.[56] The post of
Liaison Agent, however, was something more than simply a new device

for expanding the political authority of the daimyo. Many of Rokusuke's duties were related to working conditions only and were designed to ensure the completion of construction projects in a manner satisfactory to both government and the carpenters. When the government planned a construction project, for instance, it informed Rokusuke, who then met with the carpenter group and decided the actual hirings and job assignments. Consequently, the carpenters themselves were able to distribute the work load to suit their own desires. Similarly, if the carpenters had a complaint about wages or work hours, Rokusuke would present their case to the appropriate office. Finally, since, as noted above, the carpenters had organized themselves as a group with Rokusuke as their leader-spokesman even before they moved to Kanazawa, his appointment as Liaison Agent may have been simply the formal recognition of already existing duties. To view the appointment of the Liaison Agents solely as an effort to broaden daimyo political authority, then, glosses over some of the complexities of the issue. The government–Liaison Agent–tradesman structure meshed as much with the needs of the craftsmen as with those of domain governments.

Like the carpenters, swordsmiths received grants of land when they were invited to Kanazawa.[57] Some also received stipends, probably nominal sums, and all seem to have been busy with orders from the domain government and individual samurai. Toshitsune, for instance, once placed an order with seven swordsmiths for five long swords and 650 lances (*yari*). Kiyomitsu Shichiemon made swords for both Toshinaga and Toshitsune, once receiving a single order from Toshinaga for twenty long swords. Since one sword of superior quality could cost the equivalent of more than a *koku* of rice in wages alone (with the buyer paying an additional fee to cover the cost of materials), these were very sizable orders.

Some artisans were invited to Kanazawa on an individual basis. In the late 1590s, for instance, Kon'ya Shirōzaemon accepted an invitation to move to Kanazawa and a guaranteed monopoly on the dyeing of all government clothing purchases.[58] Apparently this was a large volume of business, for the daimyo periodically instructed Kon'ya to farm out part of the work whenever a backlog of orders built up. After Shirōzaemon died, his son Magojirō took over the family business. The family history records that when Toshinaga retired to nearby Takaoka in 1605, he took Magojirō with him and, according to the family history, granted him several thousand square meters of land to use for his shops and residence. That may be somewhat of a family fiction, however, since Kon'ya lived on a much more modest site when he returned to Kanazawa following Toshinaga's death. Still, his business continued to prosper, and Magojirō was appointed Dyer Liaison Agent (*kon'ya-gashira*), a position probably equivalent to Rokusuke's as Carpenter Liaison Agent.

The chartered merchants and artisans constituted an upper layer of elite townspeople. More precisely, it was a double layer, since the artisans were never able to acquire all of the economic, political, and social privileges that the merchants obtained. Artisans, on the whole, received considerably smaller land grants, and they did not have the freedom of a Hiranoya, an Echizen'ya, or a Kashiya in selecting the locations. The Liaison Agent position was neither as powerful nor as prestigious as City Elder or head of the Office of Currency Control, positions monopolized by the chartered merchants. Nor did any of the artisans establish the kind of personal relationship with the daimyo that Kamiya and Kashiya so thoroughly enjoyed. There were also distinctions, of course, among the chartered merchants themselves. Kōrinbō, for example, never received all the economic privileges of a Kanaya or Hiranoya, but then the Kashiya family never achieved the multiplicity of political appointments that distinguished the Kōrinbō family. Still, their various social and political privileges, as well as their designation as purveyors to the daimyo, did set this body of merchants and artisans apart from other townspeople and secure their place at the apex of *chōnin* society.

In addition to the elite merchants and artisans, thousands of other persons migrated to Kanazawa without any guarantee of success and depended upon their own wits for survival. Unfortunately, those persons did not leave family histories. Nor do domain records tell us very much about them, since the government paid slight attention to their commercial activities during those early years. We do know that certain merchants, such as a Sakaya family who dealt in sake and lamp oil, were able to lay the basis of family fortunes which enabled their descendants to later compete with chartered merchants for posts in city administration.[59] The Dōgan'ya family of confectioners, who became locally famous for their unbaked sweet cakes (*namagashi*), also prospered.[60]

What is perhaps most significant about these commoners is that they made their livelihoods by supplying goods and services to the civilian population. As the commoner population of the city expanded, it began to generate its own consumption demands. Those requirements stimulated all kinds of business activities and sent new ripples of growth throughout the city's economy. While Rokusuke worked on government construction projects, for instance, other carpenters built and repaired merchant and artisan housing. Although Kashiya sold many of his creations, and Kōrinbō many of his potions, to the daimyo's family, other confectioners and druggists prospered by selling only to townspeople. In addition to Dōgan'ya, at least half a dozen sweet shops thrived in the city. Pharmacists also did a brisk business. The prosperity of the shops lends credence to the effectiveness of their cures, but the appellations attached to the medicine also had an undeniable allure: *shisetsu* (literally, purple snow) and *kibamanbyō* (a name that implies an all-purpose cure for senility and for the infirmities of older women).[61] Gradually, the garrison town economy was giving way to a web of commercial activity whose purpose was to supply the consumption demands of the civilian population.

Occasionally, we catch longer glimpses of how the arriving townspeople took advantage of the new economic opportunities open to them. As early as 1601 a certain Araya asked, and received, government permission to catch *ayu,* a troutlike fish, on four rivers close to Kanazawa. In exchange for this privilege, which constituted a monopoly right, Araya was assessed a yearly fee equivalent to approximately 4.3 *koku* of rice, and was instructed to take from the river and present to the daimyo any logs over 1.8 meters in length. This Araya was probably the head of a group of fishermen who sold the *ayu* in the castle town.[62] Another group of townspeople was equally enterprising. They roamed the mountain areas east of the city and collected wood and pine cones, important fuels for heating and cooking.[63] The description quoted earlier of the shops and markets along the roadway to the southeast of the castle illustrated how increasing consumption demands stimulated the growth of new merchant wards. An equally lively spot existed in the northwest, where a small bridge spanned the Asano. There, persons would gather and set up stalls to sell trinkets, cakes, and sake. Sometimes there would also be dancers, a place to enjoy a game of cards, or even a tent where customers could peep through a curtain to view a strip tease show (*nozokimi*). In the winter months, exotic animal products were available: otter, wild boar, and fur seals. Usually, it was said, the sellers would take their money and head directly for the sake stalls.[64]

Although wholesalers who possessed government-backed monopoly rights generally did not appear in Kanazawa until the late seventeenth century, such wholesalers were active in the fish business by the early 1600s. A look at their activities yields insights into both *chōnin* initiative and the ways in which merchant and government interests could dovetail. Several wholesalers (*ton'ya*) in Kanazawa had organized themselves into a group as early as 1599, and in that year requested the exclusive right to wholesale all fish sold in the city.[65] The government refused on that occasion, but it did extend official protection to this group not many years later. A 1627 ordinance addressed to the City Magistrates outlined operating procedures. The government agreed to pay the wholesalers a total of twenty *kanme* of silver (equal to the price of approximately four hundred *koku* of rice) per year for supplying fish to the Maeda family, although the wholesalers were required to rebate roughly twenty percent as an "appreciation fee." In addition, the wholesalers were held jointly responsible for paying an annual tax bill equal to approximately forty-three *koku* of rice. In exchange, they obtained the sole right to sell fish wholesale in Kanazawa. Further, the six men who represented the wholesale distributors set daily wholesale prices, and retailers were instructed to hold their markups to a maximum of twenty percent of the wholesale prices.[66] The mutual advantages of this regulation are obvious. The wholesalers received a virtual guarantee of business success. The Maeda daimyo on the other hand, were assured that a necessary foodstuff would flow into the city at reasonable price levels.

We know least of all about the persons who lived at the lowest end of the economic scale. Some men supported themselves by becoming peddlers. They crisscrossed the city hawking a wide variety of items: flowers, fruit, kitchen utensils, *tsujira* (slips of paper with prophecies about one's future), old clothing, goldfish, and "bricks" made from pine needles, which were burnt for heat. Other men eked out a living by collecting used paper and human waste for sale as fertilizer to nearby rural villages.[67] The artisans and merchants who huddled along the banks of the Asano River earned their livelihood through the manufacture and sale of low-cost, mass consumption goods such as umbrellas and straw sandles.

The absence of government documents regulating the activities of the non-privileged merchants and artisans suggests the degree to which commercial activity in Kanazawa evolved naturally, as a result of merchant and artisan enterprise. Moreover, even when regulation did occur, as in the case of Araya and the fish wholesalers, it was often a product of *chōnin* efforts to establish their own business enterprises; not a unilateral government action to impose control over business practices. It is also important to remember that by the 1620s perhaps as many as 40,000 commoners lived in Kanazawa. Only a small fraction of these, a few hundred at best, enjoyed economic privileges granted by the daimyo. Clearly, there were thousands of merchants and artisans, such as the firewood collectors and the peddlers, whose livelihood and success depended upon their own ingenuity and upon business from other townspeople. Viewed holistically, the economy of the castle town was not simply the economy of the daimyo and his retainers; rather, it satisfied a wide variety of consumption demands. It is at this level that urban commercial life developed most clearly in response to *chōnin*-based initiatives.

A RUDIMENTARY POLITICAL SYSTEM

The rapid growth of Kanazawa during the late sixteenth and early seventeenth centuries compelled the Maeda daimyo to grapple with the task of devising an effective system of urban political administration. This problem defied easy solution, however, and it was not until the middle of the seventeenth century, nearly seventy years after their arrival, that the Maeda ultimately brought to completion the administrative structure that was to serve as the basis of urban government in Kanazawa for the remainder of the Tokugawa period.

In its final form, city government in Kanazawa could be divided functionally into two principal components: one designed to rule the townspeople, and another to govern the samurai. Both became highly bureaucratic. In *chōnin* administration, a council composed of the daimyo's most important retainers decided general policy. Below this, two City Magistrates (*machi-bugyō*) executed those policies. To that end, the Magistrates supervised a City Office (*machi-kaisho*) that eventually included more than three hundred employees in nearly a hundred different job classifications. During the seventeenth century the system increasingly came to work according to fixed legal precepts. The domain government issued a vast quantity of codes and regulations which provided both the basic framework of civil and criminal law and also established the procedures by which administrators conducted the affairs of their office. In time, certain broad philosophical and ethical principles drawn from Neo-Confucian doctrine coalesced into a new theory of government and society which provided additional support for the legal and political order.

When looked at with historical hindsight, it is possible to see in the 1583 to 1630 period the initial developments that eventually resulted in the mature system of urban government. But, for a variety of reasons, this system was slow in developing. First of all, Toshiie and Toshinaga lacked any previous experience in governing a large city, and therefore they created many of the early administrative offices on a provisional basis. Duties were loosely defined and subject to frequent revision. Second, the matter of urban government was only one of the many problems confronting the Maeda at this time. They also had to design a system of rural administration, secure control over their own band of retainers, and fight for the military integrity of their domain. Third, the dramatic growth of the city's population gave rise to unanticipated problems. Laws that had seemed adequate when the city was smaller had to be revised as the population doubled, redoubled, and then doubled again in the fifty short years between 1583 and 1630. Consequently, the opening decades of Maeda rule represent a period of experimentation, a time when daimyo law was not fully expounded and when the Maeda relied on many informal mechanisms of control.

The administration of the samurai class illustrates some of these themes. By the early 1610s, almost all samurai had been withdrawn from the countryside to reside in Kanazawa. Between 1583 and 1630 the daimyo issued three separate codes regulating the samurai's urban life. A detailed examination of these codes, proclaimed in 1601, 1605, and 1612 (with a set of supplements issued in 1613), reveals that daimyo law was very limited in scope and intent during this early period. The government's chief concern was to preserve law and order and to establish procedures for the adjudication of disputes. The 1601 codes, for instance, forbade cliques; prohibited gambling and stipulated rewards for anyone who supplied information about violators; declared that retainers should not harbor thieves or ruffians among their rear vassals; announced punishments for anyone who did not appear on time for a hearing at the Office of Police and the Judiciary; and provided that all parties involved in violent quarrels were to be judged equally guilty, irrespective of who was at fault.[68]

The 1605 code, issued under Toshinaga's personal seal, prohibited the following:

> Walking on the streets at night
> Loitering on the streets
> Singing on the streets
> Playing the flute (shakuhachi)
> Street sumo
> Dancing on the streets
> Masking one's cheeks with a scarf[69]

These were all activities that could result in fighting and violence. Loitering (*tsujidachi no koto*) was actually a broad catchall term that included such behavior as calling out insults to passersby and cavorting with streetwalkers. The bans on singing, dancing, sumo, and playing the flute meant that samurai were not to engage in such activities, nor were they to gather and watch others who were doing so. The masking of one's cheeks by tying a head scarf around the lower part of one's face was a common method of concealing one's identity, and would-be criminals often disguised themselves in this manner.

The 1612 code and the 1613 supplements repeated the prohibitions against rowdyism in the streets. They also enjoined the samurai to shun "the women who walk the streets by night," and not to talk in "loud, boisterous voices" on the streets at any time. In addition, the codes decreed that all acts of violence had to be reported to the Office of Police and the Judiciary (*kujiba*) and further specified the procedures to be followed when a samurai was summoned to appear before that office. Warriors were instructed to check their long swords with the attendants at the entrance and to enter the court one at a time.[70]

The daimyo delegated a great deal of enforcement authority to many different levels of the samurai class. As described earlier, the Maeda had put into force an organization in which authority passed from daimyo to Senior Adviser to Commander to Unit Leader and finally to individual retainers. This hierarchy of command was designed to enable the daimyo to mobilze and deploy military personnel during the early years of constant warfare. After the move to Kanazawa, the Maeda simply added civil administrative functions to this system of command. The highest level of the samurai class was known collectively as the *hakka,* or Eight Houses (actually seven until 1690), and all held fiefs (later stipends) assessed at 10,000 *koku* or above. They served as Senior Advisers and military commanders during times of warfare, and staffed the top level of policy-making offices within domain civil government. They also bore responsibility for overseeing the activities of the next lower status group, the Commanders (*hitomochi*).[71] These Commanders, who held fiefs ranging from 1,000 to 14,000 *koku,* led troops in the field and received appointments to middle-level posts in civilian government. The first City Magistrates, for instance, came from this group. In addition, the Commanders were accountable for the civil conduct of persons under their command.

The example of Aoyama Shōkan can help to clarify this pattern of governance. This *hitomochi* samurai had a total of 130 rear vassal families under his direct supervision. They were divided into eight status units, each captained by a Unit Leader (*kumigashira*). The units ranged from Councilors (*karō*) to Supply Troops (*komono*), and each had a military and civil function. The Councilors served as Aoyama's lieutenants in time of warfare and helped to supervise the rear vassals in time of peace, while the *komono* became household servants in the city.[72]

It was the responsibility of Aoyama, who himself reported to a Senior Adviser, to ensure that his rear vassals obeyed the codes issued by the daimyo. If a rear vassal committed a crime involving violence, Aoyama was supposed to turn that man over to domain officials. In other cases, however, Aoyama himself could mete out punishment, subject to the final approval of the Office of Police and the Judiciary. In addition, each Unit Leader within the house band met with parties involved in a dispute and attempted to arrange a mutually agreeable settlement. If that proved impossible, Aoyama himself would enter the case. Only problems which could not be resolved at this lower level, or which involved physical violence, were turned over to the jurisdiction of the Office of Police and the Judiciary for a court settlement.

The samurai retainers did not always act in accordance with the law. One of the most sensational incidents of lawlessness involved an Ishiwara Tetsujinosuke. In 1610 the domain sentenced this minor *bushi* to death for his acts of violence in the castle town. Ishiwara's Unit Leader, however, refused to surrender custody of the man to domain officials, and instead gave Ishiwara money so that he could try to escape from the domain. After a dramatic chase through the night, domain officials caught up with Ishiwara at a border checkpoint and in a bloody fight took his head, which they presented to Toshinaga.[73] There were also several instances in which superior officers punished their subordinates without first consulting the Office of Police and the Judiciary. The fact that the domain frequently issued notices exhorting superior officers to seek such approval provides indirect evidence of such abuses.[74] Even as late as the 1670s, there were cases of retainers carrying out punishments before seeking authorization.[75]

The ordinances which applied to the merchants and artisans, like the samurai codes, were limited in scope and were primarily attempts, and somewhat unsophisticated ones at that, simply to eliminate activities that might lead to violence. These *chōnin* codes included prohibitions against wearing high wooden clogs or carrying swords (samurai perquisities), gambling, keeping dogs as pets, and spitting, urinating, or throwing garbage from the second floor of one's house.[76] Ordinances in the 1628 code repeated the article in the samurai code declaring that all parties involved in a violent quarrel be judged equally guilty. Another article in the same code stated that townspeople would be held responsible (that is, punished) for any insolent behavior toward samurai or persons visiting from outside the domain.[77] This article also reveals a certain arbitrary quality to daimyo law since the domain clearly was placing priority on the maintenance of law and order over any concern with moral justice in the abstract sense.

The emphasis on maintaining peace in the streets of Kanazawa is not surprising, however, since crime was epidemic in the early years of the seventeenth century. Indicative of the times were the periodic notices which decried increases in street crime, arson, and murder, and offered rewards, even to the accomplice, so long as he had "a change of heart" and supplied useful information. One typical signboard, not dissimilar to the wanted posters of the American West, went up in 1604 and stated that "On the night of the 13th of last month, a visiting merchant from the Kyoto-Osaka area was murdered and his body thrown into the moat. . . . Any person with information . . . should come forward. A reward of twenty gold coins is offered."[78]

Even more threatening to the general peace and security of the castle town were the gangs of *kabukimono,* that is, young *bushi* who dressed in outlandish clothing and, with swords dangling from their belts, swaggered through the streets, often looking for trouble. The 1605 ordinances against loitering and "street sumo" were directed primarily at this group. The original death sentence for Ishiwara Tetsujinosuke was ordered because of his violent acts in the city. In the aftermath of that incident, the domain rounded up and condemned to death more than sixty other *kabukimono* in Kanazawa and Takaoka, where Toshinaga had established his retirement residence. The Maeda government further underscored its intention to bring a measure of order to the domain's urban centers by announcing a schedule of fines for retainers who harbored *kabukimono* among their rear vassals.[79]

During the 1583 to 1630 period, we see the beginnings of an administrative apparatus specifically designed to handle *chōnin* affairs. The first recorded appointment of a City Magistrate, for instance, came in the 1590s when first Shinohara Ikkō and then Murai Bungo no Kami, two *hitomochi* class samurai, were chosen to oversee the affairs of the townspeople.[80] A few years later, the daimyo named a number of lower-ranking samurai to serve as the Magistrates' Constables (*machi-dōshin*) and Junior Assistants (*machi-gedai*) in order to assist the Magistrates.[81] But this administrative structure was still in the formative stage. The City Magistrates, for example, received dual appointment as Rural Magistrates. One of the chief concerns of Rural Magistrates at this time was to impose new taxing mechanisms, and a similar interest in urban taxation, rather than strictly a concern with political administration, may have prompted the first appointment of Magistrates in Kanazawa.[82] Moreover, the office of Junior Assistant was allowed to lapse after a few years and was not revived until later in the seventeenth century.[83] Finally, the functions of all three offices were only very hazily defined, and the Junior Assistants appointed in the middle of the seventeenth century did not know what duties their predecessors had performed.

Essentially, the Maeda daimyo relied heavily on *chōnin*, all of them chartered merchants, to handle the details of urban administration. In later years, the domain would give the title City Elder (*machidoshiyori*) to these men, place them under the administrative jurisdiction of the City Magistrates, and carefully define their duties and prerogatives. But in the early seventeenth century, urban administration was carried out in a more informal, ad hoc manner. Individual townsmen would be called to the castle to meet with the daimyo, or to the home of the chartered merchant Takeya Nihei, whose residence served for a time as a City Office, to confer with the City Magistrates about administrative problems.[84] The list of those invited to such meetings is familiar: names like Echizen'ya, Hiranoya, and Kamiya. Each of their family histories notes with pride that the daimyo sought their advice and help in managing the city.

Perhaps the most intriguing story of daimyo reliance on chartered merchants is that of Kitamuraya Hikoemon, who purveyed medicines to the Maeda family. When Toshiie was in Kyoto in the early 1590s he summoned Hikoemon there and inquired about affairs in Kanazawa. Tokugawa Ieyasu was also present at the meeting and asked Toshiie about the merchant. Toshiie replied, "He is a *machidoshiyori* in Kanazawa. He is a man of wisdom, and manages the affairs of the city." Ieyasu asked permission to employ Hikoemon in a similar capacity in Edo, and for generations thereafter the merchant and his descendants served as one of the three City Elders in the shogun's home city.[85]

Many important aspects of urban administration were delegated to townspeople. The office of Ward Representative (*machi-kimoiri*) and the

Groups of Ten Households (*jūningumi*) provide examples. The daimyo
began to appoint Ward Representatives from among influential townspeople beginning in the late sixteenth century. In 1605, there were ten
such appointees and more were added as the population expanded. The
government assigned those men to specific wards, where they witnessed
documents related to the buying and selling of houses, resolved disagreements concerning succession to family headship, settled disputes and
quarrels, reported census figures, investigated commodity prices, and
assisted in tax collection.[86]

Within each ward, households were organized into Groups of Ten
Households, although the number in any one unit might exceed that
number. The Groups of Ten Households were functional equivalents of
the Household Groups established in rural villages. In both cases, the
Groups represented surveillance units and reflected an effort by the
daimyo to extend his authority and laws over the commoner populace,
since members of each Group were supposed to report any unlawful
activity by their neighbors. But the Groups performed a number of
important civil functions as well. In Kanazawa they conducted conciliation talks in the case of commercial or land disputes and when quarrels
threatened neighborhood tranquillity. If no mutually satisfactory settlement could be reached, then the Ward Representative was called in for
another round of negotiations. Only if that failed did the dispute move up
the ladder for settlement by samurai officials within the City Office.[87]

One can note, at this time, certain themes in daimyo policy toward the
merchant community that indicate the balance between control and protection that became a constant factor in daimyo-commoner relations. For
example, many ordinances safeguarded merchant and artisan interests.
One clear example from the early period was the clause in the 1613 codes
which stipulated that the samurai would be presumed at fault in any
business dispute involving a samurai and a townsperson.[88] At that time
samurai households customarily paid merchants for purchased items on a
periodic basis, and disagreements about the amount due were not uncommon. Another problem was that very low-ranking rear vassals who worked
as kitchen servants and lived in dormitories on the master's residence did
the daily shopping for the master's entire household. The rear vassals
occasionally ordered items for their own personal use, but included those
items in the master's bill. This practice led many samurai to claim that
they had been charged for goods that they had never received. According
to the 1613 codes, the merchant's version of the bill was to be assumed
correct and payable, although the samurai could take the issue to the
Office of the Police and Judiciary if he believed he had enough evidence to
prove that the merchant was in error.

Another illustration emerges from the 1627 directive concerning fish wholesalers, which stipulated that retail prices be restricted to a twenty percent markup over the wholesale level. Retailers were also obligated to keep a daily record of sales and to submit the record monthly to city officials who would confirm that the price guidelines were being respected. This was deliberate price regulation with the obvious intent of assuring the residents of the castle town an adequate supply of a basic food commodity at reasonable prices.

The above is clear evidence that the townspeople and the Maeda daimyo shared certain mutual interests. It was to everyone's advantage to have a safe city and to solve commercial and neighborhood disputes. This was one reason that the Maeda could delegate administrative and judicial functions to the townspeople. Even after the reforms of the middle seventeenth century produced a more tightly and comprehensively governed city, the townspeople would continue to play an important role in the administrative process. As in the case of city planning, domain authorities had full rights of autocratic rule, but the body of shared interests between the authorities and the townspeople made for broad areas of compromise and cooperation.

A SPIRITED URBAN SOCIAL LIFE

Social life in early Kanazawa was an outgrowth of the times, a product of the dynamism and vigor that accompanied the early decades of city building. As the warfare of the late sixteenth century wound down, a gay and lighthearted feeling of exuberance swept across the city, infecting all who lived there as things new and different unfolded before them. Nowhere was this more clearly evident than in kabuki drama, immensely popular in Kanazawa in the 1610s and 1620s. The first performance of kabuki supposedly took place in Kyoto in the late sixteenth or early seventeenth century when a woman named Okuni performed some suggestive dances and skits near the Kamo river. Within a few years, Kanazawa's residents were enthusiastically greeting troupes of touring kabuki performers and were delighted to discover that most of the actresses had an equally exciting side profession. Unfortunately, gangsters often traveled with the troupes and outbreaks of trouble with Kanazawa's own young, adventurous elements were inevitable. When the violence reached new levels in 1611 and 1612, Toshitsune issued bans against the traveling players.[89]

But such prohibitions were unpopular and, once the violence died down, Toshitsune withdrew them. When Toshiie's widow Hōshun'in, who had been sent to Edo in 1599 as a hostage, returned to Kanazawa in 1614, Toshitsune himself sponsored a series of kabuki performances for her entertainment. At that time three daimyo ladies—Hōshun'in, Gyokusen'in (Toshinaga's widow), and Tentokuin (Toshitsune's wife)—

were living in the castle and competing in hosting parties, the entertainment often centering around kabuki performers especially invited for the occasion. "Every night the castle became a lively and cheerful place," reported one observer.[90]

Kabuki's popularity was infectious.[91] Gyokusen'in, her daughter in tow, often joined the crowds at the outdoor theaters set up along the Sai and Asano rivers. On several occasions she even invited some players back to the castle and showered them with gifts. When tales of such largesse reached Osaka and Kyoto, whole troupes immediately packed their bags and headed for Kanazawa. The most popular of those in the late 1610s was a group of thirty women performers. Some took deliberately provocative names such as Jūgoya, "The Fifteenth Night." To others, Kanazawa's faithful added the nicknames, Yōkihi and Rifujin, the Japanese pronunciation of the names of two legendary Chinese beauties, Yang Kuei-fei of the T'ang period and "the Lady Li," consort of the Han emperor Wu Ti. In their skits, the young women of the kabuki troupe performed both female and male roles. "Although they are really women," wrote one fan, "in clothing and deportment they are just like young males. In their performances, they mix dancing with short comic routines and are extremely entertaining." And they won the hearts of Kanazawa. Hundreds of townspeople and samurai swarmed to the theaters daily, despite stiff ticket prices. Devotees sent gifts of sake and cakes, and fan letters by the basket load. When the plays ended in the early afternoon, the actresses were usually seen boarding palanquins dispatched by the samurai and wealthy townsmen who had engaged their services for the evening. One samurai supposedly complained (or was he boasting?) that after just a few liaisons, one actress had cost him as much as he normally spent on a whole year of falconry. There were even some, whispered another observer, "who take their wives' silk kimono and give them to the actresses; but there is no need to repeat their names here."

Other entertainments also flourished in the first two decades of the seventeenth century. *Jōruri* (a form of ballad drama) and *ayatsuri* puppet and theatrical troupes played before large houses. Jugglers, acrobats, and many dancing troupes passed through the city—the most popular was Aburaya Yojirō's team of "spider dancers," a group of tightrope walkers and acrobats. The arrival in the early 1620s of a kabuki troupe composed exclusively of young men, many of whom were male prostitutes, sent new ripples of excitement across the city. More traditional sorts of prostitution thrived along the Asano River, to the north of the castle. On the opposite side of town were the "bathhouses," in reality brothels and houses of assignation, where one could hire a private room and engage the services of a "bath attendant" (*yūjo*). That area, noted one diarist, was not inferior to the entertainment sections in Edo, and was alive at night with the merrymaking of both samurai and townsmen.

The effervescence and unbridled gaiety of the early seventeenth century was never more intense than during the "Ise fever" of 1621.[92] From the sixteenth century on, periodic crazes swept Japan, and people from all walks of life gaily set out on pilgrimages to the shrine at Ise, on the peninsula southeast of Kyoto. The shrine visit itself was actually only one highlight in a long sequence of excited planning, drunken send-offs, adventures on the road, and a debilitating round of welcome-home parties. In 1621, such a craze hit Kanazawa, and even those who stayed home made the most of the long, warm summer days. It all began innocently enough in the early spring when groups of *chōnin* children began dancing through the streets to Shinmei shrine on the west bank of the Sai River (see map 5). Soon adults and minor *bushi* joined the children in the streets, and as the fever intensified, even high-level samurai became caught up in the excitement. Revelers—townspeople as well as all grades of samurai—nightly filled the streets between the castle and Shinmei shrine. By summer, women in the castle, including mistresses of the Maeda daimyo, were dressing in newly made kimonos and joining the throngs. One song popular that summer started, "The long ages of war are over, let's play, let's play; if there is no wind, there are no waves; the realm is at peace." To the men's refrain, "Should we provide for you a knightly horse, or would you prefer a royal palanquin?" the women replied, "We want neither a horse nor a palanquin," and all concluded with "Take the hand of the one you love, the realm is at peace under the emperor." One high-ranking samurai drew crowds with his imitation of a Chinese dancer, and Murai Hida no Kami, an important government figure, seemed always to be around outside of his office hours.

Kabuki and puppet plays reached new heights of popularity that summer. The daimyo provided funds to Shinmei shrine to erect stages and to pay performers. Other troupes spread out along the riverbanks, and sometimes it seemed as if the theaters overflowed with every shopkeeper and off-duty samurai in town. Joining the *chōnin* and *bushi* spectators were farmers from rural areas of the domain, drawn by the excitement touched off months earlier by the children of the townspeople.

By the 10th month, as the days shortened and the night air took on a chill, the gaiety began to wind down. Exhausted but happy, the people of Kanazawa smugly agreed that their own experience was equal to any tales they had heard about the famous festivals at the Sannō and Asakusa shrines in Edo.

A fondness for noh drama and *sadō,* or the tea ceremony, characterized an incipient elite culture in Kanazawa practiced by the Maeda daimyo. The early Maeda shared an enthusiasm for tea with other daimyo, and wealthy merchants of Kyoto and Osaka patronized the tea ceremony as well. In fact, Toshiie learned the rudiments of the tea ceremony from two famous masters, Sen no Rikyū and Oda Uraku, while he was in Fushimi in attendance on Hideyoshi in the early 1590s.[93] Toshinaga periodically entertained his chief retainers at Kanazawa castle, and Toshitsune was often the guest of the retired shogun, Tokugawa Hidetada (who was also Toshitsune's father-in-law), at tea ceremonies held in Edo.[94]

The Maeda daimyo also enjoyed noh drama. Toshiie's fondness here, too, seems to date from his stay in Fushimi when he attended many of the performances hosted by Toyotomi Hideyoshi. At one of those, Hideyoshi, Toshiie, and Tokugawa Ieyasu supposedly performed some of the comic interludes, or *kyōgen*. In the 9th month of 1593, Hideyoshi spent a night at the Maeda mansion in Kyoto and Toshiie arranged some noh performances for his enjoyment, with Toshiie himself acting a couple of roles. Later Maeda daimyo established a tradition of authorizing noh performances to commemorate favorable events. In 1600, for instance, Toshinaga had noh performed to celebrate the victory at Sekigahara and the award of new territory to Kaga domain. The performance was actually staged in Komatsu, but many samurai and townspeople from Kanazawa attended. In 1617, Toshitsune honored his infant son's first shrine visit to Kannon by providing funds for a noh production.[95]

Yet even at this elite level there was a certain blending of cultural tastes. Toshiie, for instance, periodically authorized noh performances which townspeople were free to attend, to be held on the banks of the Asano and at certain temples. Following the initial performance at Kannon in 1617, the Maeda daimyo annually, until 1869, presented funds to the shrine for noh performances to be held on the 1st and 2nd days of the 4th month. Some *chōnin* wards in the city also made contributions, and the townspeople attended the performances on the 2nd day.[96]

Like kabuki, the noh theater brought together the social classes in Kanazawa. During this early period, the samurai and townspeople shared many of the same cultural interests. They watched the same dancing groups, enjoyed the same puppet troupes, and patronized the same "bathhouses" along the banks of the Sai River. And, in the summer of 1621, they danced in the streets together.

These aspects of social life help us to recall that in many ways the years from 1583 to 1630 constituted only the formative period of Kanazawa's growth as a castle town. Urban political administration, for instance, remained somewhat provisional and makeshift, and the daimyo leaned heavily on informal mechanisms of governance. The more rigid status system that characterized later Tokugawa Japan had not yet fully matured, and social mobility was still possible. Elevation to samurai status as in the case of Musashiya Gonbei was not common in Kanazawa, but almost all of the privileged merchants claimed *bushi* origins. Likewise, the thousands of commoner migrants to the city came principally from rural households. Moreover, the violence of the early seventeenth century symbolized a society that was still relatively open and undergoing profound changes. The fighting at kabuki theaters in 1611 and 1612, the murders on the streets, and the trouble that came when *kabukimono* loitered on street corners illustrated the degree to which the Maeda daimyo were as yet unable to extend a full measure of police control over the urban population.

Certain problems hindered the city-building efforts of the Maeda daimyo. One was the explosive population expansion that took place during the years 1583 to 1630 as Kanazawa grew from a small community of a few thousand individuals to a major urban center of at least 50,000 persons. When one also considers that the urban mortality level was probably higher than the birth rate, and that numerous persons stayed in Kanazawa only a short time before returning to home villages or moving elsewhere, then it is safe to assume that an average of nearly a thousand migrants a year probably arrived in the city. The high level of migration relates to other issues, for so much movement and flux would complicate any attempt to develop an elaborate administrative system. Similarly, with this much migration, it is unlikely that a new government would be able to strictly control all the uses of urban space.

The Maeda daimyo also had to expend a great deal of energy simply surviving as daimyo, and this too interfered with their ambitions to create new urban institutions. Toshiie actually spent very little time in Noto or Kanazawa, living instead in the Kyoto area where he could stay close to his mentors, Oda Nobunaga and Toyotomi Hideyoshi, who could help him ensure the integrity of his territorial holdings. Toshinaga and his chief advisers spent time in the field in the mid-1580s and again in 1600, and were tied down for a time in the crisis of 1599. Despite generally more peaceful conditions, Toshitsune was in Osaka for the 1614–15 campaigns and after that journeyed often to Edo to solidify his relationship with the Tokugawa shogun.

These conditions would change over the course of the next half century. As the Maeda daimyo and their chief advisers settled more completely into their castle town home, they would turn their attention toward the problem of consolidating daimyo authority over the residents of the castle town. From this would flow a variety of changes. The chartered merchants and artisans would discover the impermanence of privilege, and the carefree gaiety evident in the summer of 1621 and in the popularity of kabuki would not survive the next phase of Kanazawa's development. The transformations of 1583 to 1630 had been profound and far-reaching, but more changes lay ahead. In 1670 the descendants of Chō and Yokoyama, Kamiya and Kōrinbō, would still live in Kanazawa. But they would lead very different lives from those of their forefathers, and Kanazawa would become a different kind of city.

THREE
THE YEARS OF
CONSOLIDATION, 1630–1670

In 1600 Tokugawa Ieyasu took a major step toward achieving national military hegemony when he defeated a number of his most serious rivals at the Battle of Sekigahara. Three years later, he assumed the position of shogun, and, as was the custom for the man who held this post, he began to accept pledges of submission from daimyo throughout the country. Ascension to this office symbolized Ieyasu's intention to become the effective national ruler in yet another way, for this was the post from which the Minamoto and Ashikaga families before him had ruled Japan. In 1605 Ieyasu officially retired and passed the title of shogun to his son Hidetada, thus assuring that the office would become hereditary within the Tokugawa family. Finally, in the battles of 1614 and 1615 at Osaka, Ieyasu eliminated any further military threat to his position, and the Tokugawa family stood supreme in Japan.

With their military position secure, the Tokugawa rulers took additional measures during the first half of the seventeenth century in order to more fully extend their authority over the country. These actions built on the achievements of Nobunaga and Hideyoshi, and eventually resulted in the creation of a new structure of national political authority. Historians later coined the term *baku-han* to describe this system, thus recognizing that it was composed of two elements, the shogunate (*bakufu*) and nearly 250 individual daimyo domains (*han*). As the name suggests, this early modern form of government was a unique blend of centralized and decentralized authority.

On the local level, daimyo governments enjoyed a certain degree of independence in the management of domain affairs. The daimyo, for instance, were free to decide the organizational structure of their bands of retainers. In addition, domain rulers decided the kinds and amounts of taxes that residents paid to domain coffers, issued any laws they deemed necessary and appropriate, captured and punished criminals, and maintained the domain's fighting forces.

In counterpoint to this local autonomy, the shogunate enacted numerous policies which centralized power in its own hands. The shogun, for instance, co-opted foreign policy prerogatives and assumed responsibility for national defense, thus becoming a kind of chief of state. Tokugawa policy also sought to isolate the daimyo from the emperor, the ultimate source of political legitimacy. On the one hand, the Tokugawa rulers provided the emperor and court nobles with sustenance lands and treated them with an outward show of respect. On the other hand, they made certain that the emperor would have no opportunity to participate actively in affairs of state. The shogunate built a castle, Nijō, near the imperial palace in Kyoto and garrisoned it with a large force. Tokugawa liaison officials controlled the emperor's appointment schedule and screened all messages and reports sent to him. In 1615, the shogunate issued a seventeen-clause code that delegated to its officials the right of prior consent over all high court appointments, regulated contact between the emperor and the great temples, and restricted the emperor essentially to literary and artistic pursuits.

The Tokugawa shogun employed similar tactics in their drive to bring major religious institutions under their domination. Outwardly, the Tokugawa were respectful. Yet in reality the shogunate subjected the religious institutions to various controls. During the middle ages, some temples had held proprietary rights to vast tracts of land. Then in the late sixteenth century Oda Nobunaga broke the military power of these temples, and, in time, the land holdings of temples and shrines became dependent on the approval of military lords. The Tokugawa continued this practice, and in the process dramatically reduced the amount of land held by religious bodies. Only a few received grants of 10,000 *koku* or more, equivalent to the holdings of the country's smallest daimyo.

In order to extend its control over the daimyo, The Tokugawa shogunate institutionalized many of the practices begun by Hideyoshi. All daimyo, for instance, held their lands through grants of investiture from the shogun. Moreover, during the early decades of the seventeenth century, the Tokugawa shogun often confiscated holdings or transferred daimyo to new domains. Although such actions became less frequent with the passage of time, only a few powerful daimyo such as the Maeda remained in one location throughout the entire Tokugawa period. Beyond this, each daimyo swore a personal oath of allegiance to the shogun. A public code (*buke shohatto*), issued in 1615 and amended in 1635, regulated the private conduct of daimyo, prohibited them from forming cliques, limited the size of domain military establishments, and specified that the shogunate's regulations be regarded as the supreme law of the country.

The most ingenious control device was known as the *sankin kōtai* (alternate attendance) system. The custom of personal attendance on one's superior and the submission of hostages as a symbol of loyalty had a long history in Japan and had become fairly common practice during the sixteenth century. Maeda Toshinaga, as noted earlier, had dispatched his mother to Edo to serve as a hostage following the crisis of 1599. The third Maeda daimyo, Toshitsune, became one of the first daimyo to journey to Edo on a periodic basis to pay his respects to the Tokugawa.[1] A decree issued by the shogunate in 1633 institutionalized the practice. From that date, daimyo were compelled to alternate their residence between Edo and their home domains, to build elaborate mansions in Edo, and to leave appropriate retinues, including their wives and children, in the shogun's city on a permanent basis. From the shogun's perspective, this system of alternate residence permitted the shogunate to maintain close surveillance over the daimyo and to keep them fully informed of all shogunal ordinances and demands.

The system of alternate residence, moreover, had a number of significant consequences concerning the exercise of authority by the daimyo within their own domains. Since the daimyo were now absent from their domains at least half of the time, they came to rely more and more on important retainers and the emerging domain bureaucracies to manage the affairs of their realms and their urban centers. Similarly, the close personal relationships which had characterized daimyo—chartered merchant relations began to dissolve under these new conditions.

Perhaps the most profound effect of the new system of alternate residence was the strain that it put on daimyo finances, especially when considered together with the occasional extraordinary levies made by the shogunate. The experience of the Maeda daimyo was fairly typical. Although details for the middle seventeenth century are not available, by the end of that century their journeys to Edo and the expenses associated with maintaining the nearly three thousand persons from Kaga who lived year-round in the Edo mansion often consumed at least one-third and sometimes as much as one-half of all annual domain expenditures.

The occasional special levies were also burdensome. The Tokugawa rulers demanded military assistance during the sieges of Osaka castle in 1614–15, and economic aid when they later rebuilt the castle as a shogunal stronghold. Additional assessments on the daimyo enabled the shogun to build the castles of Edo, Sunpu (Ieyasu's place of retirement, in modern Shizuoka), and Nijō in Kyoto. When fire damaged the Edo castle in 1636, 1657, and 1658, daimyo contributed to the cost of repairs. The shogunate also made fairly regular exactions for the construction of roads, bridges, and waterways.

These sorts of expenses contributed greatly to growing domain indebtedness. As early as 1635 ruling officials in Kaga domain resorted for the first time to what was called a *goyō* levy when they asked certain wealthy merchants such as Kamiya, Kanaya, and Echizen'ya to make special cash contributions to domain coffers.[2] From the middle of the seventeenth century the daimyo government promoted the development of new paddy fields (*shinden*) in order to expand the domain's revenue base. These efforts added more than 250,000 *koku* to Kaga's productive capacity between the years 1646 and 1711.[3] Despite this achievement, however, domain indebtedness continued to mount, and, by the end of the seventeenth century, annual domain expenses amounted to twelve to fifteen percent more than Kaga's yearly revenues. After nearly all of the potentially productive land had been brought under cultivation in the early eighteenth century, the Maeda daimyo turned to borrowing funds from wealthy merchants in Edo and Osaka. By the 1760s, the total of the outstanding loans probably amounted to more than twice the sum of all annual domain revenues, and by the next decade Kaga could not even keep up with the interest payments.[4]

Although such excessive deficit spending became most pronounced during the eighteenth century, the cash requirements dictated by the shogun's levies and the system of alternate residence did make themselves felt on Maeda policies within Kaga domain as early as the middle of the seventeenth century. The need for increased and predictable sources of revenue provided one of the primary reasons for implementing a set of rural reforms, known by the general name of *kaisakuhō*, which was carried out on a district (*gun*) by district basis during the decade of the 1650s. The reforms were three-pronged. First, the domain stripped the retainers of all remaining vestiges of authority over their own fiefs. From the 1650s on, retainers were no longer allowed to administer fiefs directly or to determine tax rates. Instead, they now received annual stipends drawn from domain granaries. Consequently, although domain registers continued to list a fief of record for direct retainers, in fact all administrative and taxing authority was exercised by officials within the domain bureaucracy. Second, during the late 1640s, the domain began to resurvey all paddy lands in order to clarify peasant holdings and to uncover any unregistered fields. Third, the domain government revised the procedures for assessing rural taxes. Prior to the 1650s, samurai fief holders, and domain representatives for lands whose revenues went directly into domain coffers, traveled through the rural villages each year, inspected the rice crop, and set the tax rate for each village in accordance with the projected yields for that year. Under the new system, the government announced an uniform tax rate for all paddy fields. Although the daimyo could change that rate whenever he so desired, the Maeda very rarely increased the rate that was set in the 1650s by more than a few percent.[5]

Although the creation of an uniform tax rate and the requirement that all tax proceeds be paid directly to the domain government did provide the domain with a more stable revenue base, the *kaisakuhō* reforms were inspired by other, more complex motivations as well. Placed in a broader context, the *kaisakuhō* reforms can be seen as one part of a larger set of policy initiatives undertaken during the years from 1630 to 1670. The objective of these programs was to bring to completion the process, begun in the late sixteenth century, of dividing society into broad status groupings and extending the formal and bureaucratic authority of government over each of the groups. The *kaisakuhō* reforms were the rural component of this program and represented a culmination of Maeda efforts to sever the personal relationships between fief-holding samurai and peasant villagers and to bring each status group under more comprehensive government control.

Toshiie and Toshinaga took the initial steps toward this objective in the late sixteenth century when they issued class separation edicts, conducted sword hunts, and surveyed land. The creation of the offices of Village Headman, Senior Village Headman, and Rural Magistrate further advanced the principle of direct daimyo rule. Later ordinances continued to chip away at vassal prerogatives. In 1615, for instance, the domain gave Rural Magistrates the power to investigate peasant complaints about fief holders, and a 1631 ordinance specified that fief holders who wished to increase the rate of land taxation should first seek the approval of the Rural Magistrates.[6] Now, in the 1650s, government officials eradicated all of the remaining personal bonds and replaced them with the more impartial and bureaucratic authority of domain government.

The imposition of the *kaisakuhō* reforms held certain advantages for the farming population, who were thereby saved from the arbitrary exactions of individual fief holders. These had largely stemmed from the growing financial problems of the samurai class. After the samurai settled in the castle town and began to participate in its commercial economy, they needed increased revenues. Signs of what would a century later become rather acute impoverishment among some members of the samurai class appeared in the early 1630s when the domain issued the first sets of frugality laws.[7] By the next decade the financial condition of some retainers had deteriorated to the point that the domain began advancing loans to them.[8] In response to the need for additional income, some fief holders raised taxes to unprecedented levels, and peasant complaints to the domain government became commonplace. By establishing a system of uniform tax rates, the *kaisakuhō* rural reforms freed the peasantry from the whims and needs of individual fief holders. Gone too after the implementation of the *kaisakuhō* reforms was the power of samurai to adjudicate civil or criminal wrongdoings within their fiefs. This practice had led to abuses and had become an additional source of peasant grievances. Instead, the peasants were now brought under the umbrella of the impartial law of daimyo government, law which applied to all rural villagers regardless of place of residence.

But the *kaisakuhō* rural reforms also had an adverse impact on some rural residents, and it is at this juncture that the relationship between the 1650s reforms and urbanization becomes most noticeable. Although many villagers escaped from the harsh and extremely high tax rates imposed by some fief holders, the documents indicate that the new uniform government rates were higher on the average for the entire domain than the old rates. Moreover, the surveys had uncovered some fields which farmers had previously managed to keep off tax rolls, and this discovery also increased the overall tax burden. The late 1650s and the early 1660s became a period of considerable suffering for certain elements of the farming population.

This period of distress was an exception to a century of generally increasing rural prosperity. Historians have documented the way in which new seeds, better tools, and the increased use of fertilizers helped to improve agricultural productivity throughout the seventeenth century. After the *kaisakuhō* reforms of the 1650s, the land taxes in most villages in Kaga domain remained fairly stable throughout the rest of the Tokugawa period.[9] Consequently, productivity increases, as well as the yields from formerly marginal fields brought under cultivation by individual farmers, accrued to the farmer. Indeed, signs of rural prosperity—new and better houses, improved diet, luxurious clothing—were readily visible in Kaga during the last third of the seventeenth century.

But the sudden increase in the tax burden during the 1650s made life precarious for some farmers on the lower end of the economic scale. Hard-pressed too were households with second and third sons if arrangements could not be made for these sons to be adopted by heirless neighbors. In more normal times, these sons might have stayed on at home, helping out with chores and being cared for by their eldest brother after he succeeded to the family headship. Now these less fortunate sons joined their poorer neighbors in seeking refuge in Kanazawa. During the 1650s and early 1660s, the physical area of the castle town increased dramatically, and the city's population topped the 100,000 mark.[10]

Just as the *kaisakuhō* reforms decisively separated samurai from peasant, new legal codes in Kanazawa attempted to draw clear lines between the samurai, on the one hand, and merchants and artisans on the other. Ordinances, for instance, defined the types of clothing appropriate for each status group. The ultimate result of these programs was the so-called system of "rule by status" (*mibunsei*), based on the four-class division of samurai, peasant, artisan, and merchant, although legislation usually referred to the merchants and artisans together simply as *chōnin*. To consolidate its authority over these groups, the government issued new laws that extended its involvement beyond the previous concern with merely maintaining law and order. It created new political offices and redefined the duties of existing ones, enforced new controls over certain commercial activities, and paid greater attention to the social activities of the city's residents.

In implementing these reform programs, the Maeda were duplicating what was happening in nearly all of the 250 domains throughout Japan during the middle seventeenth century. As daimyo extended more complete control over their holdings, and as they in turn were subjected to closer oversight by the shogunate, Japan entered the era known as the "Great Peace" (*taihei*). To be certain, outbreaks of domestic violence occurred throughout the Tokugawa period as urban and rural commoners alike protested instances of unjust administration or severe tax policies during periods of economic distress. But for nearly two hundred years, until the early nineteenth century, Japan was free from any foreign military threat and enjoyed a remarkable degree of domestic tranquillity.

In Kaga, the inauguration of the Great Peace meant that the Maeda no longer had to be as sensitive to the military security of their castle town. Consequently, domain government became less concerned with manipulating the use of urban space in accordance with defense needs. Similarly, a decline in daimyo and samurai reliance on the privileged merchants and artisans who supplied military equipment led to new policies which changed some aspects of economic life in the castle town. Desires for internal stability also transformed attitudes toward the wide open character of urban social life and resulted in new government controls over the theater and the entertainments associated with the bathhouses.

NEW NOTIONS OF URBAN PLANNING
AND THE REALITIES OF GROWTH

On the morning of the 14th day of the 4th month in 1631, a fire broke out in a merchant's home near the Sai River bridge. At first it spread through the commoner sections near the river, and then, driven by strong winds, the fire turned northward and burned through huge swatches of merchant and samurai housing before working its way into the castle itself. The day was not without its lighter moments. When Toshitsune and his son were fleeing from the castle, they stopped in front of the main gate, and each insisted that protocol required the other to proceed first. Finally, in exasperation Imaeda Minbu and Okumura Kawachi no Kami grabbed Toshitsune and dragged him to safety. By the time the fire had burned out, however, the tragedy had become all too real, for the conflagration destroyed well over a thousand homes in the castle town and large portions of the castle itself.[11]

In 1635 another major fire broke out, again to the south of the castle, and burned for two days before it was finally extinguished. Damage was even more widespread than in 1631, with thousands of homes lost. Sections of commoner housing closest to the castle were among those which suffered the most damage, and many major retainers were burned out.[12] Following these two fires, Toshitsune began to reconstruct, and then to reorganize, the castle town.

Following the 1631 fire, the government constructed a new canal, and this project recapitulated in part a concern with defense needs. The course of the canal implied a military purpose. It began upriver on the Sai and, once in the castle town, curled around the residences of major retainers before entering the castle precincts.[13] Moreover, the shogunate itself expressed concern about the canal. The retired shogun, Hidetada, was seriously ill, and the shogunate feared that his death might undermine the still fragile Tokugawa hegemony and result in open warfare among the daimyo. Consequently, when the shogunate found out about the canal and also learned that Toshitsune had formed a new, elite army corps, it sent several strongly worded messages to Kanazawa which implied further action unless Toshitsune could explain his behavior and motives. Beyond this, the rumors surrounding the fate of the head of construction, Itaya Hyōshirō, also suggest a military motive. Numerous seventeenth-century documents allege that this *chōnin*, who was hired because of his previous experience on similar projects, was put to death in order to keep the exact course of the canal a secret. This was only rumor, however, and an Itaya family history written some generations later stated that Hyōshirō retired to Komatsu after finishing the project and lived out his life in peace.[14] Moreover, Toshitsune claimed that the canal had no military significance. When the shogunate made inquiries about the canal, Toshitsune provided them with a written description of its course. He also dispatched his most trusted retainers to Edo to deliver apologies and to explain that the reason that the two recent fires in Kanazawa had been so destructive was lack of water at the right places to combat them. The new canal, the envoys insisted, was built simply to rectify that situation, and, they added, the new army corps was formed merely in order to reward those Maeda retainers who had been sent to take part in the earlier campaigns at Osaka castle.[15]

The canal was the last major domain construction project of the seventeenth century. The mixed civil and military motives behind its construction marked the early 1630s as a transitional period when new conditions of peace were overtaking the older era of military insecurity. After the

canal was completed, Toshitsune's government carried out a major reorganization of the castle town. As that reorganization proceeded over the
course of the next two decades, it clearly revealed new domain concepts
concerning the use of urban space, concepts that were closely related to
the idea of rule by status.

One principal thrust of the post-1635 policy was to require those
retainers who still possessed living quarters inside the castle to move to
new locations outside of the castle walls. This was actually an extension of
policies initiated in the early 1610s when the Chō and others were moved
to the west of the castle. Following the 1635 fire, Toshitsune put new
vigor into the program, and within the next few years almost all of the
retainers remaining inside the castle compound had to give up their
residences, although one particularly favored adviser, Tsuda Genba,
stayed until the 1660s. Most of these men were important members of the
bureaucracy, and the domain government relocated some merchant and
artisan housing adjacent to the moats in order to provide them with
residences close to their offices in the castle.[16]

Nearly two decades later, in the late 1650s and the 1660s, the domain
completed the final disposition of samurai housing by creating geographically discrete residential quarters for each status group among the minor
warriors. Some of these men were direct retainers of the daimyo, such as
the *machi-ashigaru* (City Foot Soldiers), a status group which staffed subordinate posts within the City Office. Their families received residences
grouped together to the south of the castle.[17] The Falconers, who trained
and looked after the daimyo's hunting birds, also acquired new houses.
Previously, these men had lived on the supplementary residence of Maeda
Heibu, but in the early 1660s the government moved them en masse to
new quarters near the Asano River.[18]

The domain also created residential wards for low-ranking warriors who
were rear vassals of Maeda retainers, establishing in the 1660s Yorikimachi as a distinct residential ward for the families of that status group,
for example. Previously, these men and their families had lived on their
masters' supplementary residential land or in rented lodgings in the *chōnin*
sections of the city. Now the domain carved out a separate ward on farm
land to the northeast of the castle for all *yoriki,* regardless of whom their
individual masters were. In a similar fashion, the ruling authorities set up
separate wards for Foot Soldiers (*ashigaru*), Pages (*kobito*), and most other
low-ranking *bushi* status groups.[19]

As domain policies concerning warrior housing unfolded between the
1610s and 1660s, they revealed several interesting points about the shifting
nature of daimyo government motives over that half century. Before the
1630s, the daimyo transferred samurai residences for military reasons, as in
the earlier Chō example. But with the onset of the Great Peace, their

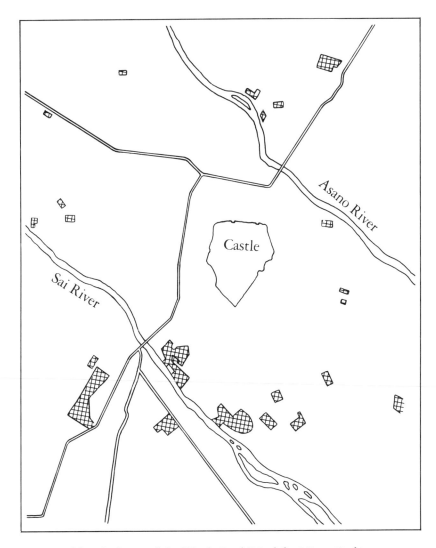

Map 8: Some of the Wards Established for Minor *Bushi*

motives changed. After 1635, the use of urban space became increasingly intertwined with the government's attempt to divide society into status groups. By the middle of the seventeenth century a new ideal had emerged: the distance of a samurai's residence from the castle ought to be proportional to his status within the warrior hierarchy. The daimyo became the sole inhabitant of the castle, and this symbolized his preeminent status. The homes of many important samurai were clustered on the eastern and northern sides of the castle, lesser retainers lived beyond this inner circle, and the lowest-ranking *bushi* tended to live farthest from the castle.

The creation of separate sections, such as Yorikimachi, for minor *bushi* helped both to define more completely the subgroups within the larger samurai class and to reinforce the notion of rank and position within the warrior hierarchy. Other motivations were also at work. Some of the *bushi* who moved into the new sections had previously rented lodgings in commoner wards, and the residential transfers geographically separated those warrior families from the merchant and artisan status groups. Other minor warrior families moved off their masters' residential holdings in order to take up lodgings in the new sections. The daimyo had previously supplied the masters with supplementary grants to provide this housing space, but now the minor *bushi* received their residences directly from the daimyo, and this enhanced daimyo authority. Moreover, by physically separating low-ranking rear vassals from their masters, the domain could hope to loosen personal ties and thereby subject all samurai to the more direct application of daimyo rule.

Military motives also ceased to be a factor influencing daimyo policy toward religious institutions. After 1630, the domain sponsored the construction of only one new shrine, Gongendō (also known as Tōshōgū), which was built in the 1640s and dedicated to the memory of Tokugawa Ieyasu.[20] The government erected the shrine in the northwest corner of the castle, a location of convenience rather than military significance. Similarly, only one temple of note was relocated after 1630. In 1660, the domain moved Nyoraiji from its home at the base of Mount Utatsu to a new site just in front of Tentokuin temple.[21] Nyoraiji and Tentokuin were both "official" temples where the Maeda family worshiped, and the new location meant that the family could visit both temples, as well as nearby Hōenji, in a single visit.

Daimyo policy toward the merchant and artisan sections of the city following the fires of 1631 and 1635 reflected many of the same concerns. After these fires, domain officials ordered the removal of several of the commoner wards adjoining the northern side of the castle to new sites in order to provide housing space for the high-ranking samurai who were being forced to vacate their residences inside the castle.[22] Ultimately, those affected included several dozen privileged merchants, perhaps as many as 200 ordinary merchants, and all of the residents of Carpenters', Swordsmiths', and Coopers' Wards.

The forced transfers illustrated the immense powers that the Maeda daimyo could exercise in determining the use of urban space. Yet several qualifications should be noted. This was the first and only instance when the daimyo ordered *chōnin* residential transfers on a massive scale. Secondly, the moves affected only a small percentage of the urban com-

moners, a few hundred families out of a total merchant and artisan population of several tens of thousands. Finally, the government ensured that
most of those who were transferred received land equal in quality and
value to that which they gave up. The privileged merchants chose their
own new residences, for instance, and the carpenters moved to bustling
areas near the Sai and Asano river bridges. Even the ordinary, non-
privileged merchants fared well. Most were moved only a very short
distance, and their shops remained close to old customers and major

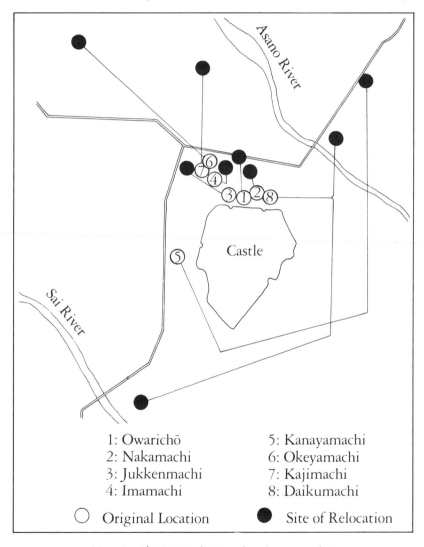

1: Owarichō   5: Kanayamachi
2: Nakamachi   6: Okeyamachi
3: Jukkenmachi   7: Kajimachi
4: Imamachi   8: Daikumachi

○ Original Location   ● Site of Relocation

Map 9: *Chōnin* Wards Transferred in the 1630s

concentrations of population. Others were given land along the northern extension of the Hokuriku highway, an area that was rapidly becoming one of the more prosperous in the city. Moreover, the domain cushioned the unpleasantness of the uprooting by providing aid to those who had been burned out in the conflagrations. Thus, although the transfers of the 1630s represented a clear example of the arbitrary and autocratic poten-tialities of daimyo rule, they were carried out in a manner that reduced possible *chōnin* antagonism and satisfied merchant needs for residential sites which offered good business prospects.

Following the 1631 and 1635 fires, the domain government in-creasingly used in its ordinances and documents terminology that dis-tinguished between samurai land (*buke chiiki*), temple and shrine land (*jisha chiiki*) and commoner land (*shōkōnin chiiki*). Furthermore, urban government divided the commoner wards into the Original Wards (*hon-machi*), the Seven Wards (*shichikashō*), and the Ordinary Wards (*ji-shimachi*).[23] The Original Wards–Ordinary Wards nomenclature was commonly used in other Japanese castle towns as well. Historians usually claim that the Original Wards were the home areas of the chartered merchants and received this designation because of the residents' special relationship with the daimyo. The people living in these wards usually enjoyed exemptions from land taxes but were subject to corvée levies. The Ordinary Wards, on the other hand, were theoretically settled later by ordinary, non-privileged merchants and artisans. The name derives from the fact that the residents had to pay land taxes (*jishigin*), although they were in general exempt from the corvée levied in the Original Wards. The Seven Wards were not typically found in other castle towns. In Kanazawa they constituted a middle layer between the Original Wards and Ordinary Wards, and they included such sections as Saigawa-aramachi, Taka-michimachi, and Kanayachō. Thus, by the end of the 1630 to 1670 period, the ruling authorities in Kanazawa had not only begun to position some retainers so that their place of residence corresponded to their stand-ing within the samurai hierarchy, but had also begun to use nomenclature which referred to the status differences between samurai and townspeople and which drew further attention to distinctions within the *chōnin* class itself.

Reality, however, often belied the theoretical arrrangements provided for in the reorganization of the castle town. In the first place, the resi-dences of some important, high-ranking samurai were more distant from the castle than those of relatively minor *bushi*. The important Chō family, one of the Eight Families, lived in geographical proximity to middle-level retainers like Emori and Okuda, noted on map 10. Maeda Gonnosuke and Maeda Bizen no Kami (see map 5) resided still further out, further from the castle even than the wards for minor *bushi* established in the 1660s. The reason, of course, was that different samurai received their residences at different times, and under different conditions. The daimyo placed the Chō and the two Maeda families to the west and north of the castle in the 1610s for defensive purposes, long before notions of status and proximity to the castle became criteria for deciding samurai residential locations.

Moreover, in Kanazawa the Original Ward—Ordinary Ward division did not merely reflect daimyo-imposed status distinctions among the merchants and artisans. It is true that most, if not all, chartered merchants lived in one or another of the Original Wards. But so too did hundreds of other merchants who came to Kanazawa without privileges. In the Genroku period (1688–1704) there were forty wards designated as Original Wards.[24] Some of those had first been settled by nonchartered merchants in the late sixteenth and early seventeenth centuries, wards such as Jukkenmachi, Yasuechō, Imamachi, and Ishiuramachi. In all, the forty Original Wards contained 2,285 households in 1697, many times the total number of chartered merchants in all of Kanazawa.[25]

In Kanazawa, the criterion used to distinguish among urban wards was business success. "The Original Wards," stated a government document, "are those wards where business flourishes. . . . Wards are classified according to their degree of prosperity."[26] The most prosperous wards were called the Original Wards, the next level were referred to as the Seven Wards, and the remainder were known as the Ordinary Wards. The number of wards in each category changed over time, in accordance with changing business conditions. Out of the slightly more than one hundred wards in the city, the number of Original Wards fluctuated between the high thirties and the low forties, while the actual number of wards in the "Seven Wards" category increased from the original seven to thirteen in the mid-seventeenth century, and then to eighteen by the end of the Tokugawa period. One of the last to be designated as one of the Seven Wards was Okobitomachi (Pages' Ward), which was founded in the 1660s as a special ward for this minor *bushi* strata, but which later became the home of many merchants. To have one's ward designated as an Original Ward or as one of the Seven Wards was a mark of honor. The honor, however, was not derived from daimyo-imposed criteria exclusively. It did not originate in the residents' special relationship with the daimyo, nor did it depend upon economic privileges or favors they received from him. Rather, the honor came from the recognition that one, and one's neighbors, had succeeded as *chōnin,* as successful businessmen.

Most wards, regardless of their classification, contained a mixture of commoner and *bushi* residences, and this too was at variance with the ideal of separate living areas for each of society's status groupings. Not uncommon was the pattern shown in map 10, a area slightly to the northwest of the Chō residence. This sort of intermingling was even more pronounced in some other wards. Precise figures for the seventeenth century are not available, but at the end of the eighteenth century fifty-nine percent of the

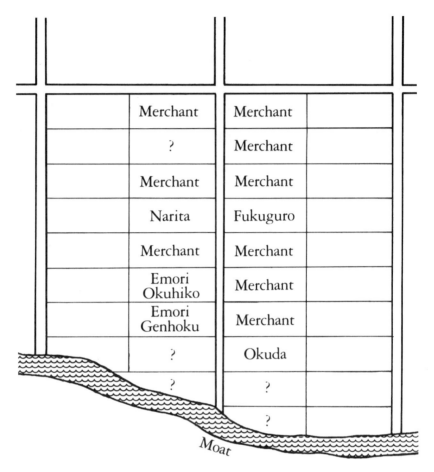

	Merchant	Merchant	
	?	Merchant	
	Merchant	Merchant	
	Narita	Fukuguro	
	Merchant	Merchant	
	Emori Okuhiko	Merchant	
	Emori Genhoku	Merchant	
	?	Okuda	
	?	?	
		?	

Moat

Map 10: A Mixed Commoner-Samurai Ward

houses in Ishiuramachi (an Original Ward), fifty-six percent in Saigawa-aramachi (one of the Seven Wards), and forty-three percent in Zaimokumachi (an Original Ward) belonged to members of the samurai class.[27]

One reason for this sort of pattern was that different parts of the city were settled at different times. Such was the case with the example in map 10. There samurai like Okuda and Emori received grants of residential land when the entire area was still uninhabited, and merchants then moved in to establish shops at a time when conceptual distinctions between samurai land and *chōnin* land were still vague. In addition, the special wards created for minor *bushi* in the 1660s were never spacious

enough to house all of the low-ranking warrior families. The *bushi* population of wards such as Saigawa-aramachi consisted of rear vassals and servant families who could not be accomodated in the special wards or on
their master's residential holdings.

The residential intermingling was most pronounced in the wards which
developed from *aitaiukechi* during the late 1650s and the 1660s.
Aitaiukechi, a term referring to land whose use was decided through
negotiation between private individuals, specifically designated rural land
which samurai, merchants, or artisans rented from farmers.[28] After
Toshitsune died in 1658, the retainers who had accompanied him to
Komatsu when he established a retirement residence there some twenty
years earlier returned to Kanazawa. The domain was obligated to provide
residential land for these families, and with most of the land within
Kanazawa already occupied, it expropriated more than a hundred acres of
farm land for this purpose.[29] This was called *goyōchi* (also *hairyōchi*), land
whose use was determined by the domain government. The returning
samurai, however, faced the problem of securing lodgings for their own
rear vassals and servants. Some probably found homes in the special new
urban wards that the domain was creating. But there were always more
potential residents than homes in those wards, and in any case, lodgings
also had to be provided for the service personnel (*hōkōnin*), for whom there
were no special wards, if they could not be accommodated on the master's
residence. Consequently, in 1661 the domain proclaimed that samurai,
merchants, and artisans could lease farm land, and this land was referred
to as *aitaiukechi*.[30] In large part, this proclamation simply confirmed what
had been happening the previous few years. In 1659, for instance, one
retainer had leased about three acres of farm land on the north side of the
Asano River, and many of the Eight Families had rented tracts of rural
land.[31] But the 1661 proclamation, by recognizing a fait accompli, released people from fears that they might be charged with violating older
ordinances which forbade the permanent alienation of rice producing
lands, and it resulted in a dramatic increase in the number of private
rental agreements.

A large number of commoner immigrants also took up residence on
aitaiukechi lands in the late 1650s and 1660s. Some came to Kanazawa for
the same reasons that had stimulated earlier migration: because of economic opportunities and a chance to improve their lot in life, and because
of the social appeal of city life. But it is impossible to put aside the
sequential relationship between the implementation of the *kaisakuhō* rural
reforms and the sudden spurt in migration, not only to Kanazawa but to
local towns such as Jōhana as well. In the four-year period from 1660 to
1663 alone, arriving would-be merchants and artisans leased well over
300,000 square meters of farm land on the fringes of Kanazawa.

This sudden influx of new residents caused administrative problems. In 1665, Village Headmen from areas around Kanazawa where *bushi* and townspeople had settled sent in petitions to the domain government. The newcomers interfered with agricultural activities, and the farmers had asked the Village Headmen to make certain that the nonfarming population observed the ordinances and did not interfere with the farmers' pursuit of livelihood. But village officials felt helpless because the *bushi* and merchants did not consider themselves farmers and would not obey ordinances or the orders of rural officials. In response, the domain quickly transferred to the jurisdiction of the City Magistrates more than 1,600 nonfarming households in areas contiguous to the city.[32] These new urban residents helped to push Kanazawa's total population over the 100,000 mark.

The rapid transformation of *aitaiukechi* land into urban wards helped to preclude the possibility that the use of all urban space would conform with status and substatus distinctions. These new wards became residential hodgepodges with merchants, artisans, day laborers, minor samurai, and *bushi* servant personnel living side by side. A few examples are illustrative. Of forty-one households in Asanogawa-kawayokemachi, two are known to have belonged to artisans, two to merchants, three to day laborers, and twenty-eight to low-ranking warriors (*ashigaru* and *hōkōnin*). Of the fifty-six households in Asanomachi whose occupants can be identified, seven were artisans, twenty-eight were merchants, six were day laborers, and ten were *bushi*. For Ushirokanayachō, the figures were nine artisans, two merchants, fourteen day laborers, and thirteen *bushi* (of a total of fifty-five households), and for Daijume-kawaramachi, the numbers were ten artisans, twelve merchants, twelve day laborers, and twenty-two *bushi* (of fifty-nine households).[33]

In a theoretical sense only, then, the urban layout of Kanazawa came to reflect the assumptions of a status-based society. On maps of the day, blocks of land for townspeople, samurai, and religious institutions were neatly drawn in different colors. Similarly, the Original Wards–Seven Wards–Ordinary Wards nomenclature and the principle relating samurai rank with proximity to the castle can be seen as illustrative of the gradations within the major urban social classes. To the extent that these conditions prevailed, they can be associated with the daimyo's desire to bring the city under the same discipline he was applying to the status groups. But one must be careful not to infer from the old maps more order than actually existed. The realities of residential land use were more complex, and often directly violated the ideal. This was so because much of the city grew organically, in response to the economic and social needs of its residents, not as the result of daimyo-centered planning alone.

THE GROWTH OF BUREAUCRATIC
URBAN GOVERNMENT

Between the years 1630 and 1670 the ruling authorities of Kaga domain instituted significant reforms in urban government that complemented the changes made in rural administration. These measures built upon the developments of the formative years before 1630 and brought to completion a comprehensive administrative organization and a body of legal codes which were to provide the basic structure of urban governance throughout the eighteenth and early nineteenth centuries.

The bureaucratization of daimyo government went on at all levels during the middle third of the seventeenth century. When the third daimyo, Toshitsune, retired in 1639, he turned the realm over to his son Mitsutaka. This man, the fourth Maeda daimyo, died suddenly in Edo in 1645, however, and Kaga domain passed to his infant son, Tsunanori, who was less than two years old. Consequently, Toshitsune reassumed effective control of domain government, ruling until his own death early in the 10th month of 1658. Within a month of Toshitsune's death, a document issued under Tsunanori's seal stated that the affairs of the realm would be placed in the hands of a Council of Advisers who would decide general policy in twice-monthly meetings and also manage the day-to-day affairs of the domain. Shortly thereafter, a document bearing the seal of the shogun Tokugawa Ietsuna, himself still in his teens, instructed Maeda Tsunanori to administer his territory by holding consultations with this set of advisers.[34] This institutionalized a practice which had been evolving for many decades. The first three Maeda daimyo had been forceful personages but had usually conferred with important retainers when making major decisions, and Toshitsune had come increasingly to rely on these men to manage domain affairs after he started to alternate his residence between Edo and Kanazawa. But the instructions issued in 1658 went further than this; they elevated Tsunanori up and out of the system, making him in many ways a figurehead ruler. Born and raised in the Maeda mansion in Edo—he did not even journey to Kanazawa until his late teens—Tsunanori would never play the direct role in government that his forefathers had. The top echelon of his advisers had emerged as the real decision makers in Kaga domain.

This Council of Advisers, usually referred to as the *yoriaishū*, in effect functioned as the highest level of urban government since it drafted legal codes and oversaw the activities of the City Magistrates. The procedures for selecting City Magistrates were formalized during the middle third of the seventeenth century. Whereas *hitomochi*-level samurai had served as Magistrates earlier, men from the next lower *heishi* level held the post from 1641 until the office was abolished following the Meiji Restoration. Moreover, from the middle seventeenth century the Council of Advisers, not the daimyo as previously, appointed the Magistrates, who now reported directly to the Council. In addition, appointees now served only as City Magistrates and did not receive dual appointments as Rural Magistrates.[35] Office tenure was not fixed, and the Magistrates served as long as the Council approved of their performance.

In 1659 the Council issued a proclamation that defined and systematized the duties of the two City Magistrates.[36] The Magistrates were instructed to administer the affairs of the townspeople, to ensure that townspeople observed the city ordinances, to investigate incidents of physical violence and to punish criminals (conferring with the Office of Police and Judiciary on difficult cases), to make certain people paid their debts (and that interest rates did not exceed 1.7 percent per month), and to oversee the collection of urban taxes. In addition, the Magistrates supervised all other officials involved in urban political administration. For this, they received an salary equivalent to approximately two hundred *koku* of rice, paid from the tax assessments levied on the townspeople.

The Constables (*machi-dōshin*) and Junior Assistants (*machi-gedai*) assisted the City Magistrates. The names of these samurai offices first appeared in late sixteenth- and early seventeenth-century documents, but appointments were not made on a systematic basis, nor were duties routinized, until the 1640s and 1650s.[37] There were usually four Constables, although they numbered as many as seven or eight at times. They assisted the Magistrates in all aspects of urban administration, but bore special responsibility for preserving public peace. To this end, they maintained permanent guard houses in some parts of the city and conducted nightly patrols throughout the *chōnin* sections of the castle town. From 1656, the salary of a Constable was fixed at fifty *koku* of rice, paid from *chōnin* tax levies.

The three to six Junior Assistants each received a salary of slightly over thirty *koku* per year. The full range of their duties is not clear, but documents state but that they were in charge of purchasing supplies which the various domain offices ordered from merchants, and that they oversaw the maintenance of roads and the bridges which crossed the moats and rivers within the city.[38] It is likely, however, that the Junior Assistants had broader supervisory duties since the City Office grew eventually to employ over three hundred persons.[39]

The establishment of a City Office (*machi-kaisho*) symbolized in physical terms the increasing bureaucratization of urban government. In earlier times, city officials had met informally at the home of the merchant Takeya Nihei, but by 1640 the domain government had provided the officials with their own set of office buildings, situated to the northwest of the castle. These included business offices, a prison, and interrogation rooms.[40]

In addition to the urban administrators who were samurai, townspeople continued to play a significant role in managing urban affairs, even during this period of increased centralization of authority. The post of City Elder (*machidoshiyori*) was the highest to which a townsperson could aspire. The term *machidoshiyori* appeared in documents as early as 1594, but appointments at that time were made on an ad hoc, temporary basis and usually for the purpose of carrying out only one specific task. A 1594 letter from Maeda Toshiie to two unnamed "City Elders," for instance, thanked them for their cooperation and for the aid of the townspeople in constructing bridges across the Sai and Asano rivers.[41] As we saw earlier, the Maeda daimyo during the early seventeenth century generally relied more upon chartered merchants such as Kōrinbō and Kitamuraya than upon official appointees for advice and assistance in managing many aspects of urban administration.

From the late 1640s or early 1650s, the post of City Elder became an official and permanent part of the expanding bureaucracy. In 1651, the domain appointed twenty men as City Elders; ten began duties immediately, and the remaining ten formed an off-duty reserve.[42] As might be expected, many were the sons and grandsons of those who had in early years met informally with the daimyo or at the home of Takeya to discuss urban affairs, men with names like Kamiya, Kanaya, and Hiranoya. They were joined by other chartered merchants: Morimotoya Hachizaemon, Sangaya Kurōbe, and Asanoya Jirōemon.

Chartered, or *goyō*, status, however, was not a prerequisite for office holding. A sizable number of nonchartered merchants, men who had made their mark in the business world and who lived in the finer parts of the city, received appointments as City Elders during the seventeenth century. Included among these were Izumoya Hikoemon from Imamachi, Kusuriya Shōbei (Tsutsumichō), Tsubata Yosaemon (Owarichō), Sasaya Jūbei (Kawaramachi), Tsuruya Ichirōemon (Nakamachi), Ishiuraya Ihei (Zaimokuchō), Imaichiya Nihei (Tatemachi), and Taiya Ichibei (Zaimokuchō). The City Elders were men who possessed administrative skills and enjoyed a high reputation, defined largely in terms of commercial success. Appointees remained in office as long as they met those standards. The domain encouraged one Kamiya to remain in office for twenty-nine years, and one Hiranoya for twenty-six, but released one Kōrinbō from service after just three years. In the late eighteenth century, the City Elder Echizen'ya Kiemon (related to the Echizen'ya Magobei family), the seventh generation of his family, fell into business ruin, sold his home and shop, and moved into rented lodgings. He was immediately removed from office.[43]

The City Elders performed a variety of duties.[44] They received written requests and complaints from townspeople, attached their own opinions, and then submitted the paperwork to the samurai officials at the City Office. They also checked tax receipts and submitted statements that the proper amount had been collected. The Elders accompanied the Constables who investigated the crimes of merchants and artisans and then sat in on any hearings. Finally, they helped to supervise the activities of other commoners who worked at the City Office. In a more general way, they were expected to promote good behavior and filial piety among the townspeople, to mediate civil disagreements between commoners, and to encourage diligence by merchants and artisans.

The City Elders received salaries and certain perquisites as payment for these services.[45] Their salary consisted of two portions: approximately five *koku* of rice paid from domain coffers, and a slightly lesser amount taken from commoner tax proceeds. They also received exemptions from city taxes. In addition, the Elders had certain ceremonial perquisites. They could use palanquins, were received at the castle by the daimyo during the New Year's ceremonies, and, in brief ceremonies held at the entrance to Kanazawa, presented greetings on behalf of all the townspeople to the daimyo when he returned from Edo.

The City Elders were assisted by the Inspectors (*yokome-kimoiri*), first appointed in 1659. The City Elders nominated these men from among the Ward Representatives (*machi-kimori*), and the City Magistrates confirmed the appointments. The Inspectors helped to supervise the activities of the Ward Representatives, worked with the Elders in verifying tax receipts, and investigated any *chōnin* charges of maladministration by city officials.[46]

The office of Ward Representative (*machi-kimoiri*) also became institutionalized during the middle third of the seventeenth century. As noted earlier, Toshiie appointed some men as Ward Representatives as early as 1598, and a 1627 document listed six such men, including a Kanaya and a Kitamuraya.[47] From the middle seventeenth century, however, the number of appointees became more set. In general, there was one Ward Representative for each one or two Original Wards and a total of eleven appointees for the more than fifty Ordinary Wards.[48]

Appointed to wards other than their own place of residence, the Ward Representatives assisted the Inspectors and City Elders.[49] The Representatives, for example, compiled census reports, examined commoner complaints about exorbitant and unfair prices, held conciliation talks in commercial disputes, and investigated suspicious deaths. They also worked with the Household Groups—conferring with persons who wanted to

draw up wills, helping to settle petty quarrels, and monitoring the negotiations when someone sold or bought a house.

In 1666, the Representatives sent a petition to the domain.[50] In this,
they pointed out that they had to put in long hours and appear almost
every day at the City Office or the Office of Police and the Judiciary.
Thus, they concluded, they ought to receive a regular salary. The domain
government agreed and fixed their salary at about one-half of the City
Elders' pay. In addition, the Representatives received exemptions from
city taxes and acquired the privilege of participating in the ceremonies
welcoming the daimyo on his return from Edo. From the 1660s and the
1670s, the domain also began to appoint assistants known as *bangashira*
(also called *banto*) to help the Representatives carry out their duties.[51]

A number of other offices on the ward level were established during the
middle third of the seventeenth century. We know most about the post of
teishuban (Ward Patrol). It is likely that persons served in this capacity as
early as the 1630s or 1640s, but it was not until the 1660s that domain
ordinances clearly specified their duties.[52] The office was rotated among
the residents of each ward, with two persons serving concurrently. The
purpose of the Ward Patrol was to watch for fire and to remind residents
to be careful about its dangers.[53] In the evening, the two-man Patrols
were supposed to stop in front of each house until the occupant assured
them that all was in order and that he would be on his guard against fire.
On days when the wind was blowing strongly, the Ward Representatives
and *bangashira* joined the Patrols and went throughout the city warning
households to exercise extreme caution, lest they accidentally start a fire.
As an additional duty, the Ward Patrols were supposed to keep a sharp
eye out for criminal activity and to report crimes to higher officials.[54]
Beyond this, each ward maintained a gate and watch house at the entrance
to the ward. Ward residents staffed the watch house and closed the gate at
night, supposedly to keep out criminals. Some wards also maintained fire-
fighting supplies at the watch house.[55]

The final new office that played a significant role in the management of
urban affairs was the post of Group Headman (*kumiaigashira*). The first
mention of this post appeared in the 1642 *chōnin* code which stated that
the Household Groups (*jūningumi*) in the commoner wards should appoint
Headmen to act as liaison agents between city officials and the Household
Groups.[56] It is likely, however, that the office was not established on a
permanent basis until the spring of 1670, when the Household Groups of
the city were divided into clusters of about ten each and a Group Headman named for each cluster.[57]

Prominent persons served as Group Headmen, and some Household
Groups invited men from other wards to serve as Headmen when they felt

that none of their own members had sufficient stature. One function of the Group Headmen was to read the *chōnin* codes to the Groups on the second day of each month (thus giving the codes their colloquial name *futsukayomi,* the second-day reading), although to what extent the Group Headmen actually carried out this tiresome task is problematical. More practical in nature were their other duties, which were essentially to help the Household Group to perform its functions. These are familiar. The Group Headmen interviewed men who were dying without heirs and helped to decide the disposition of their household property; they sat in on the negotiations when houses were sold; and, of course, they helped to settle disputes among members of their Household Group.[58]

The Household Groups, as noted earlier, had a long history in Kanazawa, dating back to at least the early years of the seventeenth century. Apparently not all urban commoners formed themselves into such groups, however, since domain proclamations issued during the 1640s instructed them to do so.[59] Interestingly enough, the *bushi* and servant personnel who lived within the commoner wards were required to join a Household Group and to participate in the Group's functions.[60] Domain regulations issued throughout the middle seventeenth century both expanded and institutionalized the duties of the Household Groups.[61] As the last, and lowest, unit of urban government, the Group carried out a variety of important administrative tasks. Many of these were noted earlier: assembling to hear a reading of the codes; reporting criminal acts by neighbors; holding conciliation talks in case of neighborhood disagreements or commercial or land disputes among Group members; and helping to enforce the provisions of wills and to decide the disposition of property when a member died without a will. In this regard, a new post entitled *hakoban,* or Keeper of the Wills, appeared, and this person was entrusted with safeguarding copies of the wills of all Group members. Another new duty for the Household Group had to do with travel papers. Any person who wished to travel outside the domain had to draft a letter specifying his date of return, have it signed by all members of his Household Group, and then submit it to the City Office in order to receive a travel permit. The Group also had to verify that a member who was moving to a different ward left no debts behind. Similarly, a samurai who gave a merchant some item (for example, household goods) to sell was supposed to have all members of the merchant's Group sign a document listing those items and their value, in order to provide protection both for the samurai in case the merchant absconded with his goods (the Group would then be held responsible) and for the merchant if the samurai later claimed that the merchant had stolen his goods or sold them for less than their fair value.

The Household Groups also became units of mutual aid and self-help.

Members, for example, were supposed to assist their neighbors when they fell on hard times economically. A 1660 ordinance specified that each Group had to maintain fire-fighting equipment, such as ladders, rakes, and rain barrels. In addition, Groups were held responsible for the prison expenses of a member who ran amok but who was too poor to pay for his own confinement.[62]

In pace with the amplification of the urban administrative apparatus, the domain issued a variety of new legal codes which expanded government involvement in the lives of Kanazawa's residents. In 1637 and 1642 government authorities issued lengthy documents dealing with governance in the *chōnin* sections of the city.[63] The 1642 proclamation can be considered the first major *chōnin* code since it was the first issued to the townspeople (through the Ward Representatives) under the seal of the City Magistrates. The 1637 document was actually a directive from the daimyo's two chief advisers, Honda Awa no Kami and Yokoyama Yamashiro no Kami, to the acting City Magistrates. Since this earlier directive does contain a number of important provisions, however, it is appropriate to consider the two documents together.

Taken as a set, the two proclamations represent an initial attempt to systematize administrative procedures and to provide a comprehensive set of ordinances pertinent to merchant and artisan behavior. However, the ordinances were essentially a codification of canons and rules that had been issued separately between 1583 and 1630. As such, the concerns of the 1642 code reflected the conditions of the earlier, formative years of castle town growth and, as noted earlier, dealt chiefly with maintaining law and order. Typical were the prohibitions against gambling, against keeping dogs as pets, and against congregating in shops and gossiping about others in a loud voice.

In 1660 the domain issued a new *chōnin* code, and, as in the past, a directive to the City Magistrates preceded the formal proclamation.[64] This code and directive established standards for urban government that would last for well over a century, until government officials issued a revised code in 1792. The 1660 code and directive (actually issued in 1659) should be seen as a part of the broader attempt to institutionalize government during the mid-seventeenth century. In the eighteen-month period from the 6th month of 1659 to the end of 1660, the government issued over twenty major proclamations which set administrative standards for nearly every important government office and established codes of behavior for all the social classes.[65] As a product of this era of government reform, the 1659 directive and 1660 code revealed many interesting contrasts to their counterparts of twenty years earlier.

One particularly noticeable feature was an expansion of government involvement in the economic life of the townspeople. One article, for instance, stipulated that interest payments be fixed at 1.7 percent per month, and another stated that samurai were not to go into business with townspeople. Another article required a representative from the City Office to visit any person who fell behind in his debt repayments or credit obligations. This was an especially important clause from the perspective of the city's merchants and artisans since it gave legal backing to all credit relationships and promised government assistance in collecting all debts and credit liabilities. Two years later the domain government extended additional protection to merchants when it promised to underwrite certain debts contracted by peasants. Farmers who lived close to Kanazawa bought household furnishings and farm tools from merchants in the city. In 1662 the domain announced that whenever a farmer's accumulation of debts interfered with his ability to pay his taxes (nengu), the domain would assume the farmer's liability and pay the merchant in full.[66]

Another feature of the 1660 code was increased government concern with what might be called public services. The domain government did not attempt to provide these services, but rather, put the burden on the townspeople. The 1660 code, for example, outlined the duties of the Ward Patrol and required Household Groups to maintain the fire-fighting equipment mentioned earlier: ladders, water barrels, and rakes. Similarly, the code prohibited throwing garbage into moats or waterways, although it did not specify how persons should dispose of that kind of waste.

Not all provisions contained in the directive and 1660 code were new. Prohibitions against gambling, prostitution, urinating from the second floor of houses, and wearing swords were repeated in the new canon. The domain was still concerned with maintaining peace in the city, but certain kinds of commoner behavior were clearly not susceptible to government regulation.

In contrast to the *chōnin* codes, the ordinances pertaining to samurai behavior showed far fewer changes during the mid-seventeenth century. The principal thrust of the samurai codes was still to eliminate behavior that might lead to quarrels and violence. Thus, almost every samurai ordinance contained the familiar prohibitions against loitering in the street, engaging in street sumo, wearing scarfs that covered the face, and "conversing with women at night and having improper liaisons."[67] As in the *chōnin* example, certain kinds of samurai behavior presented an ongoing problem to domain officials.

Nor did the domain make many changes in the samurai administrative apparatus. The ruling authorities did, of course, create separate wards for some minor *bushi* in order to make them subject to the more direct application of daimyo rule, and in 1664 they began to appoint Apprehension Officers (*kenka-oikake-bugyō*) to pursue criminals who tried to escape capture.[68] But beyond this, the earlier adaptation of the military organization for the purposes of civil administration, as well as the codes issued in the 1583 to 1630 period, continued to serve as the basic models of urban governance for the samurai class.

Perhaps one reason that samurai codes were not subject to more revision was that the level of violent crime committed by samurai had declined to acceptable levels by the middle of the seventeenth century, and the government felt it could handle crime simply by reissuing ordinances. By midcentury the main source of street violence, the *kabukimono,* had virtually disappeared as a result of the government measures described earlier. Moreover, high-level samurai had started to observe more closely the mechanisms for settling criminal cases, which called for a retainer either to turn a rear vassal over to the Office of Police and Judiciary or to seek that office's approval before he meted out punishments on his own. In earlier years some retainers had tried to protect their rear vassals who ran afoul of the law, as in the case of Ishiwara Tetsujinosuke. By the mid-seventeenth century, the behavior of Maeda Tsushima no Kami had become more typical. When Tsushima learned in 1663 that a rear vassal named Saizō was committing adultery with a household maid, he followed established procedures and reported the incident to the Judiciary. He also requested that he be allowed to punish the couple by beheading them, and after an investigation, the Judiciary gave its approval.[69]

A similar example concerns the case of Shibata Magonojō, a samurai youth who was involved in a homosexual relationship with a commoner named Shiroganeya Chōemon. For reasons that are not clear, Magonojō killed Chōemon in Magonojō's home. Magonojō and his father hid the body and tried to keep the killing a secret, but were found out by the father's superior officer, a *hitomochi*-rank samurai, who turned the two over to the Office of the Police and the Judiciary. They were sentenced to death.[70]

In addition to the codes of behavior, the domain government issued a mass of ordinances during the middle seventeenth century which attempted to regulate both samurai and *chōnin* dress and the kinds of entertainment they could engage in on festival days. The purpose of this regulation was clearly to reinforce and to help further define status distinctions. The initial steps in deciding which status groups could wear which kinds of clothing were taken in the 1630s and 1640s. A 1639 ordinance, for example, forbade Attendants (*komono*) and Keepers of the Footwear (*zōritori*) to wear silk (*kenpu*), and the 1642 *chōnin* codes prohibited garments made from silk habutae to townspeople.[71]

The major attempt to synchronize clothing with status came in 1661, the year of many other domain reforms and regulations.[72] Domain ordinances which took effect on the 1st day of the 1st month of 1661 specified the types of clothing fabrics permitted to peasants, townspeople, and each major subdivision of the samurai status group. High-level retainers such as the Eight Houses and Commanders, for instance, could wear clothing made from thirteen different kinds of silk. Persons in the more middle ranks such as the Lower Soldiers (*okachi*) and the Falconers (*takajō,* the men who trained and cared for the daimyo's hunting hawks) were only permitted to wear four types of silk as well as pongee (*tsumugi*). The more minor Archers (*yumi*) and Riflers (*teppō*), however, were restricted to pongee, cotton (*momen*), and plain cloth (*nuno*). Under the regulations, townspeople could wear plain silk (*kinu*) and pongee. The peasants, however, were instructed to wear clothes made from pongee or cotton only. As an indication of *chōnin* independence, it should be noted that the townspeople often ignored these regulations and wore whatever they pleased, and could afford. Despite problems of enforcement, however, the domain persevered in its efforts to legislate status distinctions by repeatedly reissuing the ordinances along with enjoinders that they be properly observed.[73]

The domain complemented the clothing regulations with other decrees that reinforced status concepts. At parties and for meals on holidays and ceremonial days, for example, samurai were permitted to serve guests from outside the domain a meal consisting of two soups, five vegetables, pickled vegetables, a fish, two "toasts" of sake, and cakes. For more ordinary celebrations, though, they were supposed to serve more modest meals of one soup, three vegetables, pickled vegetables, two toasts of sake, and a sweet.[74] Townspeople, on the other hand, had to be content with the lower level of indulgence, regardless of the guest.[75] Similarly, townspeople were not supposed to have carved wooden beams or doors made from cedar in their homes, because these were perquisites of the samurai class.[76] Nor could townspeople, unless they were seriously ill or were over sixty years of age, ride in palanquins, whose use was normally restricted to high-ranking samurai and certain city officials.[77] In some measure, these were frugality laws and reflected domain concern with the generally worsening financial plight of the samurai during the middle of the seventeenth century. A 1663 proclamation, for example, began "Recently there have been reports of samurai holding lavish parties . . . [although] the domain has declared that persons should be frugal," and went on to prohibit samurai from purchasing foods or supplies for banquets on credit terms.[78] The frugality that the government wanted to encourage, however, went hand in hand with the desire to create clear distinctions among and within status groups.

By the year 1670, the officials of Kaga domain had created the administrative framework and promulgated the major legal codes which provided the overall structure for urban governance that would endure for more than a century. One common argument has been that this system of government was autocratic and that the daimyo delegated certain duties to commoner functionaries such as the City Elders and Group Headmen chiefly in order to provide a mechanism for maintaining internal peace and for ensuring that commoners would obey the laws imposed on them by the state.[79] In theory, the system was autocratic, since the daimyo, or Council of Advisers once the daimyo had become more of a figurehead ruler, commanded the military, monopolized the powers of taxation, and exercised the undisputed right to legislate—the definitive ingredients of autocratic government.

But as the system of governance took shape during the middle of the seventeenth century, certain concepts and principles concerning the exercise of political authority had emerged which made government in Japan much more complex than a single descriptive term would suggest. The first of these was that ruling officials had to govern within a clearly defined framework of law and precedent. This notion began at the very apex of the political authority structure when the shogun instructed Maeda Tsunanori, as he did other daimyo, to "administer your retainers and realm in accordance with the precedents of the past. You are to rule in a manner that will not cause difficulty to the townspeople or to the peasantry."[80] Law and precedent also defined the activities of all lower administrators, and they came to rule bureaucratically. Each level in the urban administrative hierarchy in Kanazawa, from Ward Representative to City Magistrate to the Council of Advisers, carried out functions that were clearly specified by law, and each administrator was responsible to the next higher bureaucratic level.

Second, as authority came to be exercised toward legally defined status groups, each member of a group could expect a certain equality and impartiality of treatment. For instance, all merchants and artisans, regardless of wealth or place of residence, were subject to the same laws concerning debt relationships and to the same ordinances regulating clothing styles. The concept of impartiality became increasingly clear, moreover, in the documents concerning crime, and two cases can serve as examples. In the sixth month of 1664, a Foot Soldier named Iwamoto Denshichi spent part of an early morning practicing firearms on targets set up in the minuscule garden behind his residence. Unfortunately, one of his bullets went astray and killed the four-year-old son of a neighbor, an Attendant. A hearing was held at the Office of Police and the Judiciary, and it was pointed out that ordinances clearly stated that firearms could be used only at the official practice grounds. The Judiciary ordered that Denshichi have his ears and nose cut off and that he be exiled from Kaga domain.[81]

In that same year a young man named Jin'emon, the son of a middle-level samurai, became very drunk at a party one night. On the way home, a masterless samurai (*rōnin*) who happened to be on the street started to jeer at Jin'emon and to call him a drunk. A fight ensued and Jin'emon killed the other samurai. At the investigation, Jin'emon claimed that he was so drunk that he could not remember the incident. However, there was a witness, identified only as a rear vassal of Honda Awa no Kami, who stated the Jin'emon was at least sober enough to have cut down his opponent with a single sword thrust. The Judiciary ordered Jin'emon to commit suicide.[82]

A third principle that emerged during the seventeenth century was that the law applied to all persons, regardless of status. The ordinance that enforced debt relationships, for instance, applied to everyone, whether the debtor was a merchant, samurai, or peasant. The punishments meted out in two other criminal cases in Kanazawa also illustrate the point that superior status did not entitle a person to exemption from the application of the law. Sugimoto Kujūrō, the teenage son of the samurai Sugimoto Sannojō, often visited his neighbor, the son of a merchant, to play the board game *go* with that youngster and some other *chōnin* teenagers. One day a certain Tarōzaburō, the son of another neighboring merchant, insisted on giving Kujūrō unwanted advice and insulted him over and over again about his style of play. After several hours Kujūrō lost his temper and pulled his sword and struck Tarōzaburō, who died a few days later from the injuries he recieved. After an inquest, the Office of Police and the Judiciary ordered Kujūrō to commit suicide.[83]

Another case shows that, contrary to the myths of modern-day films and television, samurai did not have the unmitigated right to cut down anyone who displeased them (*kirisute-gomen*). In 1664, a commoner woman named Shima tried to kill her employer, the Mounted Guard (*oumamawari*) samurai named Iwata Heizō. During the struggle, Iwata wrestled the sword away from Shima and killed her. In the course of its inquiries, the Office of the Police and Judiciary received a letter from Shima's mother, who pointed out that Shima had actually been Iwata's mistress, although she was formally employed as a maid and maintained a separate address at a lodging house in a commoner ward. Shima's mother admitted that her daughter was not entirely sane and that Iwata had acted in self-defense. Still, the mother went on, Iwata should not have killed her daughter. Instead, he should have subdued her and turned her over to the Judiciary. That way, the mother concluded, she could have seen her daughter one last time. The Judiciary agreed with the mother and ordered Iwata into exile.[84]

Fourth, by the end of the seventeenth century, the exercise of certain administrative functions by representatives of the commoner population had come to be an assumed privilege. The list of those functions, as noted above, was lengthy: the City Elders sat in on criminal hearings, and the

Ward Representatives, Group Headmen, and Household Groups all helped to resolve commercial disagreements, adjudicate land disputes, settle quarrels, and dispose of private property. These constituted fundamental and significant judicial and police functions, made more important in the middle of the seventeenth century by the added sanction of law and by the view of domain officialdom that these lower-level offices constituted an essential component of an integrated system of urban government.

Finally, a simple passion for order and rigid control was not the sole impulse of ruling officials. Their motivations became more sophisticated than this, and it is here that Neo-Confucianism becomes important. By the middle of the seventeenth century, many of Japan's political elite had accepted certain tenets of Neo-Confucianism as a philosophical basis for their exercise of political power. As early as 1605, Tokugawa Ieyasu employed Hayashi Razan, a student of the famous Confucian scholar Fujiwara Seika, as an adviser on government and historical precedents. By the 1630s, the Hayashi family had established at their home in Edo a Confucian school which later became the official Tokugawa College. The Maeda were among the many daimyo who also employed Confucian scholars. Toshinaga received tutoring from Ōhakushi, a Chinese scholar who came to Japan. Toshinaga invited this man to Kanazawa and granted him a yearly stipend. There, he lectured Toshinaga and worked on landscape painting. At various times Toshitsune and Mitsutaka employed a number of famous Confucian tutors, including Matsunaga Sekigo and Kōsei Dōki. The Maeda also made certain that important retainers received tutoring and were exposed to the ideas of these scholars, a practice that Tsunanori continued in the second half of the seventeenth century.[85]

The significance of Confucianism is that it provided a new theory of governance for the early seventeenth-century daimyo, who were attempting to fashion order out of the turmoil of the preceding century and to create a comprehensive system of administration. Within the cosmos, the Confucian scholars argued, principle (ri) operated through force or matter (ki) to produce a human society that was both moral and based on reason and order. The specific manifestation of reason and order were the Five Relationships (between father and son, ruler and subject, husband and wife, older and younger brother, and friend and friend). The moral component was the proper observance of the obligations inherent in each of the relationships. Thus, a son owed filial devotion to his father, and the duty of a subject was to obey his ruler. In addition, the Japanese Confucian scholars taught that an ideal society was composed of a natural hierarchy of social levels (samurai/ruler, peasant, artisan, and merchant). Every individual belonged to an assigned level within this hierarchy and bore the moral responsibility not only to obey the laws of society but also to fulfill the mission assigned to his level: the samurai to rule, the peasants and artisans to produce, and the merchants to transport goods. The appeal of such a philosophy to daimyo such as the Maeda, who were attempting to create a system of rule by status, was undeniable.

But Confucianism was more than a handy tool with which the daimyo could extend their authority over people, for the moral order postulated by Confucianism stood above the political elite. A moral society was one which functioned harmoniously, and harmony came about when everyone fulfilled his obligations. These obligations were mutual. The artisan made goods; the merchant sold them. The son was filial; the father provided for his son, and protected him and cared for him. Just as the peasants, merchants, and artisans had the responsibility to be model subjects, so too did the daimyo have the obligation to be a model ruler and supply benevolent administration (*jinsei*). This burden was taken seriously in Kaga, and Tsunanori prided himself on his reputation as one of the three "model rulers" (*meikun*) of his age, the other two being the Date daimyo of Sendai domain and the Ikeda daimyo of Okayama.[86]

Under the influence of their Confucian tutors, the political leaders in Kaga came to believe that the essence of true order lay in unity, not in repression. They saw society as an organic whole in which all the members, although separated by status lines, contributed a definite share to the well-being of the entire society. Thus, the political leaders could encourage a degree of participation in the political system by all members of the status groups. For commoners, such participation—whether as City Elders, Ward Representatives, or members of Household Groups—would both symbolize the unity of society and define the expected contribution from each member. In turn, this sharing of political responsibility would lead to a higher form of moral order in which the people would voluntarily consent to the rule of domain government, would do so because that government ruled in a manner that was most beneficial for all of society. Urban government in Kanazawa, then, became more than just an expression of daimyo-centered absolutism.

This is not to deny that the system could be restrictive. The regulations that limited one's choice of clothing to what was considered appropriate to one's status certainly illustrate this. Criminal law could also be harsh, even by seventeenth-century standards. One domain ordinance, for instance, stipulated that whenever a samurai was sentenced to death, the same sentence would be extended to all sons who might inherit the family name. But the Office of Police and Judiciary was often reluctant to enforce this law. In 1674, for instance, the samurai Kawakami San'emon was ordered to commit suicide as a punishment for "unfilial acts toward his older sister." His suicide took place on the 2nd day of the 3rd month of 1674, and afterward his severed head was taken to the execution grounds in back of Teramachi to be exposed to public view. Kawakami had two sons, aged twelve and ten, who were placed in the care of temple priests while officials tried to decide what to do with the youngsters. Finally on the 1st day of the 6th month, three months after the father's death, the Council of Advisers intervened and decided that the two boys should also be ordered to commit suicide. But the Advisers went on to state that exemptions to the general rule of death for sons of condemned criminals could be made, especially if large numbers of male children were involved.[87]

In a city where buildings were wooden and packed closely together, laws against arson were strictly enforced. In the 1660s a peasant woman named Nei came to Kanazawa to work as a servant in samurai households. Over the course of several years, she worked for six employers, stole money from each of them, and set fire to their homes in order to hide her crimes. When found out, she was boiled to death in a cauldron especially cast for her execution.[88] Some twenty years later a merchant named Yaohariya Nagaemon was convicted of arson. Domain officials were uncertain of what punishment to order and wrote to Tsunanori in Edo asking whether to boil Nagaemon alive, the punishment ordered in the earlier arson case, or whether to crucify him, the standard punishment in Edo. In a terse and almost bored letter, Tsunanori replied, "Regardless of whether it is crucifixon or boiling, the result is the same. . . . To discourage crime, he should be crucified."[89]

Not only did the system occasionally resort to iron-fisted justice, sometimes it also failed to work the way in which it was intended, with the result that persons from the various status groupings sometimes received unequal treatment in the hands of court officials. In 1690, the Office of Police and the Judiciary found four samurai guilty of employing nineteen prostitutes and holding wild parties. Officials harshly punished the townsmen who had supplied the women, by decapitating some and by cutting off the noses and ears of the others and banishing them from Kaga domain. The women were taken to the northernmost section of Noto peninsula, the poorest and most isolated part of the domain, and assigned to farmers as servants for life.[90] The four samurai, on the other hand, were exiled to the rugged foothills to the northeast of Kanazawa, and later were pardoned.

Occasionally, privileged *chōnin* secured preferential treatment. In 1652 some sons of merchant and artisan families in Komatsu used a vacant samurai residence as a place to bring prostitutes and hold parties. The neighboring samurai complained to a Constable named Hirota Gendaiyū and asked him to investigate. When the parties did not stop, the samurai took their complaints to higher officials. In the ensuing investigation, it was discovered that Hirota had accepted bribes from the commoners in exchange for ignoring the complaints and not reporting the parties to the City Magistrates. The Judiciary ordered Hirota to commit suicide. It also decreed, however, that since the *chōnin* "come from illustrious families in Komatsu, they are spared any punishment." "For this," the Judiciary noted, "they are thankful."[91]

One final case, from 1719, summarizes the judicial system's bias in favor of the established elements of society, whether samurai or *chōnin*. In that year, officials in the Office of Currency Control were charged with improprieties in their official conduct and imprisoned while an investigation was carried out. One of the two commoner officials, Fukushima Shin'emon, died in prison eight months after his initial confinement, probably as a result of tortures used in trying to obtain a confession from him. The Court cleared and released the other commoner official, Kamiya Matabei, the current household head of that distinguished family of chartered merchants, and it also dropped charges against all the samurai subofficials. At that point a man identified only as Kumagae asked the Court to reopen hearings on one of the samurai subofficials named Takumi. The nature of Kumagae's lingering suspicions is not clear, but the verbal exchanges at the new hearings reveal some interesting notions about criminals. The City Magistrates defended Takumi by claiming that since he was rich and was held in high esteem it was inconceivable that he could have participated in any crime. But Kumagae pressed the point. "Is it right," he asked, "to think that only poor people commit crimes and that wealthy, respected people never do so? Can you, who have jurisdiction over the officials at the Office of Currency Control, absolutely guarantee that Takumi had no hand in this affair?" The City Magistrates admitted that they could not, but the Court decided that the evidence was insufficient to support a judgment of guilty against Takumi.[92]

The strictness of law and the imperfections of the criminal justice system, however, should not be allowed to detract from the innovative features of the new urban government. The creation of a system in which the officials who exercised authority were themselves subject to laws and regulations and were required to administer according to established bureaucratic procedures was a major accomplishment of seventeenth-century Japan. In part, it was made possible by the application of Confucian principles to government. Occasional violence was bound to occur as individual jealousies and passions over love and money bubbled through to the surface, but this is to be expected in any complex community of more than 100,000 persons. In large measure, Kanazawa became a peaceful city. People from vastly different backgrounds with a diversity of skills, talents, interests, and wealth lived together in very close proximity, and in remarkable harmony. Nationally, the shogunate had eliminated threats to the nation and helped to prevent regional clashes among the daimyo. On the local level, a system of urban governance in which all the status groups cooperated in achieving unity and order was in operation

in every castle town, and it brought the Great Peace to the cities of the
Tokugawa period.

A NEW LOOK TO ECONOMIC LIFE
AND THE COMMERCIAL CLASSES

The specific political changes discussed above as well as more general
developments such as the Great Peace had certain implications for patterns of economic growth and commercial activity in Kanazawa during
the period from 1630 to 1670. The first artisans invited to Kanazawa by
Toshiie and Toshinaga, for example, had been carpenters, roofers, and
swordsmiths—men who could build a fortress and a castle town and also
supply the warriors with essential military equipment. As problems of
military security receded during the 1630s, Toshitsune and then Tsunanori began to extend patronage to a different group of craftsmen, who
specialized in luxury goods and works of art.

Toshitsune, for instance, invited to Kanazawa the famous artisan Igarashi Dōho, who specialized in making a kind of lacquer ware known as
makie, or "sprinkled lacquer," in which gold or silver powder or leaf was
sprinkled on the object before the final coats of lacquer were applied.
Dōho was the grandson of Igarashi Shinsai, who had received patronage
from the eighth Ashikaga shogun, Yoshimasa. By the early seventeenth
century the Igarashi and the Kōami families, both of Kyoto, had emerged
as the most esteemed gold and silver lacquer craftsmen in the country.
With the Tokugawa family patronizing the Kōami, it was perhaps no
surprise that Toshitsune invited the Igarashi to Kanazawa.[93]

In the 1660s Tsunanori invited to Kanazawa a Kyoto potter named
Nagaemon to produce implements for use in the tea ceremony, which was
popular among Tsunanori and many of the castle town's samurai. In
Kaga, Nagaemon chose a residential site near Ōhi village where he
thought the clay was particularly good. His works, characterized by
strong earthen hues, took the name of that village, which was located just
to the north of Kanazawa. Thanks in part to Tsunanori's support, Ōhi
pottery became prized throughout Japan.[94]

Additional examples abound. A local artisan named Umeda Yohei went
to Edo in the early 1650s to study under Kanō Naonobu, the younger
brother of the head of the famous Kanō school of painting (*nihonga*). Later
Umeda returned to Kanazawa where the Maeda granted him a stipend and
also commissioned him to paint sliding doors (*fusuma*) and the folding
panels used as bedside screens (*byōbu*). Among the dozens of craftsmen
who received patronage from the Maeda and whose works were acclaimed
throughout the country were Igawa Zenroku, famous for his ceramics and
lacquer ware, damascene artisans such as Shiihara Ichitayū and Shimizu

Kuhei, and members of the Kyoto-based Gotō family of gold and metal carvers (*chokinkō*).[95] These artisans gave a new texture to the commercial life of the castle town, and Kanazawa became renowned as a center of taste and fine craftsmanship, a reputation that the modern city maintains even today as the descendants of many of these same craftsmen preserve the family craft traditions.

Some of the craftsmen worked in the Artisans' Workshop (*saikusho*). The Workshop had probably first been established during Toshiie's administration, with the men who worked there producing and repairing military equipment such as saddles and armor for the personal use of Toshiie and Toshinaga.[96] After the 1630s, the output of the Workshop changed markedly as Toshitsune and Tsunanori began to employ craftsmen to produce luxury items. By the middle of the seventeenth century some fifty craftsmen were employed in the Workshop, on a yearly salary of twenty to thirty *koku* each, and they produced such things as lacquer ware, paintings, and masks for noh actors. These goods were not for general sale, but became the property of the Maeda daimyo, who presented many of them to the shogun or to esteemed daimyo colleagues. Some artisans in the Workshop continued to make military equipment, but as works of art rather than as actual martial products. In the late 1650s, for instance, Tsunanori presented the shogun with one thousand pairs of stirrups, all delicately inlaid with gold and silver fittings.

The new conditions of the middle seventeenth century also affected the lives of the chartered merchants. The relationship between the daimyo and the chartered merchants, for instance, became increasingly impersonal. One sign of this came in 1645 when five privileged merchants traveled to Edo to pay respects to the new daimyo, Tsunanori. They went not as individuals, but as representatives of the entire *chōnin* population of Kanazawa. Domain officials chose the five men for this mission and temporarily designated them as Elders (*toshiyori*) for the journey.[97] Sixteen years later, Tsunanori made his first visit to Kanazawa, arriving on the 19th day of the 7th month of 1661. Over the course of the following week, the samurai came to the castle to greet Tsunanori in order of status. Protocol officials arranged for the humble Lower Soldiers (*yoriki*) and twenty-one chartered merchants to appear on the 27th, the final day. Many of the merchants' names were familiar: Kōrinbō, Kamiya, Echizen'ya, Kanaya, and Kashiya. But whereas the first three daimyo had entertained these men's forefathers at the castle as individuals, Tsunanori had the chartered merchants paraded in as a group for a simple, brief ceremony.[98]

The experience of the Kamiya family was typical. The second-generation Kamiya family head, as noted earlier, was often the daimyo's personal guest for banquets at the castle and frequently exchanged gifts with the daimyo throughout the year. All this faded off during the headships of the third- and fourth-generation Kamiya, from 1653 through the early eighteenth century, until the only Kamiya appearances at the castle were for the mass ceremonies held at New Year's, and the only gifts were those stipulated by official protocol.[99]

A number of reasons account for the increasingly formal relationship. One was simply that the character of the daimyo was different. Tsunanori was born and raised in Edo and had no contact with the "purveyors to the daimyo" until after he had been ruling for nearly sixteen years. A second reason was related to the emerging status system and political structure. Informal meetings between daimyo and important merchants, whether for pleasure or to discuss urban affairs, were not consistent with the attempt to divide society into status groups and to create new governing techniques based on bureaucratic procedures.

In another change, some chartered merchants began to suffer business reverses as the economic requirements of the domain shifted during the middle of the seventeenth century. Like many of the other chartered merchants, the Sangaya family of warriors became merchants in the late sixteenth century, supplying military equipment to Toshiie. With the end of the threat of warfare, however, government orders began to decline, and in the 1630s Sangaya Kurōbei turned to sake brewing.[100] Such shifts were not uncommon. The Kōrinbō family, whose sales of eye potions to the daimyo had probably never amounted to a great sum in any case, eventually gave up the drug business and started to sell tools. Later they changed to selling foods preserved in sugar, then opened a pawnshop, and finally turned to selling *senbei* rice crackers.[101] The Dōjiriya family, which had specialized in *mochi* (pounded-rice cakes), on the other hand, began to make and sell medicines, a business that the family pursued for many decades.[102]

Changing economic circumstances had an impact on artisan groups as well. After the 1630s, the domain and the samurai had little need for the products of the swordsmiths who had been invited to Kanazawa in the late sixteenth century. Consequently, these artisans were among the few clear losers in the reorganization of the 1630s, compelled by the domain government to move their residences from a site near the castle to the extreme northwestern edge of the city. Most harshly treated of all were the *kawata*, the outcasts who made saddles and harnesses. They were stripped of their chartered status in 1645. At that time the domain also demanded the return of their residential land, forcing the *kawata* to move into rented lodgings on the outskirts of the city.[103] This was in sharp contrast to the treatment given other chartered artisans and merchants, who were allowed to keep their residential land and tax exemptions, even after the domain no longer required their economic services.

Another new feature of economic life during the middle of the seventeenth century, touched on earlier, was the expanded intrusion of domain law into urban business affairs. In part this manifested itself in controls over some kinds of economic activities. The government, for instance, established business procedures for pawnshop owners and insisted that peddlers carry tags listing their names and addresses.[104] It also imposed wage controls for artisans working on domain-sponsored projects and prohibitions on a form of lottery known as *tanomoshi*.[105]

In the case of wage controls, the domain was acting in its own self-interest by attempting to hold down construction and maintenance costs. The motivations were more complex in the other examples, however. Pawnshops were often the outlets for stolen goods. Consequently, the ordinances stated that if a pawnshop owner took possession of goods without demanding that the person pawning those items supply a guarantor, and if the original owner later claimed the stolen goods, then the pawnshop owner would have to stand the loss. If, however, the pawnshop owner had insisted upon a guarantor, then the goods would become his property and the original owner would have to collect from the guarantor. Then, if he wished, the original owner could use the money to redeem the stolen items.[106] Determining the legal ownership of stolen goods was also the reason that peddlers who specialized in selling used articles had to carry identification tags. If someone bought an item without confirming the peddler's identity and that item turned out to have been stolen, then the buyer would have to return it to the original owner. If the buyer could prove that he had confirmed the peddler's identity, however, he could keep the goods.[107]

In other cases, the domain authorities authorized licensing procedures for peddlers in order to protect the rights of recognized wholesalers or distributors. Peddlers in Kanazawa, for instance, attempted to circumvent the fisherman–wholesaler–retail fish shop marketing route established in the 1620s by buying fish directly at ports and peddling it in Kanazawa or selling it to small "general stores" (*aimono,* literally "forty commodities"). After the wholesalers complained, a system was devised by which the wholesalers continued to distribute fresh fish but the peddlers and general stores were allowed to sell most kinds of dried and salted fish. In addition, the wholesalers were authorized to license all peddlers and shops and to determine the wholesale prices for all fish, including those sold by the peddlers.[108] Another example was the group of wholesalers in Komatsu who by the 1660s had obtained the right to sell tea at wholesale to retail shops or peddlers throughout the domain. Domain ordinances stipulated that peddlers, including those from Kanazawa, had to obtain licenses from the wholesalers. The purpose was to prevent peddlers from buying directly from producers in order to avoid the commission charged by the wholesale distributors.[109]

The prohibitions on *tanomoshi* lotteries came for a different set of reasons. In the early seventeenth century, commoners in Kanazawa formed lottery groups, with each individual member contributing a fixed sum. The group would then hold a drawing, and the winner would then have the use of the collected monies for a predetermined length of time, after which he would return that amount, plus interest, to the group. Then, the next person whose name was drawn would receive the funds, and so the process would continue until everyone in the group had a chance to use the money. The possibilities for rigging the lottery and not returning the collected funds were all too obvious, however, and in 1662 the domain prohibited *tanomoshi* lottery groups.[110] Apparently this ban was not particularly effective, since the domain amended the regulations in 1671 to read that samurai and townspeople could not join together to form lottery groups.[111] Two years later came the celebrated Shiroya Sōemon incident. In his youth Sōemon had been a Page (*koshō*) in the service of Maeda Bingo no Kami, but he resigned his post to become a *chōnin*. In the early 1670s, Shōemon conspired with eight samurai youths he knew to set up a sham lottery involving commoners. Sōemon and his samurai companions made sure that they won the drawing, and used the money to speculate in rice futures. At first they were successful and invested some of the profits in various businesses. With the remainder they rented a number of houses in Kanazawa and held some reputedly spectacular parties. About the time that the original lottery group started to insist that Sōemon return their money, the business investments began to go sour. Domain officials initiated inquiries, and Sōemon and his samurai companions, unable to repay the funds, fled the city. Domain police officials set off in pursuit and eventually caught up with Sōemon at Chirifu (modern-day Chiryū in Aichi Prefecture), a post town on the great Tōkaidō road that linked Edo with Osaka. There they killed Sōemon in a dramatic sword fight, but not before he crippled some of his assailants. "Sōemon was still young—just thirty—and was very big and very strong," the weary, battered police reported; "and," they added, "he wasn't so bad at handling his sword either." Some of Sōemon's young samurai cohorts were tracked down in Edo, and eventually all were captured. Most were punished by execution or were exiled to Noto Island, a short distance off Noto peninsula.[112]

Despite such incidents, *tanomoshi* lotteries remained popular, and in 1678 the city government recognized their popularity when it issued a law designed more simply to bring the lotteries under some measure of control. The new ordinance required lottery groups to file a statement with the city government, prohibited joint *chōnin*-samurai groups, and declared that lotteries should be formed only among relatives or neighbors for the sole intention of helping persons who were suffering from economic hardship and not for "purposes of profit" (speculating in rice futures, for example).[113] What is important to note here is that the regulations governing lotteries, as well as the new laws pertaining to peddlers and pawnshops, did not represent an extension of domain law merely for the purpose of further centralizing autocratic powers in the hands of domain government. Rather, the laws were designed to preserve established business interests and to protect merchants and ordinary residents from thieves and swindlers.

If it is easy to identify some of the new trends of the middle seventeenth century, it is more difficult to trace the major themes that first emerged in the 1583 to 1630 period. Some domain policies, such as the maintenance of transportation routes and support for the wholesalers who moved goods into the city, continued to enhance Kanazawa's economic importance throughout the seventeenth century. One daimyo activity, however, had a negative effect on the castle town's economic growth. The requirement that the Maeda daimyo join the other daimyo in maintaining a mansion in Edo, alternating his own residence between Edo and his home domain, siphoned off a great deal of wealth that might otherwise have been spent in Kanazawa. Expenditures for the required mansion in Edo increased over the course of the century, but even by the 1660s it is likely that Kaga domain was spending the equivalent of perhaps 100,000 *koku* of rice annually on this obligation.[114]

Still, the fact that new merchant and artisan wards continued to sprout up along the major arteries leading into Kanazawa indicated that the city had not yet reached any natural limit to its economic growth and development. Samurai expenditures were one of the main fuels that propelled this continued growth. Actual total samurai income from stipends amounted to more than 300,000 *koku* per year, and most of this was spent in Kanazawa. Since 1.8 *koku* is generally accepted as the minimal amount necessary to cover the basic annual costs of living—housing, food, and clothing—for one person, the assurance of an expenditure of nearly a third of a million *koku* of rice by local samurai ensured Kanazawa a certain degree of prosperity.[115]

During the 1630–70 period, we get the first glimpse of how that wealth was distributed. Samurai spanned the whole range from the very wealthy to the very poor. It is sometimes difficult, however, to calculate the precise net income of samurai since the amount that was stated on domain records—for example Honda Awa no Kami was listed as possessing a 50,000-*koku* fief—was actually the official productive capacity of the samurai's "paper" fief after the rural reforms of the 1650s. Of this "official" or "theoretical" income, the samurai actually received only the tax proceeds, or about forty percent. Thus Honda would receive a "gross income" of about 20,000 *koku*. After the rural reforms, of course, Honda did not receive this income directly from the peasants. Rather, the peasants paid their taxes to the domain granary, and the domain issued Honda a certificate entitling him to receive his 20,000 *koku* from the daimyo's warehouse.

Out of this gross income the samurai had to pay a number of exactions. For instance, he had to send gifts to the daimyo on numerous occasions—at New Year's (a cask of sake for those with an official income of 3,000 to 10,000 *koku*), at certain festivals, when assuming family headship, and when receiving an increase in "fief" size. In addition, he had to pay the domain a warehouse fee, approximately one-half percent of his gross income. Samurai also had to pay some "taxes" such as the *dashigin* (also pronounced *shuggin*), a domain levy that was used to help defray the costs of the daimyo's alternate residence in Edo. This was not a tax in the modern sense, since it was based on the concept that the samurai owed the daimyo an open-ended obligation in exchange for the lord's protection, but in effect it amounted to a tax. Since the taxes and levies were expressed in monetary terms (the *dashigin* in 1664, for example, was twenty-five *monme* per one hundred *koku* of official income) and since the price of rice fluctuated yearly, it is difficult to express these as a percentage of income, but it seems unlikely that the total of all taxes and levies amounted to more than five to ten percent of the gross income. Honda's net income, then, would come to approximately 18,000 to 19,000 *koku*.

The wealthiest samurai in Kanazawa were the Eight Families. Each of these families had an official income of more than 10,000 *koku,* which would yield a net income of about 3,500 *koku.* The luxury that this income could buy was evident in their housing styles. The Honda and Okumura residences, for instance, each boasted of dozens of rooms, expansive and beautifully landscaped gardens complete with ponds and artificial hills, and magnificent gates carved from the finest wood.[116] Interestingly enough, the architectural design of these mansions and gardens was left to the discretion of the individual samurai. The Maeda daimyo were concerned about how their urban plans met the perceived requirements of military security and the social status system, but, unlike Peter the Great who issued so many instructions about the style of houses put up on the banks of the Neva, they were not particularly interested in architecture as an urban art form. Indeed, the very concept of urban aesthetics was much less important to the Maeda daimyo than to the baroque planners of Europe.

Indirect evidence drawn from frugality laws provides additional clues about the lifestyles of the wealthy samurai. Ordinances issued in 1659, for instance, limited bridal processions to "twenty chests and ten palanquins" and prohibited brides from using in their kitchens lacquer ware decorated with gold and silver leaf.[117] Despite the regulations, however, elite samurai families continued to buy such utensils, as well as porcelains, pottery, paintings, and other works of art. Even today, the Honda family collection occupies its own two-story museum on one corner of the family's former residence.

The frugality laws also tell us a great deal about the middle-ranking samurai, those with official incomes of 300 to 3,000 koku. The 1659 ordinances forbade this level of retainers from keeping hawks for hunting, an expensive propostion when the cost of the hawks, trainers, and hunting expeditions were all included. Also prohibited in that year were the keeping of mistresses and the use in home construction of gold or silver or any "luxurious item not in accordance with one's status."[118] Later that year, the government instructed samurai not to build weapons storehouses or "any other magnificent structure inappropriate to one's status."[119] In 1663 the domain complained there were reports of samurai renting lodgings to touring groups of dancers and puppeteers and hiring these groups to perform at parties, and it ordered these practices stopped. Then two months later it threatened to send out inspectors if it received reports of samurai holding lavish parties and banquets. "This is a time," the announcement huffed, "when the domain has declared that persons should be frugal."[120]

Despite their sizable incomes, by the middle of the seventeenth century some middle-level bushi were beginning to run into financial problems. These samurai had to maintain certain prescribed standards regarding swords, clothing, and service personnel. In addition, they had to make gifts to the daimyo at prescribed times, such as presents of sake and fish at New Year's. The cost of these items, plus extras such as mistresses and banquets, drove some into indebtedness. Efforts by samurai in the 1640s and early 1650s to increase their incomes by compelling the peasants on their fiefs to pay more taxes was one reason leading to the kaisakuhō rural reforms of the 1650s. After the reforms these samurai had to live on fixed stipends, and inflation or a drop in rice prices in years of particularly good harvests could have a marked impact on their solvency. In 1658 and 1659, the domain actually bought back the stipends it had already paid some samurai at a rate higher than their real market value in order to prop up samurai incomes.[121] From the 1660s on, the domain began to make loans to samurai, although the borrowers had to sign a written pledge not to borrow from other individuals, undertake any new home construction, buy luxurious goods, drink too much sake, or own falcons without express written permission.[122]

While some middle-level samurai felt the strain of maintaining a fairly gracious standard of living, other warriors lived in much more humble circumstances. Many of the more minor ranking Lower Soldiers (okachi) and Foot Soldiers (ashigaru), for example, received a gross salary of approximately twelve or thirteen koku per year.[123] With this, the soldier had to maintain his military equipment, employ at least one or two servants, and keep up his residence, which might have four or five small rooms (in the special wards the Foot Soldiers received plots of land 165 square meters in area). If the man's family included three or four children, he would have little left for a new sword, priced at one *koku* plus the cost of materials. Since the price of a woman's outer silk jacket (*kosode*) was nearly 2.5 *koku* in 1668, the clothing ordinances restricting the Foot Soldiers to pongee and cloth may have been more of a confirmation of their economic status than a chafing prohibition.[124]

The economic strain to which the lower levels of the samurai class were subjected can be seen in the fact that even as early as the 1640s some families began to weave silk cloth as a form of household by-employ-ment.[125] Over time, the number of low-ranking samurai who supple-mented their incomes through by-employments increased. By the middle of the next century some had started to specialize. The Chō rear vassals, for instance, made paper cords (*motoyui*) that were used to style hair. They also grew apples for sale to the vegetable market. The Imaeda vassals made paper lanterns (*chōchin*) and kites, while some others specialized in toys. The Murai rear vassals grew a kind of citrus fruit (*kōji*), and other groups concentrated on peaches, apricots, and persimmons.[126]

The poorest members of the *bushi* class were the *hōkōnin* servant person-nel. Since there was an almost constant shortage of persons willing to fill these positions, prospective employers tended to bid up their wages, and the domain imposed maximum salary limits. These varied over time, but in the 1650s and early 1660s the Young Stewards (*wakatō*), the highest paid, received a maximum of 150 *monme* per year. A lower-ranking Atten-dant (*komono*) was paid between fifty-five and eighty *monme*, depending on ability and length of service, while Valets (*arashiko*) received from thirty-five to fifty *monme*.[127]

Given an absence of general price information, it is necessary to adopt two rules of thumb in order to attach meaning to these salaries. The first is that the price of rice averaged about fifty *monme* per *koku*, and the second is that it required the equivalent of 1.8 *koku* (ninety *monme*) to cover the minimum costs of food, shelter, and clothing for one person for one year.[128] Since a *hōkōnin* received housing and probably some meals from his employer, a young single man serving as a Young Steward certainly had enough income to cover his living expenses, enjoy an occasional drinking bout with his friends, and even put some savings away to use when his days of service were finished. For an Attendant, however, the extras became increasingly infrequent, and for the Valet life must have been austere indeed. Given the availability of alternative forms of employ-ment, such as artisan apprentice or clerk in a merchant shop, it is some-times difficult to imagine why a person would become a *hōkōnin*. The explanation may lie in the intangible benefits. One did have a secure, fixed income, could enjoy at least a quasi-samurai status, and might possibly travel to Edo if one's master were chosen as a member of the retinue that accompanied the daimyo on his alternate residence obligation.[129]

It would be nearly impossible to support a family on any of the *hōkōnin* salaries, however, and it is among *hōkōnin* that we see some of the bleakest examples of urban poverty. Take the case, for instance, of Kyūzaburō, an Attendant who lived in dormitory lodgings provided by his master, a middle-rank samurai named Saiga Mozaemon. Living with Kyūzaburō were his wife, his sister-in-law (named Tora), and his mother-in-law. With a maximum salary of eighty *monme,* the assumed cost of just over 1.5 *koku* of rice, life was a constant struggle for Kyūzaburō, and he finally suggested that his mother-in-law be sent out to beg on the streets as a way of supplementing family income. Tora, his sister-in-law, felt that this was intolerable and decided to kill her mother and then commit suicide. However, Kyūzaburō's brother, identified only as Roku, caught Tora just as she was about to commit the murder. A report was sent, according to established legal procedures, from the master Saiga to the Office of Police and the Judiciary. The Judiciary recognized that Tora's motive was to spare her mother from indignity, and eventually it gave Tora nearly ninety *monme* so that she could "exhibit filial piety" and care for her mother, a decision that demonstrated some of the leavening effects of Neo-Confucianism.[130]

The commoner classes also extended from the very rich to the very poor. There are no extant documents that indicate the yearly income of merchants, but if housing styles can be taken as a standard, then some merchants possessed considerable wealth. Many of the residential plots in the Original Wards measured more than sixty by thirty meters, approximately the size of a residence that a samurai with an official stipend of 1,000 *koku* received.[131] The homes themselves could also be spectacular. The Asanoya and Echizen'ya Magobei residences included elaborately carved gates, of a type not usually permitted to merchants, and platformed entranceways (*shikidai*) which rivaled in size and quality of construction those of high-level samurai. Such homes might contain more than a dozen rooms, a garden, and a detached storehouse for family treasures.[132]

It was primarily to the upper middle class and wealthy merchants that the domain addressed many of the frugality laws. Ordinances issued in 1668, for example, instructed townspeople to be thrifty when constructing homes and not to use doors made from Japanese cedar (*sugido*), have engravings carved in the woodwork, or build special libraries. Those same ordinances instructed people not to use gold or silver for children's dolls, for the miniature swords and helmets used as decorations for the Boys' Festival, or for the badminton equipment enjoyed at New Year's.[133] Furthermore, perhaps because they were driving up the prices that the samurai had to pay, commoners were instructed to pay no more than 130 *monme* for a women's silk outer jacket (*kosode*) or forty-three *monme* for a lightweight kimono (*katabira*).[134]

Contrast the above with the lifestyles of the artisans who lived in the Ordinary Wards, where property frontages averaged a modest six to nine meters. Nor were most of the economically middle and lower middle class persons who lived here able to afford the kind of homes found in the Original Wards. In the 1660s, the standard wage for a carpenter working on domain construction projects was set at 1.1 to 1.7 *monme* per day depending on his ability; that for roof thatchers was pegged at 1.0 to 1.5 *monme*.[135] If we assume that a carpenter or thatcher worked three hundred days a year, which would allow time off for rest days, festivals, rainy days, and the slack employment periods in winter, then a carpenter could expect to make from 330 to 510 *monme* per year, and a thatcher would make between 300 and 450 *monme*. In years when employment opportunities were less available or when the winter snows and spring rains interfered more with job schedules, the men would work fewer days. In a year that included only 250 work days, a carpenter would bring home 275 to 425 *monme* and a thatcher 250 to 375 *monme*.

This represented a rather wide range of wages. Expressed in terms of buying power, the highest-paid carpenter made the equivalent of more than ten *koku* of rice in a good year, while the lowest-paid thatcher made just half of that in a bad year. In absolute terms, these salaries did not match those of the poorly paid Lower Soldiers and Foot Soldiers mentioned above. Yet the samurai had heavier monetary obligations since they had to maintain more expensive houses, equip themselves with swords, hire servants, and observe certain standards of dress. Consequently, a well-paid carpenter was probably better off economically than many of the lower-ranking samurai. Certainly with an income of ten *koku* a year he could comfortably raise a family and enjoy some of the pleasures of life, a drink of sake with friends or an occasional treat from the confectionery shop for his family. The thatchers, on the other hand, were more financially pressed, but by making compromises in their standards of living—a smaller house, more barley and wheat mixed into the daily rice, more vegetables and less fish—even the lowest-paid thatcher could support a small family. But few carpenters or thatchers could afford a silk kimono for their wives. For these men, prohibitions against wearing some of the finest grades of silk or owning gold inlaid badminton sets probably carried little meaning, since they could not have afforded those items in any case.

The day laborers were part of the *chōnin* poor, and most lived in wards which emerged from the *aitaiukechi*. There rows of apartments and tiny houses sat on minuscule plots, most not more than three or four meters square. In 1662, day laborers working on government construction projects received 7 *bu* 5 *rin*, less than a *monme* a day. [136] Even if we assume that a day laborer worked 330 days a year, which would permit just two vacation days a month plus a short break at New Year's and again for the summer Festival in Honor of the Ancestors (*obon*), he could hope to make only 250 *monme*. In a more ordinary year when job opportunities were fewer or illness struck, a day laborer might earn less than two hundred *monme*—enough to provide for a wife, but a precarious income on which to raise a family. Economically, the position of the day laborer was probably not dissimilar to the Attendant discussed earlier. The day laborer had a potentially higher annual income, but he had to provide his own housing and had no guarantee of security for those years when economic conditions made his services unnecessary. [137]

A MORE PLACID URBAN CULTURE

Kabuki and other forms of entertainment such as touring groups of puppeteers and dancers continued to play before receptive audiences well into the 1620s. But by the end of that decade some of the violence that had been associated with the arrival of the first kabuki troupes in the early seventeenth century, and which had led to the 1611 and 1612 bans, had begun to reappear. Part of the problem was that theater owners customarily admitted sumo wrestlers and some samurai such as the Lower Soldiers to the theaters free of charge. The reasons for this are not clear, but it is likely that the owners were simply trying to avoid any problems with the often ill-tempered sumo giants. Whatever the reason, the policy of free admission led to other, perhaps predictable, problems. Soon some of the Young Stewards and Attendants disguised themselves as sumo wrestlers and tried to enter the theaters. When the ticket takers stopped them, the young samurai often pulled their swords and brandished them about, causing an uproar. More often than necessary, the incidents ended in bloodshed. [138]

In 1626 or 1627 the City Office ordered Chaya Sakuemon to close his theater, perhaps because his establishment on the banks of the Sai River had become the scene of frequent outbreaks of fighting. [139] A year later, however, an Inspector from the City Office noticed that Sakuemon had opened a new theater. When the Inspector interviewed Sakuemon, the theater owner assured him that Toshitsune had granted him permission to reopen. The Inspector filed a routine report which eventually reached the offices of Honda Awa no Kami and Yokoyama Yamashiro no Kami, Toshitsune's two principal advisers. They took it to Toshitsune, who in fact had never even heard of Sakuemon. An enraged Toshitsune sentenced Sakuemon to death by burning, and the punishment was carried out at the execution grounds located behind Temple Ward.

A celebrated incident of prostitution also earned Toshitsune's wrath.[140] When a Foot Soldier named Nakamura Gyōbu died, he left his widow, Imo (the name literally means "pockmarked face"), with a daughter and a young son to support. Imo arranged for her daughter, named Kichi, to work as a prostitute in the bathhouses along the Sai River. But Imo committed even more serious improprieties. She also recruited other young women of samurai background to work as prostitutes. Reportedly, they became very popular; one suspects particularly so among the merchants and artisans who frequented the bathhouses. Eventually, Honda and Yokoyama received a report on these activities, and after a conference with Toshitsune, they ordered crucifixion for Imo, Kichi, Imo's son, and three bathhouse proprietors.

These two incidents put a dramatic end to the free-wheeling social life that had centered on the theater and bathhouse districts along the Sai and Asano rivers. For the next 150 years, kabuki performers very rarely came to Kanazawa: a troupe composed of young males passed through the city in 1631, a group from Edo played a short run at a temple in Kanazawa in the summer of 1656, and troupes were reported occasionally at nearby hot springs resorts and rural villages in the late seventeenth and early eighteenth centuries.[141] Thus, kabuki virtually disappeared from Kanazawa until the domain government licensed a few theaters in the early nineteenth century, after a florescence of *chōnin* culture in Edo.[142]

Following the incident involving Imo and her daughter Kichi, the domain government in Kaga issued ordinances that prohibited prostitution and houses of assignation.[143] Prostitution never became completely extinct in Kanazawa, as is evident in the criminal cases mentioned above and the periodic reissuance of the prohibitions. However, until the domain permitted the construction of two "pleasure quarters" (*yūkaku*) at the beginning of the nineteenth century, prostitution was driven underground, and the bustling, swirling activity of the bathhouse district became only a memory.[144]

The motives which prompted the government to suppress the theater and prostitution are clear. In the first place, violence in the streets was no longer acceptable. The domain had moved forcefully against the *kabukimono* in the 1610s and was not about to tolerate a resurgence of street crime in the late 1620s. The domain had other concerns as well. In Kanazawa, elements of the theater and prostitution also cut cross-grain to government policies. The commingling of status groups that went on at the theaters and the employment of samurai women at houses of public prostitution could scarcely be condoned at a time when Toshitsune was trying to establish a society based on status distinctions. Beyond this, the first frugality laws came out in the 1630s, and Toshitsune was probably worried that the samurai were spending too much of their income on entertainment. [145] And perhaps too much of their passion as well. Indeed, the realization that many of the sons and grandsons of the military heroes of the sixteenth century had become more interested in actors and prostitutes than in maintaining their martial spirit led the shogunate to ban all female impersonators from the Edo stage in 1642. [146]

The decline of the popular culture that had characterized Kanazawa in the 1610s and early 1620s may have been due to other reasons as well. There is some indication that the puppet and dance troupes, as well as kabuki, were losing their mass appeal by the 1630s. A couple of years after Chaya Sakuemon was forced to close his theater, Toshitsune responded favorably to a request submitted by two men, identified only as Satsuma Isonosuke and Kindaiyū, to open a new theater on the banks of the Sai River, an indication that the government was willing to tolerate a more orderly theater. But Isonosuke and Kindaiyū never achieved financial success. When the fire of 1631 destroyed the theater, the government arranged for the men to receive housing and the use of stages at a temple named Ryūenji. Despite those benefits, the two men closed down their operations a short time later. [147]

By the late 1620s and 1630s, acting and dancing troupes played to what might have been a different kind of urban dweller who had a new and different view of the city. For many of the samurai and chartered merchants and artisans of the late sixteenth and early seventeenth centuries, Kanazawa was just one of several encampments that they had made during their lifetimes. Many of these men had started life in the Kyoto-Osaka area, then moved to Fukui, and later to Nanao, before finally coming to Kanazawa. Their economic livelihood and position in society depended upon their relationship with the Maeda daimyo. In the early years of the seventeenth century daimyo transfers of domain were still common, and there was no guarantee that these men would not have to pack again and follow the Maeda daimyo to a different garrison headquarters.

The situation was different for their sons and grandsons in the 1630s. For them, Kanazawa was home. The possibility that the shogun would transfer the Maeda to a new domain had become virtually nil. For the chartered merchants and artisans, economic realities had also changed. Privileged status no longer ensured business success: chartered merchants and artisans now had to sell to all levels of urban society, and consequently smiths had started to make pots and pans, and the Sangaya family had opened a sake business. The ordinary members of the merchant class also faced new conditions. In 1600 it was possible to come to the city for a few years, save some money, and return to one's home village. Domain laws against the alienation of agricultural land, however, did much to foreclose that possibility for the later generation of urban dwellers. But the appeal of rural life for the second and third generation of *chōnin* seems doubtful in any case, for they had no experience in farming or in managing an agricultural household. For them, like their privileged counterparts, the economic well-being of their families depended on how well they did as businessmen or craftsmen. Violence on the street could threaten that livelihood. Fights among sword-wielding *bushi* at theaters could spill over onto the streets. Shops might be smashed, and goods damaged. Customers would stay away. Better perhaps to forgo the pleasures of the theater and bathhouses and to obey the daimyo's laws; and thus feel more secure about one's business and less apprehensive about the danger to one's family that came with violence on the street.

The residents of Kanazawa in the 1630 to 1670 period were a more sober lot than their ancestors. As the excitement of the early seventeenth century—the emotional release that followed the end of constant warfare and the gaiety and exuberance that accompanied the first experience of city building and urban living—receded into the past, other recreational pursuits and cultural activities, some with a long history, became the dominant themes of urban social life. A restrained, even sedate, round of festivals and ceremonies came to mark the cycle of the year and the passage of time.

For the city's commoners, New Year's broke winter's monotony with a series of joyous festivities.[148] Preparations actually started late in the 12th month as families gave the house an especially thorough cleaning and invited friends and relatives for a party (*bōnenkai*) to celebrate the outgoing year. The first day of the New Year was given over to quiet family gatherings and visits to the homes of friends, relatives, and employers to offer best wishes for the coming year. The 7th day of the New Year was known colloquially as *nanakusa* (literally, seven spring flowers), and, in a tradition that went back for centuries, families would try to serve at least a small portion each of parsley, shepherd's purse, cottonweed, chickweed, henbit, turnips, and radishes. It was customary to invite relatives for dinner on the 16th day, and the New Year's celebration came to an unofficial close four days later when families consumed the last of the special *mochi* rice cake.

The 3rd day of the 3rd month was the Girls' Festival, when families set out their daughter's collection of dolls and, in the evening, served a special dinner of rice flavored with red beans, colored rice cakes (*hishi mochi*), and a soup of freshwater clams. Two months later, on the 5th day of the 5th month, came the Boys' Festival, and parents hung up streamers in the shape of carp—to represent strength and perseverance—and exchanged presents of rice dumplings wrapped in bamboo leaves (*chimaki*) with friends and neighbors. The Star Festival (*tanabata*) enlivened the summer. Two stars, which were claimed to represent lost lovers, converged in the sky on the 7th day of the 7th month and the city's residents made a spirited day, and night, of it. Merchants decorated their shops and people throughout the city lit bonfires in the evening and then congregated in the streets for dancing. Many of the younger people ended up at the Asano and Sai river bridges and, often as not, fights broke out and many ended up in the waters below the bridges. That was perhaps a way of letting off steam before the more sober Festival in Honor of Ancestors (*obon*), observed on the 14th through 17th days of the 7th month. Those families which could afford them set out Buddhist household altars and mortuary tablets. Most families visited their temples, and children built bonfires on the banks of the Asano and Sai rivers to greet, and then to see off, the souls of the ancestors, who supposedly returned to visit during the three-day festival. Finally, in the late summer and early fall, individual temples throughout the city hosted small festivals which featured folk dances by groups of parishioners and booths selling special foods.

Samurai families observed many of the same ceremonies, but usually in a slightly different manner. On New Year's, for instance, the daimyo invited many of the samurai to the castle to exchange greetings. Important retainers such as the Commanders as well as the Confucian scholars employed by the domain came on the first day of the New Year. On the second day, the daimyo hosted lesser samurai, such as the Mounted Patrol, and still lesser samurai such as the Magistrates' Constabulary, Riflemen, and Falconers appeared for their mass audience on the third day.[149] Similarly, the Boys' Festival held an extra treat for the sons of major retainers, who were given an audience with the daimyo on this day.[150]

Other events in the yearly cycle were more clearly the province of one or another of Kanazawa's social groups.[151] The merchants, for example, held a festival on the 20th day of the 10th month in honor of Ebisu, the god of commerce. They customarily celebrated by decorating their shops with colored strips of paper, holding sales, and giving small presents to their regular customers. Smiths and other artisans who used bellows held their own festival on the 8th day of the 10th month, which began with a visit to the local shrine during the day. In the evening, masters hosted friends and employees for a meal of fish, rice flavored with red beans, and sake— although it seems unlikely that they limited themselves to the "two toasts" prescribed by law.

Some sports were solely for the samurai. To promote physical fitness and a martial spirit among the warriors, the domain maintained a horse-riding ground on the north bank of the Asano, two rifle ranges, and a drill hall for training and archery practice.[152] By domain law, *bushi* also had the exclusive right to hunt birds in mountain areas. Though some sections were open to all samurai, others were set aside for the exclusive use of important retainers, who often built small hunting lodges on them.[153] Falconry, too, was extremely popular among the wealthier samurai. The first three Maeda daimyo thoroughly enjoyed the sport and created vast falconry preserves, one just to the south of Temple Ward. Tsunanori, the most "citified" of the early Maeda daimyo, had less to do with the sport, but falconry retained its popularity among the upper-level samurai, many of whom purchased their own hawks and paid falconry masters to train and care for the birds.[154]

The themes of the new urban social life—order, tranquillity, and a growing cleavage between the recreational activities of the different status groupings—echoed some of the other changes that had taken place in Kanazawa in the years 1630 to 1670. Both the onset of peace and the desire to create a system of rule by status stimulated the formulation of new ideas about the ordering of urban space. Although reality never did completely conform to theory, the domain government began to distinguish between samurai land and *chōnin* land and to associate an individual's place of residence with his position within his status hierarchy. The government also issued new ordinances and legal codes which completed the definition of status differences between samurai and commoner. The domain also created an administrative structure, based on prescribed bureaucratic procedures and a growing rule by law, which brought a new measure of order and regulation to the status groups. These trends were reflected in the economic life of the city as well. Most merchants, such as the peddlers and pawnshop owners, began to conduct their businesses in accordance with new laws and regulations. The chartered merchants also found that their lives had changed. The first and even the second generation had had political responsibilities and social privileges not unlike those of some important samurai. Now, if a chartered merchant helped to administer the city, he did so within an official capacity and in accordance with established procedures. And, if he had the opportunity to so much as see the daimyo, it was now in a formal and impersonal setting.

The current heads of the Kōrinbō and Kamiya households lived in a far different city than that of their grandfathers and great-grandfathers. Yet the next thirty years, from 1670 to 1700, would bring still another set of changes to the lives of these families, changes that gave final shape to the political, social, and economic institutions that would be characteristic of Kanazawa throughout the eighteenth century.

FOUR
THE YEARS OF CLOSURE,
1670–1700

On the national level, changes occurred in the second half of the seventeenth century and the early years of the eighteenth century that signaled a close to the first one hundred years of growth under the Tokugawa shogunate. These brought to fruition the transformations of the first half of the seventeenth century, and resulted in the formation of the basic political, social, and economic institutions that historians identify with the mature phase of Tokugawa society. The remainder of the Tokugawa period was not stagnant, for economic and social change took place continuously throughout the eighteenth and early nineteenth centuries, but those later changes occurred within the institutional framework that had emerged during the course of the seventeenth century.

The shogun's government had assumed its basic shape by the middle of the seventeenth century, but another half century or so was needed to refine the procedures and principles of governance. One notable development was the expanded application of Neo-Confucian precepts to the conduct of government officials. The fifth shogun, Tsunayoshi (ruled 1680–1709), was a fervent supporter of Neo-Confucianism. After his installation as shogun in 1680, Tsunayoshi heard three lectures a month from the Confucian scholar Hayashi Nobuatsu, the head of the Hayashi family school first established in 1630, and occasionally he assembled daimyo and government officials for lectures. In 1691 Tsunayoshi converted the Hayashi school (known as the Shōheikō) into an official government college when he ordered the establishment transferred from the family residence at Shinobugaoka in the Ueno district to a new location at Yushima.[1] In time, the further reliance on Confucianism as a guide for political and administrative conduct produced a style of government that has been called "rule by moral suasion" (*bunji seiji*).

Increased impersonality and bureaucratization in administration constituted a second prominent trend in the late seventeenth century. A proliferation of offices and a further functional differentiation of duties went on at all levels of the shogunate. The changed role of the daimyo himself symbolized these changes. The first three shogun—Ieyasu, Hidetada, and Iemitsu—had been vigorous leaders who had taken a direct hand in governing and in creating the basic administrative apparatus of the shogunate. The fourth (Ietsuna, ruled 1651–80) and fifth (Tsunayoshi) increasingly withdrew from affairs of state, and actual administrative duties passed into the hands of shogunate officials. Tsunayoshi, for instance, relied heavily on the Senior Councilor (*tairō*) Hotta Masatoshi and, after Hotta's assassination in 1684, on the Chamberlain (*sobayōnin*) Yanagisawa Yoshiyasu. Freed from the chores of governing, Tsunayoshi turned his interests toward cultural pursuits such as literature, the fine arts, and the study of Neo-Confucianism.

The continued growth of urban consumption centers such as Edo and Osaka stimulated a great deal of the economic development and change that took place during the second half of the seventeenth century. Edo's population doubled during the period, for example, and reached its peak of more than one million by the 1720s. Throughout the country, many castle towns approached Edo's growth rate in percentage terms and, like the shogun's capital, reached their maximum proportions in the early eighteenth century.

In addition, economic and commercial development was related to the ever-increasing volume of agricultural output. Some of the agricultural gains came from an expansion of the land base, as both the shogunate and individual daimyo carried out vast reclamation projects. Improved productivity and better crop yields also played a role. The seventeenth century witnessed dramatic advancements in the types of available tools and seeds, a more intensive use of fertilizers, and an expanded circulation of books on farming methods. In all, the total assessed productivity of the country leaped from about eighteen million *koku* of rice in 1597 to more than twenty-six million by 1700.

Rising productivity had a number of important consequences. Farmers were able to concentrate more of their energies on growing commercial crops such as cotton, tea, hemp, mulberry, indigo, vegetables, and tobacco for sale to the urban markets. Regional specialization also became a feature of economic life in Tokugawa Japan, as villagers around Osaka, for instance, began to specialize in cotton and farmers in northern Japan raised horses and cattle for use as draft animals. Throughout the country, individual rural households and even whole villages began to develop by-employments or simple rural industries. Common products included paper, charcoal, ink, pottery, lacquer ware, and spun silk.

The continued growth of urban consumption centers and the concurrent expansion of cash farming and rural handicraft industries provided new opportunities for wholesalers and transportation agents (*ton'ya*) who engaged in interregional trade. Such wholesalers had been active throughout the seventeenth century. In Kanazawa, as noted earlier, a group of fish wholesalers had started operations in the 1620s, and in Osaka rice, vegetable, fish, lumber, and oil *ton'ya* were already in operation by 1650. From the 1660s on, however, wholesalers appeared in ever-increasing numbers in major cities. In Osaka, nearly four hundred different kinds of *ton'ya* were in existence by the late 1670s. In Kyoto wholesale drapers like the Echigoya (Mitsui) maintained large purchasing establishments and even contracted for the textile output of whole districts. The formation of the Group of Ten Wholesale Guilds (*tokumidon'ya*) in Edo in 1694 marked its arrival as the most important group of merchants in the nation's largest city.[2]

The political authorities expressed a growing uneasiness over this increased commercial activity. On six separate occasions between 1648 and 1670, for example, the shogunate issued edicts against the unauthorized formation of merchant associations. In part, this apprehension was based on philosophical concerns. To Tokugawa political leaders, a fundamentally agrarian economy had come to be the ideal to emulate. They increasingly envisaged a society in which the samurai ruled, the peasants and artisans produced, and the merchants handled the minimum amount of trade and distribution consistent with society's continued well-being.

But the uneasiness of the political elite also sprang from practical considerations. In the early half of the seventeenth century, daimyo throughout the country had encouraged the economic development of their castle towns as part of a broader policy whose purpose was to make the domains impervious to economic or military assault from the outside. By midcentury conditions had changed. The domains were now going concerns, and the efforts of government were directed toward maintaining them as cohesive, integrated economic units and, at the same time, completing the final phases of political consolidation. Too much commercial development could cut cross-grain to these objectives. As wealth flowed into the countryside to pay for commercial crops or the products of rural handicraft industries, daimyo feared farmers might become unconcerned with rice production or worst yet, lazy, spendthrift, and disobedient. In Kanazawa, for instance, the domain government issued announcements periodically throughout the second half of the seventeenth century stating that farmers were to concentrate on agricultural activities and forbidding them to own "luxurious" clothing or to spend money on their houses for such frivolous items as separate studies, doors made from cypress wood, or woodwork with elaborate carvings and engravings.[3]

From the government's perspective, too much commercial development could also have adverse consequences within the cities. Writing in his office diary in the middle of the seventeenth century, one of Kanazawa's City Magistrates, Wakida Kuhei, had these thoughts:

Merchants deal in goods. They buy and sell things which people need in their daily lives—food, shelter, and clothing. Merchants transport goods from one area to another. . . . They accumulate money. They lend out money and make a profit. Merchants who have a plan of operations and a good sense for profits do a large volume of business and make a great deal of money. When they have a favorable destiny, they can become rich in a single generation. Among the newly rich are some whose descendants are lazy and lack a profit sense, and they squander all of the accumulated wealth. In these troubled times, samurai households are suffering vicissitudes and changes of fortune. Persons who excel in business have become society's heroes. . . . A samurai can inherit [his father's] fief, but he cannot inherit his father's standing as a great man.[4]

This was another source of government anxiety. The ruling officials were attempting to complete the final implementation of the four-status system, in which merchants were supposed to occupy the lowest rung of the Neo-Confucian hierarchy. But in some cases their business successes had given them wealth and a reputation inconsistent with their theoretical position in society.

Despite government's growing misgivings about commerce, it also realized that some degree of commercial development was both necessary and desirable. The daimyo had compelled their retainers to take up residence in the castle towns, and they were forced to rely upon merchants to move crops and goods from the rural hinterlands into the cities. To obtain cash for their trips to Edo and for their mansions in the country's largest city, the daimyo needed to market their tax rice. The Maeda daimyo could most easily sell their tax rice through the large markets in Osaka, a move which led to further reliance on merchants to arrange the transportation and marketing facilities. A prosperous castle town could also enhance a daimyo's prestige among his peers. Part of Maeda Tsunanori's reputation as a model ruler came from the widely held beliefs that Kanazawa was not only well governed, but that it was also a thriving city of well-fed and contented townspeople.

Consequently, shogunate and daimyo policy never attempted to suppress commercial development totally. Rather, their policies reflected something of an alliance, a symbiotic relationship, between government and elements of the merchant class. On the local level, that kind of relationship had first manifested itself in the diamyo-chartered merchant liaison of the early seventeenth century. Under the changed conditions of the latter half of the seventeenth century, it became most clearly expressed in the relationship between government and licensed associations of wholesalers as well as of organizations merchants and artisans on the retail level (*nakama* or *kabunakama*). These associations were organized by commodity or trade—wholesalers dealing in the same line of products, merchants in one kind of business, craftsmen who produced the same kind of goods. When licensed by the shogunate (or by the domain government on the local level), the members of an association received a monopoly right over their business or trade. The associations generally issued a fixed number of membership shares (*kabu*) to association individuals or households, which permitted the bearer to engage in that activity. In addition, the association, as a corporate group, elected officers, decided regulations, held membership meetings, adjudicated internal disputes, and established procedures for selling and bequeathing membership shares.

The shogunate launched its policy of licensing these protective associations in 1662 when, through the office of the Osaka City Magistrate, it authorized the formation of an association of money changers in that city. By the end of the century, the shogunate had authorized the formation of at least twenty-four associations of wholesalers in Osaka and ten in Edo. By licensing merchant associations and granting them monopoly rights to a specific commodity, the ruling authorities hoped to keep commercial activity within certain prescribed channels and to control and direct its development within those boundaries. Since the associations submitted their regulations and lists of business procedures to the government, officials acquired a mechanism for regulating these trades. Government could also rely on the associations to settle trade disputes, control prices, and ensure an adequate supply of essential goods to the urban centers. In addition, government expanded its revenue base by charging annual licensing fees to the associations.

The merchants and artisans fortunate enough to receive permission to establish an association also realized certain obvious benefits. The most significant was the monopoly right itself, a major aid to business success. The formation of an association also enabled the members to reduce competition both from outside and among themselves, to manage their own affairs, and to police their own activities.

Later, during the course of the eighteenth and early nineteenth centuries, the position of the protective associations underwent drastic change. As rural commerce and handicraft industry continued to grow, new commercial facilities and marketing networks developed in the rural production centers. Increasingly the protective associations became outsiders, unable to meet the challenge of rural-based entrepreneurs. Still, the urban-based protective association remained a significant economic institution until well into the middle of the nineteenth century. Some of the families, such as the Mitsui, remain in business today.

The peace and steady commercial growth of the seventeenth century also gave rise to a *chōnin*-oriented culture, at least in the three great metropolises of Edo, Osaka, and Kyoto. For the first time in Japanese history, a prosperous merchant class had acquired the financial means and the leisure to assert its own cultural independence. The result was an

urban culture which, although drawing artistic inspiration from aristocratic cultural tradition, became distinctly popular and bourgeois. It was
a culture that focused on the entertainments and activities of the "floating
world" (*ukiyo*) of brothels, theaters, and houses of assignation set in the
pleasure quarters: the Yoshiwara in Edo, the Shinmachi in Osaka, and the
Shimabara in Kyoto. Its themes were the sensual, the erotic, and the
immediate.

This *chōnin* culture reached its first florescence at the end of the seventeenth and the beginning of the eighteenth centuries, an era generally
referred to as the Genroku cultural epoch (after the era name Genroku,
1688–1704), and expressed itself in a number of innovative forms, including a new genre of fictional writing, the *ukiyo-zōshi* (stories of the
floating world), and woodblock prints. The themes expressed in these
print media played on the concerns most relevant to merchant life. The
woodblock prints, for instance, dealt intimately with the life of the theater and pleasure quarters. Many of the early prints were actually advertis-
ing circulars for theaters and brothels, but even in later years, after the
print had evolved into a more serious art form, artists continued to
concentrate on courtesans and kabuki actors, the most romanticized figures of the floating world.

Kabuki and the serious puppet theater (*bunraku*) also blossomed into
maturity during the Genroku cultural epoch. Kabuki was more popular in
Edo, while the puppet drama flourished in the Osaka-Kyoto area. But
strong ties linked the two dramatic forms. The greatest writer for both the
puppet and kabuki theaters was Chikamatsu Monzaemon (1653–1724)
whose most famous play was *The Love Suicides of Sonezaki (Sonezaki shinjū)*,
first produced in 1703 and based on actual events in Osaka. The story told
of a soy sauce salesman who rashly lent to some unreliable acquaintances
money which his employer originally had entrusted to him for safekeep-
ing. Disgraced when he was unable to collect the debt and return the
money to his employer, the salesman sought solace from his lover, a
courtesan of the pleasure quarters, and together they decided to commit
double suicide. In later plays, Chikamatsu continued to explore the emotional life of lower-class townspeople and the tensions that existed between one's duties and obligations (*giri*) and one's sentimental and human
attachments (*ninjō*).

The popular, bourgeois activities associated with the floating world did
not displace all other cultural pursuits, for in the world of the shogun and
many daimyo an aristocratic ideal still lingered. They patronized noh
drama, perpetuated the architectural styles of the earlier Ashikaga period,
and patronized a style of literati painting (*bunjin-ga*) that reached its
zenith under the artists Yosa Buson (1716–83) and Ike no Taiga
(1723–76).

Yet what was most novel and creative in Tokugawa Japan was the popular commoner culture of the townspeople, which arose spontaneously, in response to merchant interests and social needs. The popular culture was literally a creation by and for the merchant and artisan classes. Its fruition in Edo, Osaka, and Kyoto added a new and vigorous element to the nation's cultural heritage. In time, this culture would spread into the regional castle towns, although, as we shall see, its arrival in Kanazawa was considerably delayed.

THE CULMINATION OF PHYSICAL GROWTH AND THE FINAL EXTENSION OF POLITICAL AUTHORITY

The rate of population growth in Kanazawa declined rapidly throughout the final decades of the seventeenth century and then came to a halt at the beginning of the eighteenth century. In 1667, the merchant and artisan population had stood at just under 60,000 persons. Continued, but slower, growth of areas on the fringe of the city showed up in the 1697 census, which recorded a commoner population in Kanazawa of 68,636 persons. But just thirteen years later, in 1710, that figure dropped to 64,987.[5] At that time, the total city population amounted to approximately 120,000 persons, including samurai, priests, and outcasts. This was Kanazawa's maximum growth as a preindustrial city, and until the 1870s its population would not vary significantly from that figure.

One reason for the decline in the rate of population growth was the announcement by the ruling officials that samurai and chōnin could no longer rent land from farmers. The aitaiukechi form of rental arrangement had been the principal source of urban expansion in the early 1660s. But this kind of urban sprawl caused problems. Farmers complained that their holdings were broken up and that access to fields was becoming increasingly difficult. Quarrels erupted between farmers and those who made their livelihood in the city. The Village Headmen became upset when the nonfarming residents refused to listen to their instructions and ignored the laws issued by the Rural Magistrates. These sorts of problems had led the domain to incorporate some aitaiukechi areas into the city in 1665. But the next year, as conditions worsened, the government proclaimed that farmers could no longer rent land to samurai or townspeople.[6]

At first, the prohibition was not totally effective, and samurai and townspeople continued to lease land on the rural fringes of the city, although at a much reduced level.[7] The domain, however, refused to back off from its policy, and in 1669, three years after the original prohibition, the government declared that it would henceforth confiscate any new land

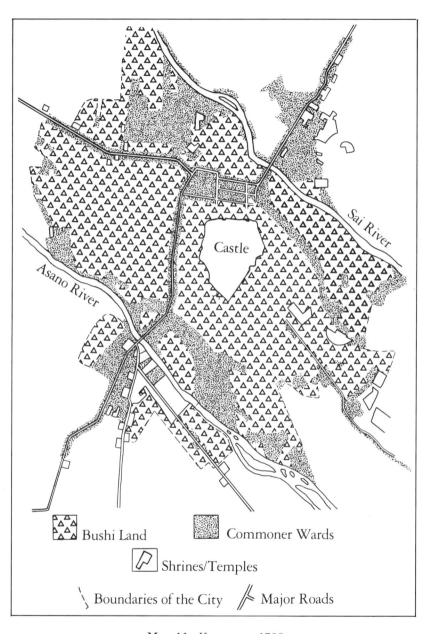

Castle

Sai River

Asano River

Map 11: Kanazawa, 1700

rented by samurai. In 1684, officials again announced that samurai were not to rent from either farmers or townspeople resident in the rural fringe areas, and in 1682 and 1689 the government required Village Headmen to submit oaths swearing that persons in their villages would not rent to samurai, priests, or townspeople.[8] Although never completely effective, these measures, based more on moral suasion than compulsion, did help to put an end to urban expansion.

Some of the long-time, established residents of Kanazawa also began to oppose further urban growth during the second half of the seventeenth century. Artisans started to fear that continued migration to the city would expand the urban labor pool, thereby harming their own economic opportunities. In 1683, the Council of Advisers announced that in recent years many "useless" artisans had arrived in the city, with certain harmful consequences and no "advantages." Consequently, they declared, any artisan who wished to migrate to the city would have to submit to "an investigation" (that is, receive official permission).[9] On the same day, the City Magistrates issued a statement that any migrating artisan who had an "elaborate set of tools" (that is, who might threaten an already-established artisan) would not be permitted to rent lodgings in Kanazawa.[10] In later years, the city government issued similar ordinances covering other kinds of occupations. From 1695, for example, all nonresidents who wished to sell medicines in the city were required to secure permission from a representative of Kanazawa's own druggists.[11] Three years later, domain officials announced that any person who wished to migrate to Kanazawa to become an apprentice or a shop clerk had first to receive the permission of the City Magistrates.[12]

A final factor that led to the end of Kanazawa's century of urban growth was the rise of local towns (zaimachi) that offered competing job opportunities. As local handicraft industries developed in these towns, they attracted rural migrants who might otherwise have chosen to live in Kanazawa. Although the evolution of villages into local towns was essentially a nineteenth-century phenomenon, as early as 1700 the government of Kaga domain recognized the commercial growth of fifteen villages by redesignating them as towns (machi) and placing them under the jurisdiction of their own Town Magistrates.[13]

In urban political administration, too, the years from 1670 to 1700 represented the culmination of a century of institutional development. Urban government in Kanazawa had assumed its basic structure by the middle of the seventeenth century, and the developments of the final decades of that century simply extended and modified the system within the already existing framework. After 1686, for instance, membership on the Council of Advisers was officially limited to the household heads of the Eight Families.[14] On a lower level, the Constables complained that they did not have time to do all their assigned work, which included overseeing the purchase of domain supplies, and the government added new officials, *machi-dōshinnami,* to assist them.[15] The domain also reduced the number of City Elders from ten to four, but gave them the additional privilege of attending the memorial services held for the various Maeda daimyo.[16] As the city grew, the number of Ward Representatives in the Ordinary Wards was increased—to eleven in 1679, to fourteen in 1686, and then to fifteen in 1687.[17]

Of greater significance was the further elaboration of Neo-Confucian principles of government.[18] Tsunanori expanded the practice of employing Confucian scholars and personally received instruction from Hayashi Gahō (the son of Razan) and Kinoshita Jun'an (1621–98), who later tutored the Tokugawa shogun. Tsunanori invited a number of Confucian scholars to Kanazawa and placed them on stipends. These included Kinoshita and Matsunaga Nagamitsu, a disciple of the famous Confucian teacher Matsunaga Sekigo. Beyond this, Tsunanori also arranged for the major samurai to receive tutoring from these scholars and even provided lecturers for the lower-ranking samurai.

The establishment of a system of Poorhouses (*hiningoya*) in 1670 gave concrete expression to the Confucian injunction that good government was benevolent government. An increase in the number of beggars had accompanied the expansion of the city's population in the early 1660s. At first officials dealt with the problem by registering the beggars and requiring them to return to their home villages, where presumably their families or Household Groups would assist them. The number of beggars in Kanazawa continued to increase, however. Then a summer of heavy rains and floods in 1669 destroyed fields with a total productive capacity of nearly 60,000 *koku* of rice and sent a wave of impoverished persons into the city. Throughout the winter of 1669 and into the early summer of 1670, the domain distributed rice through relief stations set up at various temples around the city.[19]

Once the immediate crisis had peaked, officials began to construct permanent facilities to house indigent persons. During the 6th month of 1670, the government erected a series of forty-five shelters (*koya*) at Kasamaemachi, on the southeastern edge of the city. The shelters were officially opened on the 22nd day of the 6th month, and by the middle of the 7th month more than 1,700 persons had taken up residence in these Poorhouses, which were placed under the administrative jurisdiction of the City Magistrates.[20]

Over the years, the number of persons lodged in the Poorhouses varied considerably. After a decline in the 1670s, the number expanded throughout the decade of the 1680s, when more structures were built. In 1699 a total of 4,455 persons lived in the Poorhouses. This represented a peak, however, and the numbers gradually declined to about 1,100 by the year 1717.[21]

The Poorhouses were established for the domain's impoverished, regardless of their place of permanent residence. The only year for which good information exists concerning the geographical origins of the residents is 1699. In that year, officials admitted 3,685 persons to the Poorhouses. Of these, 996, or twenty-seven percent, claimed the city of Kanazawa as their place of permanent residence. An additional 1,300 persons (thirty-six percent), however, came from rural areas immediately adjacent to the city, and may have included a large number of merchants, artisans, and day laborers who rented land on the rural fringes of Kanazawa.[22]

Generally, admission was through petition, countersigned by one's Group Headman, Ward Representative (or Village Headman in the case of a rural resident), and City Magistrates (or Rural Magistrates). Typically, the petition stated that the person desiring admission was poor, that he had no chance to immediately improve his lot and that his family, if any, and Household Group were unable to provide him with assistance.[23] Occasionally, however, persons simply showed up and asked to be admitted, and officials of the City Office also brought in starving people and abandoned babies that they found in the city.[24] In addition to the poor of Kaga domain, any traveler from outside the domain who became ill and had no one to care for him could take up lodgings in the Houses, and, when vacancies permitted, the domain sometimes interned criminals convicted of minor offenses.[25]

Life in the Poorhouses was secure, although not easy. Each house covered about 130 square meters and held forty persons. Residents received a food allowance of rice, miso, and salt. The daily rice allowance of three *gō* (about half a liter) for men and two *gō* for women was enough to supply a person's minimal calorie requirements, although the diet must have been monotonous. In addition, each resident received a daily allowance of firewood for cooking and heating, a clothing allotment consisting of a thin kimono for summer and lined cotton garments for winter, and common utensils such as ladles, brooms, and hand buckets. The domain also employed doctors to provide medical care. The residents who were physically able had to work. Principally, the people in the Poorhouses produced scrub brushes, rain gear, and other similar items from straw and hemp, for sale in the castle town.[26]

Residents in the Poorhouses could seek release at any time, as long as they could assure officials that they would not become wards of the domain again in the near future. Generally a resident was released when a relative or friend guaranteed financial support and help in setting up a new household. The domain also tried to arrange employment as agricultural workers for residents and released those who took jobs with established farm families. The rate of turnover was quite rapid. In 1699, for instance, 3,685 out of a total 4,525 residents (eighty-one percent) either left the Poorhouses or died during the course of the year.[27]

For some, the Poorhouses led to a different kind of opportunity. As the domain government reclaimed land and opened up new paddy fields, it offered people in the Poorhouses the chance to settle in the new villages. In the early 1670s, for instance, persons from the Poorhouses founded the village which became known as Kisabata. The domain supplied the land and also provided the new settlers with houses, household furnishings, tools, firewood, salt, and foodstuffs.[28] During the same decade, 104 persons from the Poorhouses settled the new village of Nagasaka. Again, the domain provided houses, furnishings, and tools. At first, this land was only marginally productive and for five years, until the village became self-supporting, the domain government also exempted the settlers from taxes and supplied them with an annual rice allowance.[29]

Contemporaries saw the Poorhouse system as an example of benevolent government and enlightened rule. Scholars and other daimyo praised Tsunanori, and the Poorhouse system contributed to Kaga's reputation as the best-governed domain in Japan.[30] Certainly the Houses provided an alternative to starvation, and some residents gained a second chance in life as settlers in new villages. But the ruling officials were motivated by more practical concerns as well. In the 1660s, government leaders feared that an increase in the number of impoverished persons might lead to outbreaks of crime and perhaps even to organized, violent demonstrations against the government. The Poorhouse system provided the domain with the opportunity to bring these persons under closer government supervision. Moreover, the government could expect to profit eventually from the new villages as they became self-sufficient in rice and began to return tax proceeds to the domain. The establishment of the system of Poorhouses, then, offered an additional example of the complex mixture of protection, control, and self-interest that characterized government policy toward Kanazawa's residents during the seventeenth century.

Official policy toward the outcast groups revealed yet another aspect of urban governance. In Kaga domain, there were several such groups, including the leather workers described earlier. Perhaps numerically largest was the group known as the *tōnai* (literally, within the wisteria).[31] Very little is known of the origins of the *tōnai* except that some lived in Kanazawa in the late sixteenth century, and Toshiie employed them as janitors and groundskeepers at the castle.

The government began to expand its authority over the *tōnai* during the first half of the seventeenth century. First of all, it officially recognized two men, a Ninzō and a San'emon, as Tōnai Headmen (*tōnaigashira*), a position that became hereditary within the two families. Ninzō and San'emon were charged with overseeing the activities of their fellow *tōnai*, and they maintained confinement cells in their homes to jail outcast thieves. The domain also defined and formalized the duties that the other *tōnai* could perform. Some were employed by the government at the Office of the Police and the Judiciary, where they took care of prisoners, cremated bodies, and kept the execution grounds clean. Others served in a police capacity. The *mawaritōnai* (Rural Patrol) were assigned to specific rural areas and were supposed to report vagrants, criminals, and beggars to domain officials. The *miakashi* performed a similar function in Kanazawa and were also instructed to report on the "seasonal prostitutes" who came into the city during the winter months. The domain also employed some *tōnai* temporarily, as in the 1660s when the *tōnai* helped to distribute relief rice. The salaries which the domain paid the *tōnai* for these services are not fully known. The two Headmen received the equivalent of about ten *koku* of rice each, and the Rural Patrol earned one *koku* for each one thousand *koku* of official productive capacity of the villages they patrolled. Finally, the domain provided the *tōnai* with two residential areas, one to the north of the Asano River and a second on the banks of the Sai River, slightly north of the bridge.

The domain government intensified its control over the *tōnai* during the second half of the seventeenth century. In 1677, a government order stated that *tōnai* were forbidden to rent lodgings outside of their own segregated residential areas. A second set of ordinances issued the same year prohibited them from serving in unauthorized occupations, such as servants in temple compounds or samurai households.

The domain also extended its authority over the professional beggars.[32] Little is known of this group before 1652, when the domain appointed seven men to act as the Beggars' Headmen (*hiningashira*) and placed them under the oversight of the Tōnai Headmen. It is likely that these seven families were already the leaders of the beggars' subcommunity, which numbered about six to seven hundred persons, and that the 1652 ordinance formalized their duties. Specifically, the Headmen were instructed to dispose of the bodies of any beggars who died within the city, in particular bodies found near the bridges or in front of temples and samurai residences. In addition, the Headmen had to chase beggars off the streets whenever the daimyo or a member of his family visited a temple, and they were supposed to patrol the castle town after a fire to make sure that no beggars engaged in looting. In exchange for these services, the Headmen received small grants of residential land, about 165 square meters each, and probably a small salary.

In 1691, the Tōnai Headmen forwarded a message from the Beggars' Headmen to domain officials. According to this message, the Beggars'

Headmen were concerned about the number of persons who in recent years had started to "intermingle" with the "established" beggars. The message went on to suggest that professional beggars ought to carry "tags," in effect licenses to beg, and that no other persons should be allowed to mix with the professional beggars. The tags would be issued only to those who intended to beg permanently, and to their children. The domain quickly seized this opportunity to bring the beggar community under more comprehensive control and ordered that professional beggars be so licensed.[33] In Kanazawa, the word *hinin*, which previously had meant any beggar, took on the new meaning of those persons who were now a part of a hereditary caste of professional beggars.

Another outcast group was known as the *monoyoshi*, which might be rendered as "the beggars who bring good fortune."[34] This group of thirty to forty households lived in the area behind Shinmei shrine. Their origins are unknown but they probably resided in Kanazawa from at least the late sixteenth century. Certainly they were fiercely independent. They had their own separate headman for liaison with domain officials and consistently pointed out how they were different from other beggars. In fact, they were only part-time beggars. The families produced sandals and rain clogs for sale in the city and also cared for lepers. On certain days generally regarded as being auspicious, however, the *monoyoshi* would assemble in front of samurai and commoner homes.[35] If they received money or food, they would then call out favorable sayings and greetings. If not, the samurai or *chōnin* would be showered with insults. The *monoyoshi* even had their own festival, during the first ten days of the 11th month, in which they dressed as lepers and wandered the streets of Kanazawa begging money in exchange for a verbal charm that would protect the giver against the dread disease.

In time, the domain brought this group under tighter control, too. First it compelled the *Monoyoshi* Headman to report to the Tōnai Headman, and then it restricted the number of occasions when the *monoyoshi* could gather in front of houses and clamor for presents of food or money. Finally, in 1691 the domain added the requirement that *monoyoshi* families carry license tags.[36]

The above groups were outcasts in the philosophical sense that they were not part of society's four status groups of samurai, peasant, artisan, and merchant. It is here that the impersonal, institutionalized authority of government impinged most forcefully and oppressively upon the individual. It might be argued that government action accommodated the interests of these outcasts. The licensing procedures protected the professionals' begging rights, and many *tōnai* received employment and land grants from the domain. But these were hereditary castes. Once a person acquired a license as a beggar, his station in life became permanently fixed. He had to remain a beggar, and his children were supposed to follow that occupation. Nor was there a free choice of place of residence, for an outcast had to live on the land assigned to him. Various kinds of outcast groups had existed throughout the middle ages in Japan, and many had worked at the same kinds of occupations as Kanazawa's outcasts. The discriminatory practices of the earlier period had been enforced by social practice and custom. To this, the Maeda government added the full weight of law and public authority.[37]

Seen in another perspective, the extension of domain authority over the outcast groups and the urban pooor signaled the maturation of urban political administration. All residents of the castle town had now been brought under the administrative authority of the city government, and until the abolition of Kaga domain itself in the early 1870s, that government would continue to function within the theoretical and bureaucratic framework that had evolved over the course of the dynamic seventeenth century. As in the case of population growth, the final decades of that century had witnessed an end to an era of city-building.

THE RISE OF THE "NEW MERCHANTS"

The continued growth of Kanazawa's urban population in the middle decades of the seventeenth century as well as the emergence of rural centers of handicraft production gave rise in Kaga domain to the same kinds of economic opportunities that interregional wholesalers and forwarding agents were enjoying on the national level. As in Osaka and Edo, groups of wholesalers in Kanazawa formed associations and acquired monopoly rights from the domain to wholesale specific kinds of commodities and commercial crops.

Such associations were not entirely new to Kanazawa in the 1670 to 1700 period. An association of fish wholesalers had been active in the city from at least the 1620s, and associations of oil, tea, cotton, and flour wholesalers had come into being by the middle of the seventeenth century. Some of these associations participated in interregional trade. The association of tea wholesalers, for instance, arranged for tea to be imported from other domains, added their fixed markup (three *rin* per 0.6 kilogram), and sold the tea to peddlers who then retailed it throughout Kaga domain.[38] By the 1650s, two associations, one in Komatsu and another in Kanazawa, were importing various kinds of cloth and processed cotton from the Osaka area.[39]

The 1680s, however, witnessed a sudden expansion in the number of licensed associations of wholesalers and forwarding agents. All of these new associations were based within the city of Kanazawa, and they specialized in commodities which would eventually be retailed within the castle town. With government-sponsored monopoly rights, most of the association members prospered, so much so that they became known as the *shinkō chōnin,* "the newly arising merchants."

Notoya Kuhei, Isobeya Mataemon, Hishiikeya Han'emon, and Shimizudaniya Den'emon were among this new breed of merchants. In 1683 these four men requested monopoly rights for handling the wholesale phases of paper production. Specifically, they requested that villagers throughout Kaga domain sell exclusively to them all the trees used as raw materials. The four men would then sell the trees to producers and arrange for peddlers to receive the manufactured paper for retail sale in Kanazawa and other consumption centers in the domain. In addition, the four men offered to advance capital to producers at the low annual rate of ten percent. To cover their own costs and profit margin, the men proposed taking a surcharge from the manufacturers.[40]

In the same year three merchants with residences in the Ordinary Wards received authorization to buy charcoal from producers in rural areas and transship it to their warehouses, where retailers from Kanazawa could purchase supplies. In addition, all charcoal shipped into Kaga domain had to be sold to these wholesalers. The three merchants negotiated the price with the producers and added their surcharge, which varied according to season but averaged about eight percent in the 1680s. Although these wholesalers offered no firm price guarantee, they did state that if anyone could privide cheaper supplies to the residents of Kanazawa, then those persons should be allowed to become wholesalers.[41]

In the fall of 1683, two merchants from Kamitsutsumi Ward in Kanazawa sent a petition to domain officials. They pointed out that the cost of cotton imported from Osaka had increased sharply and suggested a plan for growing the plant in Kaga. The plan itself was outlined in somewhat confusing language, perhaps because of laws against the alienation of farm land and possible domain reluctance to see any land taken out of rice production. At one point the two merchants stated that they would import seeds from Osaka, arrange to rent the use of nonproductive fields from farmers, and employ farm wives and children to grow the crop. Later the two men suggested that they would actually sell the seeds to the farmers, offer advice on how to grow the crop, and guarantee to buy the entire harvest at a price to be negotiated between themselves and the growers. In either event, the two men planned to sell the cotton to local weavers and the cotton seeds to oil manufacturers. The ultimate goal, aside from personal profit, was to bring down the retail costs of cotton products in Kanazawa, and the two men appended a long list of figures outlining projected costs and profits on expected sales in order to demonstrate that their plan would in fact result in lower consumer prices.[42]

Other sorts of wholesale merchants also received monopoly authorizations in 1683. In the 11th month, for instance, three Kanazawa merchants received the exclusive right to wholesale fish oil (*gyoyu*), which was made by boiling sardines and sea smelt in order to extract the oil for use in lamps.[43] Earlier in the year some Kanazawa merchants had received a monopoly on the essence of a kind of sumac, which was processed into a lacquer base and into wax for candles.[44]

In one instance, a new association came into being to procure for government offices in Kanazawa supplies of ink, paper, and firewood. Farmers around the castle town produced these items as a form of by-employment, and, until 1683, the farmers brought the commodities into domain offices whenever they had the spare time to do so. In the spring of that year two merchants from Kanazawa petitioned for the exclusive right to purchase these goods in rural areas and resell them to government offices in the castle town. By working at this business full time, the merchants promised the domain a steady supply of goods. They also guaranteed lower prices through transportation savings, since the men could collect the goods in one circuit through the countryside, whereas previously individual producers had brought the items into the city. The domain first checked with the rural producers to see if they objected to the new system. The farmer-producers replied, in effect, that the older system was very inconvenient for them since they often had only small amounts to sell and had to travel long distances to collect the goods and deliver them to domain offices. Thereupon, the domain issued the authorization to the two urban merchants.[45]

Aside from the wholesalers, other kinds of business groups also formed protective associations. The association of pawnshop owners, mentioned above, was one example. Associations of sake brewers, soy sauce producers, oil producers, and druggists also came into existence during the middle of the seventeenth century.[46] Like the wholesale groups, these were closed associations. In order to engage in that line of business, one needed a *kabu*, or license, and licenses could be acquired only through the permission of the association members.

During the latter half of the seventeenth century, an association of rice brokers (*komenakagai*) started operations.[47] Following the *kaisakuhō* rural reforms of the 1650s, all the samurai in Kanazawa were placed on the stipend system. Twice a year they received certificates which entitled the bearer to draw a specified amount of rice from the daimyo's warehouse. The rice brokers purchased the certificates from the samurai, and then they sold the certificates to others (usually to persons speculating on the future price) or actually drew the rice from the granary and sold it on the city market. In time the government became concerned about the effects of futures speculation on prices, and in 1681 it began to license the rice brokers. It also required anyone who wanted to become a rice broker to supply two guarantors and to secure the permission of the established brokers, although children of the established brokers were allowed to enter the business freely. In 1683, the government extended additional controls over the brokers when it established the post of Rice Broker Liaison Agent (*komenakagai-kimoiri*) and required the five appointees to maintain a record of all transactions completed by the rice brokers.

In very broad terms, the protective associations could be divided into two types: those established by the government to police a trade (pawnbrokers) and those authorized at the request of the merchant group (almost all of the wholesale associations). In either case, however, the government and the merchants derived certain clear benefits, just as when associations were authorized in Osaka or Edo. The merchants received monopoly rights and a means of reducing intragroup competition. They were also free to coordinate their own activities and to police their own membership. The government, on the other hand, acquired a degree of regulatory control. Whenever a person received permission to enter an association, for example, he had to submit a pledge to adhere to established business practices.[48] Through licensing practices, the government was also able to provide protection to business enterprises that were important to the overall economy and well-being of the city. Finally, the government gained a new revenue source from the annual licensing fees it charged the associations.[49]

It is possible that reduced competition on the wholesale level resulted in higher prices for the final consumer in some cases. But, in general, savings on economies of scale, as in the example of the merchants who supplied products to government offices, probably kept prices down. Moreover, the government usually specified the amount that wholesalers could add to their purchase price to cover costs and profit margins. In addition, government officials expected retailers to keep their markups at a reasonable level. To this end, the government maintained a close watch over both wholesale and retail prices. At one point, for instance, it ordered a reduction in the wholesale price of charcoal.[50] In 1693, the City Magistrates closed some tofu shops temporarily because their prices were "unethical."[51] In the 1650s the government heard complaints that some retailers in Komatsu who purchased wooden buckets from wholesalers in Kanazawa were selling those buckets at excessively high prices. It immediately ordered the wholesalers to submit receipts and price lists and instructed the retailers to compile a register of the prices charged in all retail shops. Officials then required the retailers to submit a pledge that they would charge the proper prices.[52]

In marked constrast to the "newly arising merchants," many of the older chartered merchant and artisan families continued to suffer the economic decline which had first become noticeable at midcentury. In increasing numbers artisans gave up their residential grants, moved to scattered locations in the city, and earned their livelihoods by selling solely to other townspeople.[53] Others gave up the old family business for new occupations. Most is known about the plight of the swordsmiths. In the first half of the seventeenth century this group had prospered, some-times receiving orders for dozens of long swords and hundreds of lances. As noted earlier, however, very few orders came in after the 1650s. In 1720, when the domain decided to order some new swords, no one kenw what price to charge. No one, in fact, could even remember the last time that the craftsmen had made swords, and the City Magistrates had to order a search of the records in order to find out what the standard prices had been in the past.[54]

As their business declined in the second half of the century, many smiths gave up their residences and moved to other parts of town where they made pots and pans for *chōnin* customers. One group of eight smiths applied for permission to gather firewood and brush from domain forests, which they then sold in the city. The domain withdrew its permission in 1706, however, probably to let the forests grow back. Ten years later, the same eight men send a petition to the City Magistrates. "There have been no orders for swords from the domain or from the samurai retainers," they wrote, "and we are starving and our business prospects are poor. . . . We would like to request that you negotiate on our behalf . . . to get permis-sion [for us to collect firewood] restored."[55]

Perhaps the most revealing case, however, concerned the Kiyomitsu family. In the early decades of the seventeenth century Kiyomitsu Shichiemon was constantly busy with domain business, once even receiv-ing a single order for twenty long swords. His grandson lived in the Poorhouses. In the late 1670s Kiyomitsu Chōbei, his mother, his sisters, his sons, and his younger brothers all applied for permission to enter the Houses. There Kiyomitsu worked at a variety of crafts and even forged a few swords before his death in the late 1680s. His son Chōemon con-tinued to live in the Poorhouse, and a Kiyomitsu resided there as late as 1721.[56]

The decline of the chartered merchants was more gradual. Some, such as the Sangaya family, had fallen into economic difficulty by the middle of the seventeenth century. The decline quickened during the second half of that century and became steepest during the eighteenth century. In 1818, the old privileged merchant families asked the domain government to draw up a list of "families of distinguished lineage" (*iegara honretsu*) and to make appointments of City Elders and heads of the Office of Currency Control only from the names on this list. The domain compiled with the request, but only eighteen families received this recognition.[57]

Some very familiar names were missing from the list, men such as Tōfuya, Dōjiriya, Takeya, and Echizen'ya Kiemon. The original Echizen'ya Kiemon, a brother of Echizen'ya Magobei, had received chartered status, a grant of residential land, and tax exemptions from Toshiie. The family enjoyed a close personal relationship with the first three Maeda daimyo, and Toshinaga often visited their home. Family headmen also served in the Office of Currency Control and as City Elders. By the early eighteenth century, however, the family's sake-brewing business had failed, and they sold their shop and house. The family was stripped of its charter and was no longer appointed to serve in any administrative capacity.[58]

The Tōfuya family lost its monopoly rights in the middle of the seventeenth century. In 1666, nine City Elders, all the Ward Representatives from the Original Wards, and nine Ward Representatives from the Ordinary Wards submitted a petition to the City Office requesting that the tofu business be thrown open to everyone. If this were done, the men argued, the number of shops would increase and retail prices in the city would fall. A month later the City Magistrates gave their approval, and the Tōfuya family, whose founder had brought back the secret of making bean curd from Korea, now had to compete with ordinary merchants. Sixty years later the family gave up their residence, originally granted more than a century earlier, and themselves became ordinary merchants.[59]

The Dōjiriya family had made *mochi* rice cakes and had been purveyors to the daimyo from the 1610s. When the *mochi* business later failed, the family turned to making drugs. By the nineteenth century this business, too, was in trouble, and the family asked the daimyo for loans.[60] In the early seventeenth century, the Takeya residence had served as a meeting place for the City Magistrates and the twonspeople who helped to manage urban affairs. In 1801, the family head was imprisoned, and the Takeya lost all of their former privileges.[61]

Some old chartered families continued to prosper. The Nakaya family of druggists, for example, had originally received its charter from Toshiie, who often asked the family head for advice about how to run the city. Later family heads often served as City Elders; one Nakaya or another held the post for a total of sixty-one years between 1725 and 1870, when the post was abolished. For generation after generation, one Nakaya after another successfully managed the family enterprise, located on the main north-south road that ran through the castle town, and, in fact, they remain in business today at the same location.[62] The Miyatakeya (Kameda) family, to cite another example, survived first as innkeepers and then as druggists.[63] The Kamiya family, one of the most distinguished of the chartered merchants, went bankrupt in the 1770s, but the domain continued to employ them within the City Office, and the family later reopened its shop.[64]

But the few successful chartered merchants stood in sharp contrast to the majority of privileged merchants and artisans, who fell on hard times after the middle of the seventeenth century. By the early eighteenth century their heyday was past. As the commercial and financial requirements of the daimyo changed, men such as Sangaya, Kiyomitsu, Dōjiriya, and even Kamiya found that their original family charters meant less and less. Family fortunes had come to depend on how well they did as businessmen, not upon their relationship with the daimyo. Those who lacked the requisite business skills were soon eclipsed by the "newly rising chōnin" of the trade associations.

The overwhelming majority of the city's merchants and artisans, of course, ran their shops and businesses without receiving any special economic privileges. This sort of independent business initiative had been evident in the early seventeenth century among the artisans who settled along the Asano and townspeople who gathered firewood for sale to the urban centers. It continued to be a constant theme of urban life throughout the Tokugawa period, and the case of Tsuruya Buhei, Tachibanaya Shōemon, and Yoshida Shichibei provides a final example. By the late seventeenth century, visits to onsen, or hot springs, had become very popular among Kanazawa's townspeople and samurai for both recreational and health reasons. In the summer of 1705, the three merchants named above prowled the foothills around Kanazawa searching for a suitable place to build a new onsen. At Tatsunokuchi, fifteen kilometers southwest of the city, they discovered a natural hot spring stream. Unfortunately, a cold water stream flowed into it and diluted the water temperature. Undaunted, the three men returned later in the year, after winter had set in, and were delighted to find that the cold stream had disappeared. After making inquiries in the neighborhood, they learned that farmers used the cold stream for irrigation in the summer and, for this purpose, had previously built a dam upstream which they opened in the summer but closed after the harvest. The three chōnin felt that they could construct a waterway that would divert the cold stream away from the hot stream yet still make the cold water available to the farmers. Back in Kanazawa, the men submitted a petition to the City Magistrates outlining their plans. They stressed that their project would in no way interfere with agricultural productivity and also pointed out that, if successful, the domain would profit from the business taxes levied on the new enterprise. Additionally, they noted that all the venture capital was theirs and that if the business did not succeed, it was they who would suffer the loss. Finally they wound down to their major point. The Tatsunokuchi area was under the jurisdiction of the Rural Magistrates, and the three townsmen wanted the City Magistrates to intercede on their behalf and negotiate permission for the project. The City Magistrates did so, and the men soon set to work on their project.[65]

The late seventeenth century, then, was a period of both continuity and change. Examples of independent merchant enterprise and ingenuity repeated themselves throughout the seventeenth century. The creation of protective associations expressed that ingenuity in a different form as the organizers seized the economic opportunities available to them and then sought out alliances with government. In addition, the associations represented a new way of organizing commercial life and provided another example of the integration of interests between daimyo government and members of the merchant and artisan class.

A VARIEGATED URBAN CULTURE

At the same time that Louis XIV was adding to his princely fame by helping to develop the Opera in Paris, the fifth Maeda daimyo, Tsunanori, was gaining equal renown within his own country as a great patron of the noh theater. The Maeda family had always been fond of this form of theatrical entertainment. Toshiie and Toshinaga had sponsored a number of performances in Kanazawa, and the noh presentations at Kannon on the first two days of the fourth month had become an annual tradition under the patronage of Toshitsune and his wife Tentokuin. The early Maeda daimyo had also started the practice of inviting noh performers to their castle town. Toshiie granted a stipend of four hundred *koku* and a plot of residential land to Takeda Gonbei, the third son of Konparu Shichirō, the head of a famous Kyoto family of noh actors whose history dated back into the middle ages.[66] The Maeda also extended their patronage to a branch of the Hōshō, a famous noh family who had settled in Edo.[67] Two local families which had achieved prominence in the Kaga area before Toshiie's arrival, the Motohashi and the Namiyoshi, came under Maeda patronage as well, receiving stipends and residences.[68]

But noh really came to the fore as one of the predominant cultural activities in Kanazawa during the administration of Tsunanori, who sponsored hundreds of noh performances. It became traditional, for example, to include noh in the memorial services held on the anniversaries of the deaths of past daimyo.[69] Noh chanting became part of the New Year's ceremonies when the daimyo was in residence at the castle. Beyond this, Tsunanori had noh performed to celebrate almost any special occasion, such as when the Maeda were entrusted with overseeing the administration of the territory known as Hida Takayama.[70] Special performances were also held when a new Maeda daimyo made his first journey to Kanazawa. Takeda Gonbei acted the main roles for two days of noh when Tsunanori first came to Kanazawa in 1661, and all the major retainers were in the audience for the performances held in 1725 to greet Yoshinori, when he succeeded his father, Tsunanori.[71]

In Edo, noh gave Tsunanori the opportunity to mingle with his daimyo peers and even with the shogun himself. Tsunanori was a frequent guest at shogun-sponsored noh performances held at Edo castle, and, in turn, he hosted fellow daimyo and the shogun at the family's Edo mansion.[72] This round of hosting and counterhosting could sometimes take on exaggerated dimensions. On the 26th day of the 4th month of 1690 the shogun, Tsunayoshi, invited Tsunanori to the Tokugawa castle for a noh performance and made Tsunanori a gift of a large folding screen. To celebrate this invitation, Tsunanori gave a party, complete with noh, for a number of daimyo on the 10th day of the 5th month. Three days later, he hosted yet another gathering to which he invited his high-level retainers who were in the city, and after the noh performance, he exhibited the screen for all to admire. Back in Kanazawa, Tsunanori held yet another set of parties on the 13th and 14th days of the 11th month and invited a total of 105 retainers. Again the screen was exhibited and noh performed. These parties were less decorous than the ones in Edo, however. "Because it was cold and snowing," concluded one report, "there was much drinking and revelry."[73]

Tsunanori's relationship with the noh families in Kanazawa was somewhat different from that of his forefathers. He continued the stipends to the Takeda, Hōshō, Namiyoshi, and Morohashi families. The Takeda, however, moved back to Kyoto, although in return for their stipend they continued to journey to Kanazawa and, on occasion, even to Edo to act in noh dramas sponsored by Tsunanori. The daimyo took the Hōshō family to Edo, and they were the principal actors in the dramas staged at the family mansion. This set of moves reflected Tsunanori's personal tastes. Toshiie and Toshinaga had enjoyed the Konparu style of noh acting, which the Takeda family had brought to a creative peak in Kyoto. Tsunanori, however, was more fond of the Hōshō style, popularized in Edo by the main branch of that noh family. The Namiyoshi and Morohashi families continued to serve the Maeda in Kanazawa, and they alternated in taking the leads in the plays presented annually at Kannon on the first two days of the 4th month.

Tsunanori expressed his interest in the traditional arts and scholarship in a variety of ways. He carried on the family interest in the tea ceremony (*sadō*), for example. In the 1660s, Tsunanori had tea houses constructed for his own use, and invited to Kanazawa Sen no Sōshitsu and Kanamori Muneshitsu, descendants of famous Kyoto tea masters, to teach the finer points of tea.[74] Nearly 300 blind musicians who specialized in the traditional drums and zither (*koto*) lived and performed in Kanazawa, and Tsunanori often invited them to the castle to stage performances.[75] Tsunanori also put together one of the greatest personal libraries in Japan. He sent agents throughout the country to purchase or make copies of books, and he collected works of Korean, Chinese, and Dutch origin. To these he added his own works, a total of perhaps a hundred volumes of poetry and essays. It is unclear exactly how many volumes Tsunanori's library held—he gave many away as presents and others were destroyed in the periodic fires of the Edo period—but even in the early twentieth century, Maeda family descendants still retained several tens of thousands of volumes.[76]

It is difficult to judge the extent to which interest in noh, tea, and traditional forms of music extended beyond the daimyo's inner circle. The higher-level retainers were frequent guests for noh performances staged at the castle, and many of these men shared at least some of Tsunanori's enthusiasm. Occasionally high-ranking samurai even sponsored performances on their own, for which they hired actors and built temporary stages on the residential holdings.[77] Middle-ranking *bushi* also received invitations from the daimyo on occasion.[78] For these men, though, the highly esoteric noh may well have held less attraction than the opportunity to meet the daimyo and to enjoy his food and wine, as they did on that cold and snowy winter's day in 1690.

Townspeople had less opportunity to view noh drama. As in Edo, noh was intended principally for the *bushi* in Kanazawa, and performances staged for the enjoyment of the townspeople had to receive prior government approval. In 1657 some residents petitioned to hold noh performances in conjunction with a festival, and permission was granted.[79] Such performances were infrequent, however, probably because of *chōnin* indifference since the government does not seem to have refused any requests. Townspeople did attend the noh performances staged annually at Kannon from 1618, and these became very popular events. Temporary shops selling snacks and candy went up along the approaches to Kannon, and after the plays the persons attending stayed in the area and held boisterous parties through the night. "The mountains trembled with singing voices," wrote one eyewitness, "the city of Kanazawa was silent . . . and even peddlers did not pass through the town."[80] For these revelers, many of whom dressed in outlandish costumes, the noh performance itself was just one part of a spring festival.

Aside from noh drama and the tea ceremony, hunting and falconry remained popular samurai pastimes. Many samurai of three thousand *koku* status and above kept their own hawks, and some of them would even sneak onto the hunting preserves set aside for the daimyo's exclusive use.[81] Samurai of all levels fished for sport along the Sai and Asano rivers, angling for salmon, carp, catfish, and the troutlike *ayu*.[82] In the spring, groups of samurai organized outings to the countryside to view cherry blossoms and the other spring flowers.[83] Teahouses such as Hatsubatake, which afforded good views of the mountains to the east of the city, became increasingly popular. Samurai stopped there to enjoy the scenery and tried to capture the mood in a few lines of poetry.[84] In autumn, many of the same groups ventured out to see the foliage, and the daimyo usually invited some of his major retainers to view the fall colors in the gardens inside the castle.[85] The recreational pursuits of these "city *bushi*" offered many sharp contrasts to those of their forefathers, who had roared their pleasure on the city streets during the Ise craze in the summer of 1621.

Life had changed for samurai women, too. The lady Tentokuin had often appeared in the crowds at the kabuki theaters in the 1610s, but by the 1710s, opportunities for social recreation had become restricted for samurai women. In general, they were expected to stay in the house and not appear on the streets. Confined to their homes, women were supposed to concentrate on educational and artistic amusements such as poetry, calligraphy, the tea ceremony, and playing classical musical instruments.[86]

Many women found ways to circumvent these restrictions, as can be seen by the following statement, issued in 1729 by Yokoyama Yamato no Kami, a member of the Council of Advisers:

> Recently the wives, mothers, and daughters of samurai have been seen taking walks and strolls to temples and shrines for the purpose of amusement. In old times no women behaved like this, but recently such behavior has become common. . . . Women should not be doing this, [and] fathers, husbands, and sons will be held responsible. . . . However, there are exceptions. A woman who is married shall on occasion be permitted to visit the home of her parents. Women are permitted to go to the supplementary residences (*shimoyashiki*). Women are also permitted to go mushroom hunting . . . but they should not wear heavy makeup or take extravagant picnic lunches.
>
> Maids who are recovering from an illness are permitted to take short walks in the company of other maids.
>
> Wives are permitted to attend Buddhist sermons and lectures at temples. However, since we have heard rumors that younger women are simply using these as an excuse for frivolous pleasure-seeking, only older women should be permitted to go.[87]

The last clause was directed in part at the phenomenon of young, handsome priests, some of whom enjoyed an enormous popularity not unlike that accorded public celebrities in modern-day society. Some priests were not above capitalizing on this popularity, although such conduct could end tragically. In 1681, for instance, the government ordered that Kyōen, the head priest of Seigenji temple, be crucified in front of his temple gate for having engaged in sexual relations with one of his women parishioners.[88]

The *chōnin* culture which reached its first creative peak at the end of the seventeenth century in Osaka and Kyoto, and to a lesser extent in Edo, made only sporadic and minor appearances in Kanazawa. In 1663, domain officials noted that some samurai had been employing touring dancers and puppeteers to provide entertainment at parties and had even been providing those entertainers with lodgings. Since the domain wanted to encourage frugality, the officials announced, such practices should stop.[89] In that same year, the Rural Magistrates received a note from higher officials that rural residents had been renting lodgings to touring groups. Since the domain laws permitted villagers to put up travelers for one night, the note continued, no action would be taken against the farmers, but henceforth no lodgings were to be provided to entertainers.[90] About ten years later, in 1667, officials complained that *tōnai* and *monoyoshi* had been renting rooms to touring dancers and pointed out that this practice was strictly forbidden.[91]

In the 1690s the government agreed to license an association of bathhouse owners. Bathhouses were of two types: regular baths (*yuburo*) and a kind of steam bath (*karaburo*). The government imposed strict controls over the operations, permitting the steam baths to open only on six days each month, and closing all bathhouses at sunset. Moreover, the owners were not supposed to provide customers with private rooms where, as the government order delicately put it, "they might be served tea and tobacco." Even with these restrictions, however, the bathhouses built a regular clientele of townsmen and *bushi* servant personnel, and it is difficult to believe that at least some owners did not find a way to provide some of the other services traditionally associated with the bathhouses.[92]

The early eighteenth century was a bit livelier. In 1708, for instance, the domain again complained that samurai were providing lodgings to touring performers, and the summer of 1712 was reminiscent in some ways of the summer of 1621.[93] In the 6th month of 1712 Okada Joemon, a high-ranking samurai, sent the following letter to domain officials:

> Recently many Kanazawa samurai have been going out on the streets near their residences and even into the commoner wards without having any specific business. On these hot nights, there have been persons [wandering the streets] who have no fixed address and one cannot tell [from their dress] whether they are merchants or artisans or samurai or Young Stewards. Persons congregate at intersections and along the streets and trade insults until late into the night. Moreover, persons gather [along the riverbanks] and there is dancing. Persons of undeterminable status mingle with them. Even the Foot Soldiers I send out to investigate say that it is difficult to tell who is who. First of all, I would like to ask that the domain prohibit this kind of behavior in which people wander the streets late at night and shout out insults. . . .
>
> During shrine and temple festivals in recent years, merchants and artisans, persons who live in front of temples and shrines, and persons from rural areas on the outskirts of Kanazawa have been setting up tea shops and selling snacks, fish, and sake. . . . Numerous men and women from all social ranks join in and there is much drinking and wild revelry, especially in the shops which are enclosed by bamboo shades. I would like to ask that you take measures to end this kind of behavior.[94]

Various groups of touring performers may have been among the "persons of undeterminable status" that Okada fretted about, for the following month domain officials asked the City Magistrates to investigate rumors that touring entertainers were staying in the city. The Magistrates submitted a self-serving report which claimed that since they had proclaimed the laws vigorously, there were no townspeople who would rent rooms to entertainers.[95] Beyond this brief report, however, there is no record that the domain felt inclined to take any further official action.

With few exceptions the *chōnin* culture of the three major cities on the Pacific seaboard did not reach Kanazawa at this time. There is no evidence in government regulations, official correspondence, or the diaries of contemporaries that kabuki and the activities associated with the pleasure quarters became popular among Kanazawa's commoners; and the round of festivals, ceremonial days, and holidays described earlier remained the chief focus of *chōnin* social life in the castle town on the coast of the Sea of Japan.[96] The reasons for this are not entirely clear. Government suppression undoubtedly played a role. Officials had moved forcefully against kabuki and prostitution in the 1630s. They continued to deal out stern punishments to some persons who violated the laws at a later date, as in the case in which the Court banished nineteen prostitutes to Noto and either exiled or executed their *chōnin* procurers. Moreover, when a commoner named Ōsakaya Zenbei invited a kabuki troupe to Kanazawa in 1673 and staged some performances inside a shrine without first securing permission from the domain, he was sentenced to death.[97]

But government suppression alone is not the answer. Despite the occasionally harsh punishments meted out to men like Ōsakaya, the domain usually reacted more mildly toward violators, continually reminding them, in the spirit of moral suasion, that they were not supposed to rent lodgings to touring groups or employ them at parties. Kanazawa's merchants and artisans, moreover, routinely ignored some laws that displeased them. Clothing regulations and the prohibitions against lavish parties, for instance, had to be repeatedly reissued,[98] suggesting that if Kanazawa's residents had pushed for a theater and a pleasure quarter, some compromise with officials might have been possible, as in the case of the bathhouses licensed in the 1690s. The fact that this did not happen lends some credence to the notion that the merchants and artisans in Kanazawa during the late seventeenth century were different from their counterparts in the three major cities, and less interested in the pleasures of kabuki and the entertainment quarters.[99]

Whatever the reasons, it was not until the second half of the eighteenth century, nearly 130 years after Toshitsune had outlawed prostitution and prohibited kabuki, that a new generation of townspeople in Kanazawa came to share in the entertainments of the "floating world." By the

1760s, hot spring owners at Yamanaka, a little over thirty kilometers southwest of Kanazawa, offered regular theater performances, and customers staying at inns at the nearby Yamashiro hot spring could hire geisha and also enjoy performances of kabuki, acrobatics, and sumo wrestling.[100] From the 1760s and 1770s kabuki was staged with increasing frequency in Kanazawa, and houses of prostitution started to spring up around the city.[101] It was not until the early nineteenth century, however, that the domain government permitted the construction of two pleasure quarters, one between the Asano River bridge and Kannon, and the second behind Shinmei on the far banks of the Sai River. Licensing finally came at a time when daimyo government had less to fear from violence in the streets than in Toshitsune's day, and when a new generation of townspeople had become accustomed to traveling to Edo and Osaka and had sampled the offerings of the pleasure quarters in those cities.

For now, a variety of miscellaneous activities enlivened the social lives of Kanazawa's residents during the late seventeenth century. Traveling peddler-entertainers, whose circuits might include all of northern Japan, passed through Kanazawa. These men and women performed their juggling routines and balancing tricks on street corners and in front of shrines and temples. After they had generated some audience response, they would start hawking tooth medicine, household tools, and the like.[102] Other kinds of beggars and performers appeared on the streets. The *monkyōyomi,* for instance, read Buddhist sutras to passersby and then asked for contributions. The *saramawashi* spun dishes on the ends of long sticks and did other balancing tricks. The *onbōbanzai* were groups consisting of four or five men and women who strolled the streets with their drums and shamisen singing traditional lovers' tales, but with revised, salacious lyrics. Wandering female minstrels were called *chongari.* In Edo most *chongari* were wives of outcasts, and, tradition has it, many were beautiful women who had become outcasts following attempted double love suicides. In Kanazawa they usually gathered in front of the houses of wealthy samurai and commoners, playing the shamisen and singing lewd songs until the occupant gave them some money.[103]

There were other activities that could have taken place in almost any city at almost any time. When fires broke out, people rushed to gawk at the burning buildings. They hindered fire-fighting efforts, and the domain posted decrees forbidding anyone except fire-fighters from appearing at the scene of a fire. But the directives had little effect and had to be reissued after almost every major blaze.[104] When domain construction teams set about repairing the damage after landslides destroyed houses in some commoner wards at the foot of Mount Utatsu, *chōnin* "sidewalk engineers" were so numerous that they interfered with the work, and the City Office had to instruct people to stay out of the area.[105] Wedding trains, funeral processions, and the daimyo's hunting parties paraded through the streets, and people lined the routes to watch and gossip.[106] Commoners who were more physically inclined joined in the fishing on the Sai and Asano rivers, and Tsunanori even offered cash prizes for the first forty-six salmon caught each year.[107]

Townspeople with enough time and money took trips, often to the shrine at Ise or to Edo and Osaka. Commoners also journeyed frequently to the shrines located on two nearby mountains, Tateyama and Hakusan. These two mountains were the main nesting areas for the rare and attractive bird named *raichō,* and persons who were lucky enough to spot one of the birds while on a shrine visit routinely reported the sighting to the City Office.[108]

The emergence of noh during the second half of the seventeenth century as an important cultural activity for at least some of Kanazawa's residents added another element to Kanazawa's social life and helped to define the end of a century of cultural development. For generations to come, noh, the annual festivals and holidays, brief flirtations with kabuki, and the miscellaneous street activities would continue to provide the principal recreational pursuits for the city's inhabitants. The extension of administrative authority over the outcasts and the further elaboration of Neo-Confucian principles of governance in the closing decades of the seventeenth century symbolized, in a similar fashion, the maturation of urban government. An era of city-building had drawn to a close. In 1700, the residents of Kanazawa could look back over more than a century of sustained urban growth. Sometimes violently, sometimes peacefully; at times through cooperation, at times through confrontation; they had created a community that would endure until the intrusion of new historical forces in the middle of the nineteenth century.

CONCLUSION

A walking tour around the modern-day city of Kanazawa can impress upon us the enormous impact that the events of the seventeenth century had upon the subsequent evolution of the city. With a population of about 450,000 persons, today's city is larger than in the past, but, like its predecessor, it performs several functions. Kanazawa still serves as an administrative center, the capital of Ishikawa Prefecture, whose geographical boundaries correspond to the old Kaga and Noto portions of the Maeda family's holdings. The city remains the principal manufacturing center of the Hokuriku area as well as a large consumption center that draws on its rural hinterland for agricultural and handicraft products. With more than a dozen universities and colleges, Kanazawa is still a focal point of learning and education, and it continues to be home to the arts and a wide array of cultural activities.

To get to Kanazawa, we, like most other tourists, go by train. A limited express, the Hokuriku, departs Tokyo's old Ueno Station at 9:18 and, rolling through the night, crosses the broad Kantō plain and travels up the mountain valleys of Japan's "snow country." Just at dawn, the Hokuriku emerges from the mountains at Naoetsu and turns toward the southwest to run along the Sea of Japan, whose steely gray waves break against the rocky coast outside our dining car window. From Kanazawa's modern train station, we start our tour by taking a taxi to the remains of the old Maeda castle, which still functions as the geographical linchpin of the city's layout. Today the castle grounds are deceptively tranquil and peaceful, for they serve as the campus of Kanazawa University. Across the street from Ishikawa Gate, the only entry gate to the castle still standing today, is Kenrokuen Park. Completed in 1822 by Narinaga, the twelfth in the line of Maeda daimyo, Kenrokuen is an outstanding example of an Edo-period landscape garden. With its winding streams and its gentle hills and waterfalls, the park is often hailed as one of the three most beautiful in Japan.

But as we stand inside Kenrokuen on a warm summer's morning and look back upon Ishikawa Gate, we are impressed by the size of its turrets, by the massiveness of the adjoining stretch of stone walls dotted with camouflaged firing holes, and by the permanency of the armory with its lead-shingled roof. They quickly remind us of the castle's original func-

147

tion; Toshiie and Toshinaga built it as a military fortress. Traces of the old internal defensive enclosures are clearly visible. We can recognize as well the old pattern of outer walls and moats—many converted into modern streets and highways—and can appreciate how the castle was located to dominate strategically the high plain between the Sai and Asano rivers.

When we leave the castle and start out along the streets of Kanazawa, we can see the imprint of the daimyo on the city in many other ways. To the west of the castle is another popular tourist spot, the administrative division known as Nagamachi. Its name a compound made up of the characters indicating the surname of the old Chō family and the word for city ward, this is the area where the Maeda stationed the Chō, the Murai, and other important samurai families in the earliest years of the seventeenth century in order to complete a defensive belt around the city. We notice deep rain gutters separating the streets from the residential lots, and are somewhat startled to realize that we are looking at the narrowed-down remains of the old canals and waterways that once provided both drinking water and moatlike defenses for the samurai families who lived here.

As conditions of warfare gave way to peace during the first half of the seventeenth century, we recall, Toshitsune modified the original design of the city and attempted to bring it into greater conformity with the evolving ideals of a status-based society. Our stroll through the heart of Nagamachi takes us past old earthen walls and wooden gates, perquisites of the former samurai class, which even today, by city ordinance, the residents are bound to preserve. Some gates are larger than others, some more elaborately carved—all helping to bring into clearer focus the important relationship between symbols and status in old Kanazawa. Later, after a relaxing few moments at a conveniently located teahouse, we walk through a few blocks in one of the nearby wards established in the 1660s for lower-ranking warriors. This area, we note, is rather more distant from the castle than Nagamachi, and still today the plots of land are smaller, the gates less ornate, or even nonexistent.

As we continue clockwise through the maze of streets around the perimeter of the castle, we discover reminders of daimyo intervention in the economic life of the old castle town. In Ōmi Ward we browse through some of the hundreds of tiny shops selling fish, vegetables, and fruit that sprawl over several square blocks on the site where the daimyo first agreed to establish a central market more than 350 years ago. Beyond the market we spot the beginning of the highway that Toshitsune built to the port of Miyanokoshi. It is still used to transport foodstuffs to the urban market, but now also carries a reverse flow of swimmers to beaches on summer weekends. Pawnshops still flourish on the back streets and call to mind the daimyo laws regulating business practices and interest rates. We run across wards whose names echo the past: Stonecutters' Ward (Ishibikichō), Lumber Merchants' Ward (Zaimokuchō), and Carpenters' Ward (Daikumachi). Today office workers, taxi drivers, and school teachers live here, in contrast to the late sixteenth and early seventeenth centuries, when the Maeda daimyo established these residential areas in order to provide incentives to the skilled artisans whom they hoped to lure to their castle town.

We follow the streets of Carpenters' Ward down to the banks of the Sai River, lined now with concrete levees to prevent flooding. On sunny days fishermen still test their luck in the Sai's clear waters, and, in the first flush of summer's warmth, an occasional group of university students, more interested in fun than profit, will try their hand at panning for gold and perhaps recall the origins of their city's name.

Across the Sai stands Temple Ward, established by daimyo fiat and still home to dozens of temples. It is a disappointing sight. When the temples were first ordered to relocate here, their immense worship halls and extensive grounds formed part of the city's defenses. Today, however, the grandeur is missing. The temple buildings seem small, the grounds reduced in size—some are even used as parking lots. The world has become a more secular place than it was in the seventeenth century, and as parishioners have become less generous and have decreased in number, temple authorities have resorted to selling or renting their land in order to remain solvent.

We leave Temple Ward rather quickly and, recrossing the Sai, work our way northward in search of those temples which had a special relationship with the Maeda family and which still, we hope, retain some of their former elegance. They are difficult to locate. Nyoraiji is so small that even the people of the neighborhood seem unaware of its existence; Tentokuin temple, built in honor of Toshitsune's wife, is under repair and we are its only lonely visitors; Hōenji is uninteresting except for a small cemetery that contains some weathered and dilapidated gravestones of former samurai families.

Across the Asano River, and a little to the northwest, is Kannon, the shrine and temple complex where over the centuries the Maeda family worshiped, presented their newly born to the gods, and sponsored noh drama every spring. We climb the nearly one hundred steps to its entrance on a bluff overlooking the city, and again we are disappointed. All that remains of its former glory are a few gravestones and one shabby building, so run-down that we doubt it can survive another Hokuriku winter.

Despite Kannon's drab appearance, its hillside location provides us with a wonderful view of the city and a convenient spot to rest and enjoy the food we purchased earlier at the central market. Our walking tour has impressed upon us the way in which modern-day Kanazawa bears the marks of its daimyo heritage. But, as we linger on the steps of Kannon warming ourselves and our thoughts, we are once again struck by the idea that daimyo-centered planning cannot adequately account for certain aspects of Kanazawa's growth as a castle town. Grazing out over the city we discover buildings and recall events which demonstrate that the commoners of the castle town, as well as the outcasts and lower elements of the samurai class, were not merely objects of political authority but were also agents of historical change.[1] The people of Kanazawa possessed enormous vigor, which they used in historically creative ways: to participate in city administration, to devise new economic institutions, and to fashion a distinctive urban culture. This energy, this desire to shape their environment, sprang not from any particular intellectual or philosophical concern about the course of history, but rather arose out of the exigencies and necessities of everyday life. The principal concerns of Kanazawa's residents were to survive and, as much as possible, to prosper, given the circumstances that confronted them. It was in pursuit of these goals, and in the joy of having secured their livelihoods, that the people of Kanazawa influenced the course of castle town urbanization.

The rolling hills we see stretching out behind Kannon were one place where the townspeople created their own cultural norms during the seventeenth century. While it was the Maeda daimyo who planned and sponsored the noh festival held each spring on the stages especially constructed at Kannon, it was the city's commoners, permitted inside the shrine precincts to view noh on only one day each year, who turned the otherwise somber occasion into a rite of spring; for, as the buildings at Kannon reverberated to the dignified chants of the noh chorus, the surrounding mountains and valleys, as our old diarist noted, trembled with the singing voices of merchants and artisans whose carousing and boisterous parties went on through the night.

Across the Asano, within the city proper, the amusements of the merchant and artisan families came from the annual round of ceremonies and festival days, and from a street culture that featured touring acrobats, jugglers, musicians, and animal acts. This miscellany of street events was different from the rough riverbank kabuki and bathhouse milieu of the early seventeenth century. It also constrasted sharply with the more aristocratic cultural endeavors of Kanazawa's elite samurai population and with the floating world of the pleasure quarters of Edo and Osaka—the latter, a more rousing kind of *chōnin* culture that would not spread to Kanazawa until the eighteenth century. But these festivals and street events provided a satisfying range of cultural activities for several generations of Kanazawa's commoners during the seventeenth century.

From the steps of Kannon we can also look down at that old stretch of the Hokuriku highway which still runs between the Sai and Asano bridges. The roadway today is lined with hotels, office buildings, and shops—including a retail outlet for Ōhi pottery—and we are reminded that this area was the commercial heart of the castle town and that the merchants who settled here contributed greatly to the city's prosperity. To the right of our vantage point, along the northern banks of the Asano River, is a very different kind of area: a section of run-down apartments and tenements, a direct descendant of the impoverished quarters occupied by the unskilled artisans and day laborers who arrived during the seventeenth century. This slumlike district calls to mind not only the differences within the old commercial classes but also the difficulties that the first three Maeda daimyo faced in attempting to control the scale and texture of migration to their castle town. Back across the Asano, modern-day Kanazawa seems congested, with homes, retail shops, and small-scale factories jammed together in great disarray—not too different from the old castle town, where rich and not-so-rich merchants, and, in some cases, even merchants and samurai, lived in the same wards despite the ideals of the system of rule-by-status.

In their effort to survive and prosper, the townspeople who lived in these various sections of the city helped to create significant new economic institutions. The Nakaya, a pharmacy established nearly four hundred years ago by one of the first purveyors to the daimyo, is still in business today at its original location next to the castle grounds, and the shop reminds us that the chartered merchant–daimyo relationship depended as much on the hard work and ingenuity of the merchant as it did on the goodwill of the daimyo. Later in the seventeenth century other merchants and artisans took the initiative in forming protective associations—when Notoya Kuhei and three other men received monopoly rights on the wholesale phases of paper production, for instance, or when Itoya Matabei and Aburaya Magobei received the exclusive right to act as wholesalers for the lacquer base extracted from sumac plants.

Finally, we also recall that the merchants and artisans helped to administer their city by serving as City Elders, Ward Representatives, and Heads of Household Groups. In these capacities, they enforced laws, collected taxes, and investigated criminal cases. Their duties gave them a thorough knowledge of law and administrative techniques, and perhaps too a measure of political sophistication and leadership that historians have not yet fully appreciated. Politically, as well as economically and culturally, the castle town of Kanazawa was the product of the efforts of all the status groups that lived in the city.

It is time to end our tour, and as we make our way through the streets of the city back to the station, we engage in some final thoughts about the various contributions of daimyo and commoners to the city-building process and about the nature of class relations during the seventeenth century. Perhaps surprisingly, there is little evidence of serious confrontation between classes, or more appropriately, between status groups; nor is there much evidence of conflict between upper and lower elements within any single status group during the seventeenth century in Kanazawa. Later, the situation would change: in the early eighteenth century samurai elites would act to prevent ambitious lower-ranking members of their class from holding important administrative posts, and by the end of that century the grievances of the lower samurai against a system that seemed to deny them the possibility of personal advancement would become pronounced. In the early nineteenth century a similar contest arose between established and newly wealthy merchants for control of the office of City Elder, and by mid-century many townspeople were questioning the entire structure of political rights within the city.

Yet, aside from the occasional street-corner brawl or other act of violence between samurai and commoner, the seventeenth century saw relatively little conflict that was status-based. In part, perhaps, this was due simply to the newness of the system; any emerging sense of status-consciousness was still in an embryonic stage. In addition, the delegation of certain political prerogatives to the townspeople and to lower elements within the samurai hierarchy generated a sense of power sharing, a feeling of participation, that drained off some tensions and helped to mask the ultimate rigidity and inflexibility of the system of rule-by-status. Beyond this, the daimyo, samurai, and commoners shared certain mutual interests during the seventeenth century that overcame the divisive tendencies inherent in the status system.

These common interests linked together the city-building efforts of the daimyo and townspeople and gave a distinct shape to the urbanization experience in seventeenth-century Kanazawa. In the first place, the townspeople and the ruling authorities had mutual needs and depended upon one another to satisfy those needs. In the late sixteenth and early seventeenth century, for instance, the Maeda daimyo strove to create a physically and economically secure castle town headquarters. As the military class took up residence in the garrison town, it relied on certain merchants and artisans to supply military goods, and this dependency gave rise to the first government-merchant alliance between the daimyo and the chartered merchants and artisans. In these early years, the first Maeda daimyo also instituted a variety of programs that encouraged more general economic development. They standardized weights and measures, improved transportation facilities, minted coins, and provided land for merchant shops and homes by moving farm villages and undertaking the

Sai River project. In all, these efforts created an environment in which the commoners who migrated to Kanazawa could hope to pursue their own economic interests and to achieve individual business success.

Because of this integration of interests, the domain government often responded positively to the needs of the merchant class. The sanctions granted to the protective associations provide a clear example of this. On a more general level, the ruling authorities offered a degree of official support to all merchants and artisans. Two examples of this include the proclamation issued by the government in the early seventeenth century which stated that the samurai were obligated to honor all credit obligations recorded on merchant ledgers and the announcement in the 1660s which stated that the government would assist merchants in collecting all debts. The Poorhouses expressed the government's concern for the urban poor, and its restrictions on kabuki and prostitution were designed in part to bring peace to the streets of the castle town. Artisan and merchant fears and complaints about the possible loss of business and job opportunities to newcomers was one factor behind the government decision to restrict migration to the city in the 1680s.

It was impossible, however, for the domain to protect everyone's interests all of the time. On occasion, the domain government pursued its own self-interests at the expense of those of others. The forced relocation of temples in 1616, for instance, imposed burdens on those institutions and separated them from their parishioners. It is also difficult to imagine that the merchants and artisans unanimously greeted with enthusiasm the order that they move to new residences in the 1630s.

Conflicts of interest between competing economic groups also occasionally developed, and when they did, the domain often found itself in the position of acting as arbitrator. One clear example of this came in the 1650s when peddlers tried to circumvent the established fisherman–wholesaler–fish market distribution system by buying directly from fishermen and then either peddling the fish within the city or selling the fish to small general stores scattered throughout the castle town. A number of interests were thus brought into conflict. The established wholesalers and shops in the fish markets wanted to maintain the status quo, while the peddlers and the scattered general stores favored a more open system, and it seems likely that the general consumer found the new system more convenient, too. When the established wholesalers complained to the government, the domain bueaucrats worked out a compromise that gave everyone something, but perhaps satisfied no one completely. They permitted the peddlers and small general shops to handle some kinds of dried and salted fish, and reconfirmed the exclusive right of the established wholesalers and markets to deal in fresh fish. Similar examples are plentiful. In 1659, the domain fixed interest rates, but offered to help enforce debt relationships. In the 1660s, urban residents complained about tofu prices, and the authorities decreed that this business be thrown open to everyone. In all, a very complex mix of mutual needs, common goals, shared interests, government protection, competing rights, and compromise conditioned the urbanization experience in Kanazawa.

As our train pulls out from Kanazawa Station and we catch our final view of the castle and Temple Ward, of the Nakaya drug shop and the downtown commercial center (named after one of its original settlers, Kōrinbō), our thoughts turn from Kanazawa toward cities in general. In many ways, it would seem that the historical forces that led to the formation of early modern societies in Europe and Japan also gave rise to a class of cities whose similarities cut across national and cultural boundaries. Like Kanazawa, Paris and Saint Petersburg bore the imprint of their absolutist overlords. Peter the Great impressed labor to build his northern capital and then forcibly summoned the bureaucracy and a number of important merchants to inhabit it. Louis XIV remodeled the architectural facade of Paris to make it more pleasing to his baroque eye and then reorganized the city's administrative machinery to make it more responsive to his royal will. Both men engaged as well in a form of cultural authoritarianism; Louis by granting theatrical monopolies and Peter by attempting to recreate French salon society on the muddy banks of the Neva. In France, Russia, and Japan, the seventeenth century gave birth to cities that expressed the tastes of their rulers and reflected the social and political realities of the early modern era.

This study of Kanazawa, however, has sought to demonstrate that urban commoners can play a historically significant role, even within the context of a highly statist society. The same can be suggested for the baroque cities of Europe. Although a portion of Saint Petersburg's population first came north in response to the tsar's commands, for example, thousands of others migrated there when they learned of the enormous profits that could be made. It was this sort of commercial activity that provided the economic basis for Saint Petersburg's continued existence.[2]

In Paris and Kanazawa the highest organs of the autocrat's government monopolized legislative functions and decided the distribution of political rights. But in each city, the different levels of society shared in the performance of administrative responsibilities. The heads of the sixteen *quartiers* of Paris and the City Elders of Kanazawa carried out many similar functions: reporting crimes and fires to high officials, helping to collect municipal taxes, and standing, at least in theory, as representatives of proper moral behavior.

In neither Kanazawa nor Paris did the residents live in total awe of the autocrat's laws. The domain bureaucracy in Kanazawa found it difficult to enforce sumptuary regulations concerning clothing, housing styles, and the food to be served on festival days. In Paris, Louis's minions had to constantly reissue, because they were not being obeyed, the ordinances instructing beggars to leave the city; those forbidding rowdyism in front of theaters and the carrying of firearms into the buildings; and those, like the ordinance of 1656, that prohibited public gatherings of "all women and girls of ill repute, lackeys, idlers, vagabonds and other such."[3] In both cities this sort of disregard for behavioral codes lent a certain texture to urban life. It also displayed very clearly the limits of premodern autocracy; for while enforcement of such laws would strain the capabilities of a modern bureaucracy, it was a certain impossibility for the relatively primitive administrative machinery of the seventeenth century.

And finally, the urban commoners in each of these cities created their own cultural forms. Peter the Great built zoos and attended the salons of the rich, but the sons and daughters of Saint Petersburg's merchants and artisans mostly took their amusement from popular spectacles such as magic shows, animal acts, juggling, and rope dancing—a street culture that they shared with their counterparts in the castle town of Kanazawa. The seventeenth century might still be known as the age of absolutism, but it is also important to recognize that in France, Russia, and Japan, commoners possessed a vital, constructive energy which they used to shape their urban environments.

Our journey to Kanazawa has also emphasized to us that cities are dynamic, constantly evolving institutions. In the tumultuous century since 1868, the old Japanese status groups have disappeared; the daimyo–City Magistrate–City Elder construct has been superseded by an administrative system more highly centralized than any that a seventeenth-century ruler could have imagined; the merchant purveyors to the daimyo have been replaced by a new class of capitalist enterpreneurs; and kabuki and noh have fallen victim to baseball, motion pictures, and touring rock stars. In Kanazawa, as in all other cities, the past has merged with the present to form the scaffolding for yet a new and different future.

APPENDIX ONE

THE PRINCIPAL SAMURAI RANKS

Rank	Fief Size	Military Duties	Civil Functions
Hakka[a] (Senior Advisers)	11,000– 50,000	Army commanders advisers	Council of Advisers
Hitomochi (Commanders)	1,000– 14,000	Army commanders	Temple Magistrates Head of the Office of Police and the Judiciary, etc.
Heishi (Officers)	80–2,400	Troop leaders	City Magistrates, Rural Magistrates, etc.
Yoriki (Soldiers)		Troops	Employed in various offices
Okachi (Lower Soldiers)		Troops Mounted troops	Employed in various offices
Ashigaru (Foot Soldiers)		Troops	Employed in various offices

Hōkōnin[b]
Wakatō (Young Stewards)
Chūgen (Chamberlains)
Dōgumochi (Keepers of the Equipment)
Komono (Attendants)
Yarimochi (Keepers of the Lances)
Umatori (Livery Stewards)
Norimono (Vehicle Stewards)
Zōritori (Keepers of the Footwear)
Arashiko (Valets)

a. The *hakka* (Eight Houses) and their land holdings were as follows:
Honda   50,000   *koku*
Chō   33,000
Yokoyama   30,000

(*continued on next page*)

Maeda (Nagatane line)	18,000
Okumura (Nagatomi line)	17,000
Murai (from 1690)	16,000
Okumura (Yasuhide line)	12,000
Maeda (Naoyuki line)	11,000

b. The ranks from *wakatō* to *arashiko* are referred to collectively as *hōkōnin,* a term that might be translated as "samurai servants." In Kaga, these men served on one-year contracts, and domain laws specified that they should serve for a maximum of ten years, although many were actually employed for longer periods of time. In wartime, they served as supply and quartermaster personnel, and in times of peace they worked as household servants. They did not hold fiefs, but were paid an annual salary. The documents refer to these men both as *bushi* and as *hōkōnin,* and most received some of the perquisites of samurai status, such as permission to wear one short sword. For additional information, see *Chōji tsūsai,* 1, pp. 102–04; *Manji izen osadamegaki,* 2, pp. 21–25; *Tsutsui kyūki,* 3, pp. 200–08; *KZ,* 1, ch. 7, doc. 12, pp. 260–62; and 2, ch. 9, doc. 11, pp. 343–44; and *KHS,* 2, Kan'ei 15 (1638)/2, pp. 859–60, and Kan'ei 16 (1639)/2, pp. 893–95; 3, Kan'ei 18 (1641)/2/7, pp. 2–5, and Kanbun 1 (1661)/1/25, pp. 913–15; and 6, Kyōhō 14 (1729)/intercalary 9, pp. 686–89.

APPENDIX TWO
The 1642 *Chōnin* Code

Chōnin and persons of low status (*shimojimo*)[a] must obey these ordinances which are now proclaimed throughout the city.

Chōnin are not to possess a large number of luxurious clothes. Earlier we [issued ordinances which] permitted retainers to wear silk, silk habutae, and pongee. Materials other than the above are prohibited, even for decorative purposes on sleeves and collars. *Chōnin* are to obey the ordinances issued earlier and to restrict themselves to clothing that is appropriate [to their status]. More detailed instructions will be issued later.

Chōnin, regardless of who they are, will be held responsible if they are slovenly or commit improprieties toward samurai.

It is forbidden to keep dogs as pets or to walk along the street next to samurai. Such incidents should be reported immediately to the Ward Representative who will report to the Magistrates. If the Ward Representative does not make a report, he will be held responsible. Birds (*heri*) may be kept as pets.

Chōnin are strictly forbidden to bet money on games of chance. Parents and masters should warn their charges about this. If there are violations, the parent, master, and the person who rented the premises for gambling shall be punished, regardless of the status of the violator. We will consider those who love gambling to be the same as thieves.

Behavior inappropriate to one's status as a *chōnin* or artisan is forbidden. Do your jobs well.

Chōnin are not to gather in shops and gossip loudly about others, nor are *chōnin* in shops to sit around in rude positions.

Chōnin, children, youngsters, and persons of low status shall not wear straw hats or scarves which cover the face and engage in *kabukimono*-type

---

a. The exact meaning of the term *shimojimo* is not clear. In some documents, it seems to indicate low-ranking *bushi,* while in other documents it refers to low-ranking *bushi* and townspeople.

behavior. Persons shall not loiter on the streets (*tsujidachi*), nor shall they sing ballads of noh chants in a loud voice. If an Investigator (*metsuke*) learns of such behavior, he will report it regardless of who is involved.

Chōnin, children, and *rokushaku* and *zōritori* (*hōkōnin*) shall not wear high rain clogs (*ashida*). The height of clogs and the quality of materials shall be in accordance with one's status. If someone violates this, regardless of who he is, he shall be reported to his master.

Chōnin, children, and others should be reported if they get together and behave rudely.

Persons who urinate from the second floor of houses in the city, regardless of whether it is night or day, shall certainly be punished. If a traveler at an inn commits such an act, the innkeeper shall be held responsible. This is to be explained to all children, travelers, and persons of low status. Spitting from the second floor, throwing waste water from the second floor, and opening the second-floor windows and staring at passersby or calling out rude comments to them are also prohibited.

Chōnin are not to wear long swords. They will be held responsible if they wear swords and imitate *hōkōnin* when they go sight-seeing at Hakusan [a nearby mountain], Yasue, Miyanokoshi, or any other place.

When *chōnin* go sight-seeing, men and women shall not enter the same place together. Persons of low status in the city should not be negligent [about observing this rule].

When an item is pawned, the pawnshop owner shall insist that the person pawning the item have a guarantor. If it is later discovered that the pawned item was stolen, the guarantor will be held responsible. The pawnshop owner will be responsible if there was no guarantor.

The Household Groups in the city shall appoint Group Heads (*kumiaigashira*) to act as liaison agents between officials and the Household Groups.

I have been instructed to issue these ordinances to the wards in Kanazawa. The ordinances are as set forth herein, and henceforth people are not to neglect them. If there are any transgressions, an investigation shall be held and punishments meted out in accordance with the transgression. Since the daimyo has stated that people are not to neglect the ordinances once they are issued, people must henceforth observe these ordinances at all times.

Kan'ei 19 [1642]/6/1   Nagase Gorōemon
                                                       [City Magistrate]

Source: *Kahan kokusho ibun*, 17, pp. 75–84.

APPENDIX THREE
The 1659 Directive to the City Magistrates

You are to ensure that there is always a sufficient number of horses and porters. You are to make corvée levies in accordance with domain regulations.

If there are people in the city who get into a fight, they should be stopped immediately and reported to the City Magistrates. If a large number of people are involved and it is difficult to stop the fight, the fight should be reported immediately to their landlords and neighbors, and the City Magistrates should be notified immediately.

The *yoban* and *teishuban* [Ward Patrol] should always be alert for the danger of fire. If there is a fire, the City Magistrates should take the Constables (*dōshin*) and City Foot Soldiers (*machi ashigaru*) and immediately go to the site of the fire and fight the fire. After the fire is extinguished, the City Magistrates should investigate and determine the number of houses destroyed by the fire, and then confer with [Maeda] Tsushima, [Okumura] Inaba, [Tsuda] Genba, and [Imaeda] Minbu. The persons who lose their homes will be given exemptions from some city taxes.

If there is an incident in the city that is difficult to resolve, you should confer with the Office of the Police and Judiciary (*kujiba*).

You should instruct *hōkōnin* not to be impolite and *chōnin* not to commit improprieties.

When a person is ill, he should consult with his Household Group and Ward Representative and draw up a will. A person may change his will whenever he wishes. If a person dies unexpectedly without leaving a will, the Household Group and Ward Representative should immediately send a report to the City Magistrates, who will then dispatch a Constable to inspect the deceased's household goods. The Household Group, Ward Representative, and Constable shall decide the disposition of the property.

The City Magistrates shall take care of the laws, problems, and legal matters in the Ordinary Wards. As before, Asanoya Jirōbei and Kikuya Hachizaemon shall handle the details of collecting the land taxes (*jishigin* and *jishimai*).

If someone is late paying a debt or paying for goods purchased on credit, the City Magistrates will contact that person. In addition, if payment is not made, an Inspector (*yokome*) will be dispatched [to tell that person to pay].

When pawning goods, there must be a guarantor. If there is no guarantor and stolen goods are pawned, the pawnshop owner must suffer the loss.

A person should not buy goods from a peddler he does not know. If a person wants to buy something [from an unknown peddler], he should ask the address of the peddler, send someone to verify this, and then pay the money for the goods.

The interest rate on loans shall be fixed at 1.7 percent per month.

When one rents lodgings [on a permanent basis] to someone, he should first ask that person's original home, lineage, previous addresses, and religious affiliation, even if the person seeking lodgings is a masterless samurai (*rōnin*) or a doctor. A record of this information should be made and a guarantor named. Persons who rent lodgings to disreputable people will be held responsible. Of course, renting lodgings for one night is a different matter [and this sort of information need not be recorded].

Gambling, prostitution, and keeping mistresses are strictly prohibited. Lodgings are not to be rented to dancers, *kyōgen* performers, or any suspicious persons.

Chōnin and samurai are strictly forbidden to join together and go into business.

A *chōnin* of unsavory appearance or any person of suspicious appearance should be immediately reported to the City Magistrates, regardless of the time of day.

If household goods that are confiscated for auction [a common procedure in certain types of criminal trials] are not sold immediately, the Constables and Ward Representatives shall assess their value and the City Office may use that amount of money for city expenses. When the goods are finally sold at auction, the receipts should then be used to cover the money previously spent.

Except for persons who are over sixty years of age or who are sick, *chōnin* are not permitted to use palanquins.

A report must be submitted whenever there is a fight or trouble in the Original Wards and the Ordinary Wards.

The City Magistrates are to make inspection tours of the city four times annually and issue any necessary orders.

The city [the *chōnin* as a whole] shall present twenty *mai* of silver to each Magistrate at New Year's and one hundred pieces of cash (*chōmoku*) at the Five Festivals. At New Year's three *mai* of silver shall be presented to each Constable, and fifty pieces of cash at the Five Festivals. Other than this, no other gifts are to be presented.

The Household Groups shall be responsible for prison expenses.

The ten City Elders shall receive a salary of *sannin buchi* [about five and a half *koku*] from the domain. From the *chōnin*, they shall receive five *mai* of silver each. Salaries for the Ward Representatives and Inspectors will be settled by negotiation between them and the City Offices.

There is to be no misunderstanding concerning the above.

Manji 2 [1659]/6/1

[From] Imaeda Minbu
Tsuda Genba
Okumura Inaba
Maeda Tsushima

[To] The Kanazawa City Magistrates

Source: *Kanazawa machijū gohatto no chō*, pp. 10–16.

APPENDIX FOUR
The 1660 *Chōnin* Code

Fireworks, street dancing, street sumo, loitering, and singing on the street are all strictly forbidden.

Each house and each ward shall maintain rain barrels [to collect water for fire fighting].

Each Household Group shall maintain two ladders, a water barrel, sickles, and rakes.

When the wind is blowing, the Ward Representatives, *bangashira,* and Ward Patrol (*teishuban*) shall go throughout the city and warn households to exercise caution about fire.

If a household sends a child, a cripple, or a blind person to serve as a member of the Ward Patrol [*yoban;* equivalent to the *teishuban;* the duty was rotated among the households in a ward], that household shall be held responsible.

The wooden gates to each ward shall be closed at dusk. The side gates should be closed later. The Gate Keepers should be diligent, and the gates should be opened at dawn.

The roads, bridges, and the flow of water in sewers in the city must be constantly checked.

Holes should not be dug in front of houses.

Water and so forth is not to be thrown from the second floor of houses. Nor are people to urinate from the second floor. This is to be thoroughly explained to children, travelers, and persons of low status.

Chōnin are not to wear swords and imitate *hōkōnin* when visiting shrines or going sight-seeing.

At wedding ceremonies, latticed shutters are not to be broken, nor stones thrown. If a person commits such an act, the Household Group should take that person into custody.

Houses of assignation are strictly prohibited. Keeping a mistress is forbidden.

164

The floors of smiths' shops and the Artisans' Workshop (*saikusho*) shall be built high above the ground. The roofs shall be lacquered and a barrel of rain water kept at hand. When the wind is strong, the Artisans' Workshop shall suspend operations.

Cutting bamboo along dikes and moats is strictly forbidden.

Taking plants, shrubs, or dirt from vacant samurai residences is strictly forbidden.

Persons shall not throw snow or *mizuuchi* [the water that individual homeowners and shopkeepers sprinkle on the streets to keep dust down] on passersby.

Chōnin who are entrusted with tax rice [certain merchants worked for the domain and decided when to release supplies of government rice for sale in Osaka] shall not send their wives or children to distant places.

Persons who come to the city to sell hawks should first report to Ōhara Gen'emon and Tanba Sōbei and then [if they receive permission] conclude the sale and give the hawks to the falconers.

Chōnin are strictly forbidden to wear high clogs. When the streets are bad, illustrious *chōnin* may wear them.

The above are to be strictly observed. They are to be explained to each Household Group.

Manji 3 [1660]/7/10

> [From] Satomi Shichizaemon
> Nagaya Shichirōemon
> [City Magistrates]

[To] The Ward Representatives
of the Original Wards
and the Ordinary Wards

Source: *Kanazawa machijū gohatto no chō*, pp. 21–25.

NOTES

The Japanese characters for all authors as well as book, journal, and document collection titles are contained in the bibliography. Unless otherwise noted, the place of publication is Tokyo.

Documents in published collections are usually arranged in chronological order, by title, or by chapter and document number. In these notes, references to documents arranged chronologically include the title of the collection, volume number, document date (year, month, and day, if known; with the year translated into the Gregorian calendar), and page number (e.g., *KHS*, 4, Kanbun 3 [1663]/7/3, pp. 4–17). When arrangement is by title, the citation includes the title of the collection, volume number, document title, and page number (e.g., *KKS*, 3, "Gojōnai kaji no koto," pp. 541–42). When arrangement is by chapter and document number, the note includes the title of the collection, volume number, chapter number, document number, and page number (*KZ*, 2, ch. 6, doc. 37, pp. 8–10, for example). When a collection uses none of the above arrangements, the citation includes only the title of the collection, volume number, and page number (e.g., *KK*, 3, pp. 57–58).

Most of the unpublished sources are compilations of documents. If the individual document bears a title, the reference includes the name of the collection, volume number, the title of the document, and page number (*Chōnin yuishochō*, 2, "Tōfuya Taemon," pp. 5–7). If the individual document is untitled, the reference is to collection, volume, and page number (*Manji izen osadamegaki*, 2, pp. 211–32). The pagination for all unpublished documents is the author's own.

The following abbreviations are used:

KHS   Hioki Ken, ed. *Kaga han shiryō*. Vols. 1–6. Ishiguro Bunkichi, 1929–33.

KK   Ishikawa-ken Toshokan Kyōkai, ed. *Kaisakusho kyūki*. 3 vols. Kanazawa: Ishikawa-ken Toshokan Kyōkai, 1939.

KKS   Morita Heiji, comp. (Edited and revised by Hioki Ken.) *Kanazawa kosekishi*. 3 vols. Rekishi Toshosha, 1976.

KKSS Wada Bunjirō, ed. *Kōhon Kanazawa shishi*. Vols. 1–5, 11, and 12. Kanazawa: Kanazawa Shiyakusho, 1916–33.

KS   Ishikawa-ken Toshokan Kyōkai, ed. *Kinjō shinpiroku*. Kanazawa: Ishikawa-ken Toshokan Kyōkai, 1937.

KZ   Ishikawa-ken Toshokan Kyōkai, ed. *Kokuji zasshō*. 3 vols. Kanazawa: Ishikawa-ken Toshokan Kyōkai, 1931–33.

MK   Ishikawa-ken Toshokan Kyōkai, ed. *Mitsubo kikigaki*. Kanazawa: Ishikawa-ken Toshokan Kyōkai, 1931.

OG   Kanazawa Bunka Kyōkai, ed. *Kaga han osadamegaki.* 2 vols. Kanazawa: Kanazawa Bunka Kyōkai, 1936.

All other published source collections and local histories that contain documents are referred to after the initial citation by title only.

INTRODUCTION

1. Harada Tomohiko, *Nihon hōken toshi kenkyū* (Tōkyō Daigaku Shuppankai, 1973; originally published 1957), pp. 421–32. This and the books by Toyoda Takeshi and Ono Hitoshi cited below constitute the three "classic" works on early castle town evolution. In English, many of their themes are given expression in John W. Hall, "Castle Towns and Japan's Early Modern Urbanization," in John W. Hall and Marius B. Jansen, eds., *Studies in the Institutional History of Early Modern Japan* (Princeton: Princeton University Press, 1968), pp. 169–81. For more recent studies, see Nakabe Yoshiko, *Jōkamachi* (Yanagihara Shoten, 1978); Yamori Kazuhiko, *Toshizu no rekishi* (Kōdansha, 1974), pp. 227–35; Matsumoto Jirō, "Hagi-jō no kōzō—chikujōji o chūshin ni," *Rekishi techō* 5:8 (August 1977): 26–30; Nakabayashi Tamotsu, "Kinsei no jōkamachi Tottori," *Rekishi techō* 5:9 (September 1977): 21–28; Tokuda Kojun, "Utsunomiya-jō to jōkamachi puran no kōsatsu," *Rekishi techō* 6:4 (April 1978): 36–42; and Ugawa Kaoru, "Social Structure and Land Use in Japan: The Case of Yonezawa," *Rikkyō keizaigaku kenkyū* 30:2 (September 1976): 107–28.

2. Murai Masuo, "Hōkensei no kakuritsu to toshi no sugata," in Morisue Yoshiaki et al., eds., *Taikei: Nihonshi sōsho 16: Seikatsu 2* (Yamakawa Shuppansha, 1977), pp. 118–22.

3. Ono Hitoshi, *Kinsei jōkamachi no kenkyū* (Shibundō, 1928), pp. 56–58, 163–73, and 201–05; and Toyoda Takeshi, *Nihon no hōken toshi* (Iwanami Shoten, 1976; originally published 1952), pp. 116–20. For more recent studies see Hirotani Kijūrō, "Kōchi ni okeru jōkamachi-teki keizaiken no tenkai katei," *Rekishi techō* 6:3 (March 1978): 24–29; and Sasaki Gin'ya with William B. Hauser, "Sengoku Daimyo Rule and Commerce," in John W. Hall, Nagahara Keiji, and Kozo Yamamura, eds., *Japan before Tokugawa* (Princeton: Princeton University Press, 1981), pp. 125–48.

4. Toyoda, *Nihon no hōken toshi,* pp. 161–75; Ono, *Kinsei jōkamachi,* pp. 155–63; and Matsumoto Shirō, "Toshi to kokka shihai," in Hara Hidesaburō et al., eds., *Taikei: Nihon kokkashi* (Tōkyō Daigaku Shuppankai, 1975), 3: 240–42 and 248–52. For an individual case study see Aono Shunsui, "Jōkamachi no kensetsu: Fukuyama no baai," in Ōishi Shinzaburō, ed., *Edo to chihō bunka* (Bun'ichi Sōgō Shuppan, 1977), pp. 289–312.

5. Tanaka Yoshio, "Kaga han hiningoya-sei seiritsu no jijō ni tsuite," *Nihon rekishi* 183 (August 1963): 63.

6. Quoted in F. Roy Willis, *Western Civilization: An Urban Perspective* (Lexington, Mass.: D. C. Heath & Company, 1973), vol. 1, p. 506. The classic introduction to the development of the early modern state is Carl J. Friedrich, *The Age of Baroque* (New York: Harper & Brothers, 1952), while a more recent attempt to analyze the nature of political authority can be found in the essays in Charles Tilly, ed., *The Formation of Nation States in Europe* (Princeton: Princeton University Press, 1975).

7. Peter Brock Putnam, *Peter, the Revolutionary Tsar* (New York: Harper & Row, 1973), p. 113.

8. A good introduction to the baroque city is contained in Willis, *Western Civilization,* pp. 483–528; and Lewis Mumford, *The City in History* (New York: Harcourt, Brace & Company, 1961), pp. 344–409. In addition to the specific works on Paris and Saint Petersburg cited below, N. J. G. Pounds has interesting observations on the baroque aspects of Madrid and Warsaw in his *An Historical Geography of Europe, 1500–1840* (Cambridge: Cambridge University Press, 1979), pp. 120–24; urban governance in a German city receives full treatment in T. C. W. Blanning, *Reform and Revolution in Mainz,*

1743–1803 (Cambridge: Cambridge University Press, 1974); while Edwin Y. Galantay deals with Europe's new capitals in general in his *New Towns: Antiquity to the Present* (New York: George Braziller, 1975), pp. 5–19.

9. Willis, *Western Civilization,* p. 486.

10. The information on Paris is from Willis, *Western Civilization,* pp. 504–17; Leon Bernard, *The Emerging City: Paris in the Age of Louis XIV* (Durham: Duke University Press, 1970), pp. 3–131; Orest Ranum, *Paris in the Age of Absolutism* (New York: John Wiley & Sons, 1968), pp. 252–92; and Alan Williams, "The Police and the Administration of Eighteenth Century Paris," *Journal of Urban History* 4:2 (February 1978): 157–82. Details of later reforms can be found in David H. Pickney, *Napoleon III and the Rebuilding of Paris* (Princeton: Princeton University Press, 1958); and Howard Saalman, *Haussmann: Paris Transformed* (New York: George Braziller, 1971).

11. The information on Saint Petersburg is from Willis, *Western Civilization,* pp. 497–504; Robert K. Massie, *Peter the Great* (New York: Alfred A. Knopf, 1980), pp. 355–66, 602–12, and 795–817; Putnam, *Peter, the Revolutionary Tsar,* pp. 159–65; L. Jay Oliva, *Russia in the Era of Peter the Great* (Englewood Cliffs, N.J.: Prentice-Hall, 1969), pp. 153–69; and Galantay, *New Towns,* pp. 10–11.

12. For more on this, see Toyoda, *Nihon no hōken toshi,* pp. 19–22; and Wakita Osamu with James L. McClain, "The Commercial and Urban Policies of Oda Nobunaga and Toyotomi Hideyoshi," in Hall, Nagahara, and Yamamura, eds., *Japan before Tokugawa,* pp. 224–47.

13. Among the numerous works available, see, for example, Sakata Yoshio, *Chōnin* (Shimizu Kōbundō Shobō, 1968), pp. 26–61; Nakai Nobuhiko, *Chōnin* (vol. 21 in the series *Nihon no rekishi;* Shōgakkan, 1975), pp. 211–49; Harada, *Nihon hōken toshi kenkyū,* pp. 395–97; H. Paul Varley, *Japanese Culture* (Charles E. Tuttle, 1973), pp. 113–58; and William B. Hauser, *Economic Institutional Change in Tokugawa Japan* (Cambridge: Cambridge University Press, 1974), pp. 7–32.

14. Gilbert Rozman, "Edo's Importance in the Changing Tokugawa Society," *Journal of Japanese Studies* 1:1 (Autumn 1974): 105–12.

15. See the introductory comments in Tilly, *An Urban World,* pp. 29–30.

16. Rozman, "Edo's Importance"; William B. Hauser, "Osaka: A Commercial City in Tokugawa Japan," *Urbanism Past & Present* 5 (Winter 1977–78): 23–36; and E. Sidney Crawcour, "Changes in Japanese Commerce in the Tokugawa Period," in Hall and Jansen, eds., *Studies,* pp. 189–202.

17. For a fuller discussion of these questions, see Willis, *Western Civilization,* pp. v–viii.

18. See John Butler's review essay, "A Bicentennial Harvest," in *Journal of Urban History* 4:4 (August 1978): 485–97.

CHAPTER 1

1. For more on this see Shimode Sekiyo, *Ishikawa ken no rekishi* (Yamakawa Shuppan, 1975), pp. 85–103; and David L. Davis, "*Ikki* in Late Medieval Japan," in John W. Hall and Jeffrey P. Mass, eds., *Medieval Japan: Essays in Institutional History* (New Haven: Yale University Press, 1974), pp. 221–47.

2. Some historians think that an administrative headquarters may have been established as early as 1489. For a summation of the arguments, see Kanazawa Daigaku Kanazawa-jō Gakujutsu Chōsa Iinkai, "Kanazawa-jō" Henshūiin, ed., *Kanazawa-jō* (Kanazawa: Kanazawa Daigaku Seikatsu Kyōdōkumiai Shuppan, 1968), pp. 4–5; Kitanishi Hiroshi, "Ikkō-ikki to Kanazawa Gobō," *Rekishi techō* 2:5 (May 1974): 52–55; and Tanaka Yoshio, "Kaga hyakumangoku no jōkamachi o kochizu ni saguru," in Yamori Kazuhiko, ed., *Kanazawa-Nagoya* (Kōdansha, 1977), p. 26.

3. The information on the Maeda rise to power is from Iwasawa Yoshihiko, *Maeda Toshiie* (Yoshikawa Kōbunkan, 1969), pp. 1–76; Toda Shōzō, ed., *Ishikawa ken no kinsei shiryō* (Kanazawa: Kanazawa Daigaku Kaga Han Shomin Shiryō Chōsa Iinkai, 1961), pp. 30–31; Wakabayashi Kisaburō, *Maeda Tsunanori* (Yoshikawa Kōbunkan, 1972), pp. 3–9; Kuranami Seiji, *Kaga hansei kaikakushi no kenkyū* (Sekai Shoin, 1973), pp. 3–10; and Akai Tatsurō, "Hokkokuji to kinsei kaiga," in Akai Tatsurō, ed., *Hokurikudō* (Chikuma Shobō, 1976), p. 150.

4. For further details concerning this incident, see *KKS*, 1, "Sōgamaebori fushin raiyu," pp. 357–59; Kuranami Seiji, *Kaga: Hyakumangoku* (Hachiyo Shuppan, 1974), pp. 20–25; and Iwasawa, *Maeda Toshiie*, pp. 261–91.

5. *KKSS*, 4, pp. 1017–18.

6. Daimyo domains—what contemporaries called the *ryōgoku* and what historians have come to refer to as the *han*—did not technically become part of a national political structure until Tokugawa Ieyasu became shogun in 1603. In this sense, Toshiie was not the first daimyo of Kaga domain. However, later Maeda daimyo, as well as modern historians, refer to him as the founder of the Maeda line and as the first ruler of the family's territorial holdings.

In the late 1630s the third Maeda daimyo, Toshitsune, created two branch domains for his sons. The second son (the eldest would become daimyo of the home domain) received a 100,000-*koku* domain (Toyama *han*) and the third son became the daimyo of the 70,000-*koku* Daishōji domain. In theory these were independent domains, but in practice the new domains followed closely the policies of the home domain, Kaga *han*.

7. For studies in English on the establishment of daimyo rule in the late sixteenth and early seventeenth centuries, see the following articles, all in Hall and Jansen, eds., *Studies:* John W. Hall, "Foundations of the Modern Japanese Daimyo," pp. 65–77; John W. Hall, "The Ikeda House and Its Retainers in Bizen," pp. 79–88; Marius B. Jansen, "Tosa in the Seventeenth Century: The Establishment of Yamauchi Rule," pp. 115–30; and Robert Sakai, "The Consolidation of Power in Satsuma-han," pp. 131–39.

8. The figures on the size of the warrior band are taken from Kuranami, *Kaga: Hyakumangoku*, pp. 32–35; and Tanaka Yoshio, *Kanazawa: Saihakken* (Nihon Shobō, 1970), p. 255 (hereafter cited as Tanaka, *Kanazawa*).

9. Additional information on the warrior band can be found in Kuranami, *Kaga hansei*, pp. 21–26; Shimode, *Ishikawa ken no rekishi*, pp. 130–32; and Wakabayashi Kisaburō, *Ishikawa ken no rekishi* (Kanazawa: Hokkoku Shoseki, 1972), p. 144.

10. For more information on the early fief system, see Kuranami, *Kaga: Hyakumangoku*, pp. 48–49.

11. Few documents concerning the early surveys are extant. For more details, see Toda, *Ishikawa ken*, p. 58; and Urada Masayoshi, "Shoki Maeda kashindan no jikata chigyō ni tsuite no ichi kōsatsu," *Hokuriku shigaku* 17 (1969): 1–24.

12. The best description of the new system is in Kuranami, *Kaga: Hyakumangoku*, pp. 51–61.

13. The first appointments to the new post were probably made in the 1590s. *KHS*, 1, Keichō 6 (1601)/5/17, pp. 837–38.

14. *KHS*, 1, Tenshō 19 (1591)/2/17, p. 424; and *KHS*, 2, Genna 1 (1615)/3/5, pp. 288–89.

15. This post was officially created in 1604, although it appears that officials called *daihyakushō* performed similar functions before that date. *KHS*, 1, Keichō 9 (1604), pp. 896–903.

16. The first appointments in Noto were made as early as 1582; *KHS*, 1, Tenshō 10 (1582)/8/5, pp. 162–63.

17. This system of rural administration was similar in structure and function to those created by daimyo in other domains. For a general overview of the system, see Harumi

Befu, "Village Autonomy and Articulation with the State," in Hall and Jansen, eds., *Studies*, pp. 301–14.

18. For estimates on the *bushi* population, see Kuranami, *Kaga: Hyakumangoku*, p. 45; *KKSS*, 1, p. 284, and 11, pp. 12–13; Tanaka Yoshio, "Kinsei jōkamachi shūhen ni okeru shokugyō kōsei no ichi jirei—Kanazawa hokubu aitaiukechi chiiki o chūshin ni shite," *Shizen to shakai* 29–30 (1963):39; and Tanaka Yoshio, *Kaga hyakumangoku* (Kyōikusha, 1980), p. 33.

19. This is the *chōnin* population as estimated in *KKSS*, 1, p. 281.

20. *KZ*, 2, ch. 14, doc. 17, p. 539. A census taken in 1664 yielded a *chōnin* count of 55,106; *KHS*, 4, Kanbun 4 (1664), pp. 76–78. Like all premodern Japanese population statistics, these numbers should be accepted only on the understanding that they include a high potential for error, particularly for underenumeration. For some of the problems in evaluating Tokugawa-period population statistics, see Susan B. Hanley and Kozo Yamamura, *Economic and Demographic Change in Preindustrial Japan, 1600–1868* (Princeton: Princeton University Press, 1977), pp. 37–50.

21. *Onko shūroku* (MS copy, Kanazawa City Library), 18, "Kanazawa machikazu jin'in kosū," pp. 93–100; and *KZ*, 1, ch. 3, doc. 59, pp. 110–11. An earlier census in 1697 had tabulated 68,636 *chōnin*. *KHS*, 5, Genroku 10 (1697), pp. 386–88.

22. *KHS*, 6, Kyōhō 6 (1721), pp. 253–56; *KKSS*, 3, pp. 790–98 and 842–43; and Tanaka Yoshio, "Jōkamachi Kanazawa ni okeru aitaiukechi chiiki no kōzō," *Hokuriku shigaku* 11–12 (1963): 20.

CHAPTER 2

1. The few details that are known about Oyama Gobō before 1583 are contained in *KS*, "Kashū kokufu," pp. 4–6; Tanaka Yoshio et al., *Dentō toshi no kūkan ron: Kanazawa* (Kōjunsha, 1977), pp. 7–11 and 22 (hereafter cited as Tanaka, *Dentō toshi*); and Tanaka Yoshio, *Waga machi no rekishi Kanazawa* (Bun'ichi Sōgō Shuppan, 1979), pp. 54–61.

2. Tanaka, *Dentō toshi*, pp. 6–10; and Inoue Toshio, *Ikkō-ikki no kenkyū* (Yoshikawa Kōbunkan, 1968), pp. 542. Shimode Sekiyo thinks that the Honganji headquarters were located at a slightly different spot, to the south of the Maeda castle; see his *Ishikawa ken no rekishi*, p. 167.

3. *KHS*, 1, Bunroku 1 (1592), pp. 438–39; *KS*, "Anao no kihon" and "Shiro ishigaki kojitsu," pp. 37–40; *MK*, "Kanazawa oshiro otsukuri no koto," p. 77; Ishikawa-ken Toshokan Kyōkai, ed., *Kokuji shōhi mondō* (Kanazawa: Ishikawa-ken Toshokan Kyōkai, 1970), p. 82; and Kinai Bin, comp., *Kanazawa jōkaku shiryō* (Kanazawa: Ishikawa Kenritsu Toshokan Kyōkai, 1976), "Kodensho," pp. 133–46.

4. *KS*, "Uchisōgamae no koto," p. 22; and *KKS*, 1, "Sōgamaebori fushin raiyu," pp. 357–59. A written description of the course of the inner moat system is also contained in Tanaka, *Kanazawa*, pp. 39–40; and Wakabayashi, *Ishikawa ken*, pp. 152–57.

5. *KKS*, 2, "Sōgamaebori," pp. 67–68; *KS*, "Sotosōgamaebori no koto," p. 22; and *KHS*, 2, Keichō 15 (1610), pp. 71–72. A written description is also contained in Tanaka, *Kanazawa*, pp. 270–71; and Hioki Ken, ed., *Ishikawa kenshi* (Kanazawa, 1928), 2: 366.

6. For descriptions of the various canals, see *KKSS*, 1, pp. 119–26; Tanaka Yoshio, *Jōkamachi Kanazawa* (Nihon Shoin, 1966), pp. 16–17 (hereafter cited as Tanaka, *Jōkamachi*); and Tanaka, *Kanazawa*, pp. 271–74.

7. The first known map of Kanazawa, which included a drawing of the castle grounds, was produced during the Keichō period. No original remains extant today, but numerous copies were made during the Tokugawa period and these are in the document collections at both the Ishikawa Prefectural Library and the Kanazawa City Library. One copy, for instance, is contained in *Onko shūroku*, 6, pp. 5–6. There are also sketches of portions of the castle included in numerous documents, such as the drawing of the western part of the

castle in *KKS*, 1, "San-no-maru shoshi kyodai ato," pp. 257–58. Written descriptions of the sites mentioned here can be found in the following; all in *KKS*, 1: "Chō Kurōzaemon kyūtei," pp. 214–15, "Yokoyama Yamashiro no Kami Nagachika kyūtei," p. 260, "Shinmaru," p. 271, "Sakujisho," pp. 293–94, "Tsuda Genba," pp. 418–19, and "Yokoyama Yamashiro no Kami kyūtei," p. 596. See also *KS*, "Ōseki gojōnai ni samurai yashiki no koto," pp. 67–68; *KHS*, 1, Keichō 5 (1600), p. 832; and *Kokuji shōhi mondō*, p. 7.

8. Ishikawa-ken Toshokan Kyōkai, ed., *Kame no o no ki* (Kanazawa: Ishikawa-ken Toshokan Kyōkai, 1932), "Chō-shi shimotei," p. 59; *KKS*, 1, "Chō Kurōzaemon kyūtei," pp. 214–15, and "Chō Kurōzaemon Tsuratatsu kyūtei," pp. 258–59. See also the Kanbun (1661–73) and Enpō (1673–81) period maps, each about ten meters square, at the Ishikawa Prefectural Library. An Enpō period map is reproduced in Yamori, ed., *Kanazawa-Nagoya*, pp. 2–3.

9. *KKS*, 1, "Okumura Inaba kyūtei," pp. 503–04, "Honda Awa no Kami teichi," p. 589, and "Yokoyama Yamashiro no Kami kyūtei," p. 596. See also *KKS*, 2, "Honda Awa no Kami shimotei," p. 1; and *KHS*, 2, Keichō 17 (1612)/2/29, pp. 141–42, Keichō 17/7/ last day, pp. 151–52, and Keichō 17/11/10, p. 158. See also the maps cited in n. 8.

10. *Shūri zakki* (MS copy, Kanazawa City Library), 1, pp. 49–52. For the announcement of the *yashiki-bugyō*, see *KHS*, 2, Keichō 16 (1611)/8/27, pp. 115–16. The following chart, taken from the *Shūri zakki*, lists fief sizes and the corresponding allotments. A note in the document explains that, for example, an 8,000-*koku* fief should be taken to mean retainers with fiefs between 7,500 *koku* and 8,499 *koku* would receive a residential lot measuring 35 by 40 *ken*. One *ken* equals 1.82 meters.

Fief Size	*Lot Size*	
10,000 *koku*	40 *ken* × 40 *ken*	(5300 sq. meters)
9,000	The same as above	
8,000	35 × 40	(4637)
7,000	The same as above	
6,000	30 × 40	(3975)
5,000	The same as above	
4,000	30 × 30	(2981)
3,000	The same as above	
2,500	25 × 30	(2484)
2,000	The same as above	
1,900 to 1,500	20 × 30	(1987)
1,000 to 800	20 × 25	(1656)
700 to 500	20 × 20	(1325)
400 to 300	15 × 20	(993)
200 to 150	10 × 20	(662)

11. *Shūri zakki*, 1, pp. 52–56; *Kokuji shōhi mondō*, p. 84; *OG*, ch. 1, doc. 68, p. 46; and *KHS*, 2, Keichō 16 (1611)/9/23, pp. 123–24.

12. See the maps cited in n. 8.

13. A convenient listing of the transferred temples, along with the date and the place of their relocation, can be found in Tanaka, *Kanazawa*, pp. 246–48.

14. *KZ*, 2, ch. 12, doc. 35, pp. 468–69; *KHS*, 4, Enpō 8 (1680)/2/17, pp. 591–93, and 5, Hōei 1 (1704), pp. 665–73.

15. *KHS*, 2, Genna 2 (1616)/8, pp. 382 and 3, Keian 2 (1649)/3/10, pp. 294–95; *KZ*, 1, ch. 1, doc. 47, p. 24; ch. 7, doc. 1, pp. 249–50; and ch. 7, doc. 4, pp. 253–54; *KKS*, 3, "Shinji nō kōgyō raireki," pp. 589–91; and *Kokuji shōhi mondō*, p. 94.

16. *KZ*, 3, ch. 21, doc. 27, pp. 805–06, and ch. 21, doc. 62, pp. 833–34; and *Kame no o no ki*, "Shinmeigū," p. 63. The other three shrines were Kasuga, Kajimachi Hachiman, and Tai Tenjin. For more information see *KZ*, 3, ch. 21, docs. 29–31, pp. 808–10.

17. *KHS*, 2, Keichō 18 (1613)/2/10, p. 169; *KKS*, 1, "Hōenji kyūjichi," pp. 554–56; *MK*, "Hōenji no koto," pp. 103–04; and *Kokuji shōhi mondō*, p. 93.

18. *KHS*, 3, Manji 3 (1660)/1, p. 865.

19. *KS*, "Orusui-tei no koto," pp. 46–53; and *KHS*, 1, "Tentokuin-dono tsutaebanashi," pp. 700–02.

20. *KHS*, 2, Genna 2 (1616), pp. 389–99; and *MK*, "Kanazawa machidategawari michihashi nado tsukekawaru koto," pp. 177–78.

21. It is impossible to determine on the basis of existing documents exactly where the land grant was located. Like the grants to many other chartered merchants, it is spoken of as being *kakunai*, which may be rendered as "within the enclosure" or "within the castle walls." It seems improbable, however, that these grants were actually within the walls since this space was reserved for the daimyo and his direct retainers in the other castle towns. Probably the *kakunai* grants were outside the castle walls, but inside or adjacent to the inner moats. Here, the term "castle complex" is used to refer to the area protected by and adjacent to the inner moats, while the word "castle" refers only to the central citadel enclosed by stone walls.

22. Tanaka, *Jōkamachi*, pp. 118–20, 144–45, and 147; and Tanaka, *Kanazawa*, pp. 262–63.

23. *Chōnin shochō (ihon)* (MS copy, Kanazawa City Library), 2, "Hiranoya Hansuke," pp. 102–22.

24. The men who made the selection of new residential sites were actually the grandsons of the first Echizen'ya and Hiranoya who had been invited to Kanazawa by Toshiie. When the sons and then grandsons succeeded to family headship, they received the same privileges as their forefathers. See nn. 22 and 23.

25. In several instances merchants engaged in one line of sales lived together in the same ward; examples include fresh fish retailers, lumber merchants, and salt dealers. This was not a result of the daimyo enforcing residential patterns simply for the purpose of more efficient political administration, however. The fish retailers, as we will see later, lived together in order to have better access to wholesalers, and because the domain grouped the shops together to ensure that price guidelines and other economic directives were being respected. In the case of the Lumber Merchants' Ward (Zaimokuchō), a 1603 document stated that a three-year exemption on corvée levies was to be granted to the ward's residents and that the buying and selling of lumber was to be conducted in this ward. It is not certain that the ward was ever established as intended, however, since lumber merchants are known to have lived in other parts of the city. Also, the document may simply confirm domain recognition to a ward already settled by merchants on their own, or may be a temporary grant of special privileges issued to encourage the migration of these merchants to Kanazawa. *KZ*, 1, ch. 3, doc. 7, pp. 88–89; *KKS*, 2, "Izumino machidate raireki," pp. 386–87; Kanazawa-shi Ōmichō Ichiba-shi Hensan Iinkai, ed., *Kanazawa-shi Ōmichō ichiba-shi* (Kanazawa: Hokkoku Shuppansha, 1980), pp. 10–25; and Tanaka, *Kaga hyakumangoku*, p. 31.

26. For additional details see Tanaka, *Dentō toshi*, pp. 33–34; and Tanaka, *Jōkamachi*, pp. 89–91. Also see my "Castle Towns and Daimyo Authority: Kanazawa in the Years 1583–1630," *Journal of Japanese Studies* 6:2 (Summer 1980): 267–99.

27. *KKS*, 2, "Saigawa-aramachi," pp. 111–12.

28. The quotation is from *Kame no o no ki*, "Kodachino," p. 10. For additional descriptions, see *KKS*, 3, "Taimura kyūchi," pp. 438–39, and "Tai sonraku," pp. 450–51; and *KZ*, 3, ch. 21, doc. 29, p. 808.

29. *KZ*, 3, ch. 21, doc. 30, pp. 808–09.

30. *KHS*, 2, Genna 1 (1615)/4/3, pp. 294–96; *Kame no o no ki*, "Kannonmachi," p. 114; *KKSS*, 2, pp. 567–69; and Tanaka Yoshio, *Kaga han ni okeru toshi no kenkyū* (Bun'ichi Sōgō Shuppan, 1978), p. 46 (hereafter cited as Tanaka, *Kaga*).

31. *Kame no o no ki*, "Kodachino," p. 10; *KKS*, 3, "Ishiuramachi raireki," pp. 1–2, "Shimoyasue-mura ato," p. 161, "Taimura kyūchi," pp. 438–39, and "Tai sonraku," pp. 450–51; *KZ*, 3, ch. 21, docs. 29 and 30, pp. 808–09; and *KKSS*, 1, pp. 274–75.

32. *Kame no o no ki*, "Katamachi, Kōrinbō, Kawaramachi, Furuderamachi," p. 48; *KKS*, 2, "Kawaramachi," pp. 175–76 and "Saigawabashi," p. 247. For other descriptions of the project, see *KKSS*, 1, pp. 274–75, and 3, pp. 560–62 and 593–94; and Tanaka, *Jōkamachi*, pp. 80–84.

33. There is a possibility that two of the Eight Wards were relocated in 1592 when some canals were dug. However, even if they were moved at that date, it was only a very short distance, as reconstruction of maps based on old documents makes clear, and the new locations would have been as advantageous as the old. There is also the possibility, strongly supported by Wada Bunjirō, editor of *KKSS*, that the two wards were not relocated until the major reorganization of the 1630s. Finally, it is not certain that the number of wards in existence before 1583 totaled eight in number. The documents themselves are vague and often contradictory. See: *Kokuji shōhi mondō*, p. 72; *Kame no o no ki*, "Morimotomachi [also read as Morishitamachi], Kanayachō, Takamichimachi, Kasugamachi," p. 102; *KS*, "Oyama hachimachi no koto," p. 46; *KKS*, 1, "Kanayamon," p. 230, "Kanaya demaruchi," pp. 359–60. See also the following documents in *KKS*, 3: "Minamichō," pp. 16–17, "Tsutsumichō," pp. 20–21, "Tsutsumichō tsutsumi no yurai," pp. 21–23, "Kanayachō," pp. 700–01, and "Kanayachō raireki," pp. 701–02. For a summation and evaluation of the documents, see *KKSS*, 1, pp. 260–69, and 3, pp. 649–65, and 4, pp. 1151–52; as well as Tanaka, *Kanazawa*, p. 268.

34. *Chōnin shochō (ihon)*, 2, "Hiranoya Hansuke," pp. 102–22; and Tanaka, *Kaga*, pp. 18 and 50.

35. *KKSS*, 3, pp. 704–05.

36. *KKS*, 1, "Matsubarachō," p. 354 and 3, "Eta oriato," p. 423; and *KHS*, 2, Keichō 16 (1611)/10/26, p. 127.

37. *Kame no o no ki*, "Asano kawata," pp. 105–06; and *KHS*, 2, Keichō 14 (1609), pp. 57–58. See also the documents quoted in *KKSS*, 3, pp. 741–44.

38. Wakita Osamu with James L. McClain, "The Commercial and Urban Policies of Oda Nobunaga and Toyotomi Hideyoshi," p. 243.

39. *KHS*, 1, Keichō 3 (1598)/6/3, p. 575; and *KKS*, 3, "Kamiya Kuemon tsutaebanashi," pp. 10–11.

40. *KHS*, 1, Keichō 8 (1603)/5, p. 877 and 2, Genna 2 (1616)/12/16, pp. 392–93.

41. *KZ*, 3, ch. 20, doc. 12, pp. 762–63; *KHS*, 1, Keichō 8 (1603)/5, p. 877; *KHS*, 3, Manji 3 (1660)/6/10, pp. 883–85; and 5, Genroku 8 (1695)/2/29, pp. 319–22.

42. See, for example, *KZ*, 1, ch. 4, doc. 12, p. 136.

43. *KZ*, 2, ch. 10, doc. 48, p. 628; *KKS*, 3, "Uoichiba raireki," pp. 66–67; and *Kanazawa-shi Ōmichō ichiba-shi*, pp. 10–15. Very few documents concerning the early markets are extant, and it is not clear whether the petition was for the markets near the Asano or those near the Sai. Tanaka believes that the first markets, near the Asano, opened in the late sixteenth century and that increased *chōnin* consumption demands led to the opening of the second set of markets sometime during the administration of Toshitsune. Tanaka, *Jōkamachi*, p. 74.

44. *KHS*, 2, Genna 2 (1616), pp. 398–99.

45. *KHS*, 2, Genna 6 (1620), pp. 464–65.

46. For additional details, see Hotta Shigeo, "Noshū Ninomiya eki ni okeru shukunuke ni tsuite—Kaga han kinsei shukuekisei no ichi kōsatsu," *Hokuriku shigaku* 13–14 (1965): 23–34.

47. See, for example, *KHS*, 2, Keichō 16 (1611)/6/1, pp. 104–05; *KZ*, 2, ch. 14, doc. 9, pp. 533–34; and *KKS*, 3, "Kamiya Kuemon tsutaebanashi," pp. 10–11.

48. Information about the Musashiya family is taken from *Chōnin yuishochō* (MS copy, Kanazawa City Library), 1, "Ishiguro Gonbei," pp. 5–9; *Chōnin shochō (ihon)*, 2, "Ishiguro Gonbei jiseki kyūki," pp. 80–82; *KKS*, 3, "Ishiguro Gonbei tsutaebanashi," pp. 48–51; *MK*, "Ishiguro Gonbei no koto," pp. 278–80; and *KZ*, 1, ch. 5, doc. 64, pp. 202–03.

49. *Machidoshiyori rekimei narabi ni tsutomekatachō* (MS copy, Kanazawa City Library), pp. 37–57; *KZ*, 1, ch. 5, doc. 39, p. 186, and ch. 5, doc. 63, p. 202, and 2, ch. 16, doc. 1, pp. 599–600; *KHS*, 1, Keichō 9 (1604), pp. 903–04, and 2, Keichō 12 (1607), p. 33; *KKS*, 3, "Rōsokuza ato," pp. 34–35 and "Kanaya Hikoshirō den," pp. 60–63; and those portions of the family history reprinted in Tanaka, *Jōkamachi*, pp. 124–25.

50. *Chōnin shochō (ihon)*, 2, "Hiranoya Hansuke," pp. 102–22; *KZ*, 1, ch. 2, doc. 3, p. 43; *KHS*, 1, Keichō 6 (1601)/1/20, pp. 833–34, and 2, Genna 4 (1618)/7/10, p. 431; and *KKS*, 3, "Hiranoya Hansuke teiseki," pp. 37–38, "Hiranoya Hansuke den," pp. 38–39, and "Echizen'ya Kiemon den," pp. 52–58.

51. *Chōnin shochō (ihon)*, 2, "Tōfuya Taemon," pp. 5–14; *KKS*, 3, "Tōfuya Taemon kyūtei," p. 578, and "Tōfuya Taemon den," pp. 578–79; and *KHS*, 1, Keichō 10 (1605)/9/5, pp. 921–22, and 2, Keichō 12 (1607)/1/17, p. 23. Later, other merchants were permitted to make tofu. There is some possibility that the 1605 and 1607 ordinances were issued in order to conserve supplies for military reasons, but this is unlikely since there was no military threat during those two years.

52. *KZ*, 1, ch. 5, doc. 65, p. 203; and *KKS*, 2, "Mukōda Kōrinbō den," pp. 234–35, and *Machidoshiyori rekimei narabi ni tsutomekatachō*, pp. 37–57. Tanaka, *Jōkamachi*, reprints a portion of the family history on pp. 130–31.

53. *Chōnin shochō (ihon)*, 1, "Kashida Kichizō yuisho," pp. 82–97; and *KZ*, 1, ch. 5, doc. 62, pp. 200–02.

54. *Chōnin shochō (ihon)*, 2, "Nakada Shozaburō," pp. 3–26.

55. Information about Rokusuke and the carpenters is based on *Shōunkō saishū ihen* (MS copy, Kanazawa City Library), 141, "Kanazawa daiku denshō utsushi," pp. 193–208. The Rokusuke family lineage also appears in *Zoku zenroku zakki* (MS copy, Kanazawa City Library), 40, pp. 118–24. Portions are reprinted in *KKS*, 2, "Kanazawa-kumi daiku yurai," pp. 182–84; *KZ*, 2, ch. 12, doc. 50, pp. 476–78; and *KHS*, 1, Tenshō 12 (1584), pp. 269–71.

56. For more on this dominant interpretation in the Japanese literature, see, for example, Ono, *Kinsei jōkamachi*, pp. 160–64; and Nakabe, *Jōkamachi*, pp. 161–64.

57. Information about the smiths is from *KZ*, 1, ch. 5, doc. 55, pp. 195–96; *KKS*, 2, "Kaji Yukimitsu-Kiyomitsu den," pp. 403–05 and 3, "Kaji yashiki," pp. 285–87; *KKSS*, 3, pp. 708–12; and Tanaka, *Jōkamachi*, pp. 67–68.

58. *KHS*, 1, Keichō 3 (1598)/4/21, p. 571, and Keichō 5 (1600)/5/27, pp. 741–43; and *KKS*, 1, "Tachikon'ya no den," pp. 525–26.

59. Once the family began to receive appointments to administrative offices, they were referred to as *tokken chōnin*, or "privileged merchants." Tanaka, *Jōkamachi*, pp. 213–24. Japanese historians are just starting to explore the non-privileged levels of townspeople; for one recent study, see Nishiyama Matsunosuke, *Edokko* (Yoshikawa Kōbunkan, 1980), pp. 182–200.

60. *KKS*, 2, "Dogan'ya kyūtei," p. 245.

61. *KKSS*, 12, pp. 301–04.

62. *KHS*, 1, Keichō 6 (1601)/5/24, pp. 839–40.

63. *KZ*, 1, ch. 7, doc. 38, p. 277.

64. *KKSS*, 8, pp. 161–62.

65. Tanaka, *Jōkamachi*, pp. 75–76; and *Kanazawa-shi Ōmichō ichiba-shi*, pp. 10–19.

66. *KHS*, 2, Kan'ei 4 (1627)/9/17, pp. 552–54.

67. *KKSS,* 12, pp. 297–98.

68. *KHS,* 1, Keichō 6 (1601)/5/17, pp. 837–39.

69. A retainer whose rear vassals engaged in the above activities could be fined three *mai* of silver if he had a fief assessed at 5,000 *koku* or above, and one *mai* if his fief was smaller. *Manji izen osadamegaki* (MS copy, Kanazawa City Library), 2, pp. 124–26. Reprinted in *KHS,* Keichō 10 (1605)/6/19, pp. 914–15.

70. *KHS,* 2, Keichō 17 (1612)/10/17, pp. 154–55, and Keichō 18 (1613)/8/16, pp. 178–79; and *Manji izen osadamegaki,* 2, pp. 212–15.

71. See appendix 1 for a listing of principal samurai ranks. Additional details can be found in Shimode, *Ishikawa ken no rekishi,* pp. 130–32; Wakabayashi, *Ishikawa ken,* pp. 144; Kuranami, *Kaga hansei,* pp. 21–26; and Kuranami, *Kaga: Hyakumangoku,* pp. 36–46.

72. For more details, see Kameda Yasunori, "Kaga han no baishin—hitomochi Aoyama kashindan no kōzō," *Hokuriku shigaku* 18 (1970): 29–45.

73. *KHS,* 2, Keichō 15 (1610), pp. 72–73; and *Kokuji shōhi mondō,* p. 78. The documents do not record the punishment meted out to Ishiwara's superior officers.

74. See, for instance, *KHS,* 2, Kan'ei 16 (1639)/2/20, pp. 891–93; and *OG,* 1, ch. 6, doc. 3, p. 160.

75. See, for example, the 1678 case of Imamura Zenbei, the son and heir to a middle-level samurai, in *KHS,* 4, Tenna 2 (1682)/12/11, pp. 691–92.

76. The most convenient listing of early *chōnin* laws is actually the code issued in 1642—a compilation of many ordinances issued separately at earlier dates. *Kahan kokusho ibun* (MS copy, Kanazawa City Library), 17, pp. 75–84; reprinted in *KHS,* 3, Kan'ei 19 (1642)/6/1, pp. 35–37. This is translated in appendix 2.

77. The 1628 ordinances can be found in *Kahan kokusho ibun,* 12, pp. 65–80. An edited version is reprinted in *KHS,* 2, Kan'ei 5 (1628)/8/23, pp. 577–82.

The reference to persons from outside the domain probably means samurai officials from other domains who were visiting Kanazawa on official business.

78. *KHS,* 2, Keichō 16 (1611)/8/12, pp. 113–14. See also *OG,* 1, ch. 1, doc. 48, p. 38.

79. *Manji izen osadamegaki,* 2, pp. 201–03; and *OG,* 1, ch. 1, doc. 74, p. 49.

80. Ishikawa-ken Toshokan Kyōkai, ed., *Hankoku kanshoku tsūkō* (Kanazawa: Ishikawa-ken Toshokan Kyōkai, 1932), "Machi-bugyō ninin," pp. 39–40.

81. *Hankoku kanshoku tsūkō,* "Machi-dōshin yonin," pp. 41–42; and *Keichō nenchū gohatto nukigaki* (MS copy, Kanazawa City Library), p. 1.

82. This is the observation of Professor Tanaka Yoshio, who is currently preparing a study on the early City Magistrates.

83. *KZ,* 1, ch. 3, doc. 50, pp. 107–08.

84. See, for example, *Chōnin shochō (ihon),* 2, "Nakada Shozaburō," pp. 3–26, and "Hiranoya Hansuke," pp. 102–22; and *KKS,* 3, "Nakaya Hikoemon den,", pp. 19–20, "Machi kaisho ato," pp. 44–45, and "Takeya Nihei kyūtei", pp. 398–99. Unfortunately, the documents do not record specifically what advice was asked or given.

85. *Chōnin shochō (ihon),* 3, "Kitamura Hikoemon," pp. 79–96. For more on Kitamura in Edo, see Nomura Kentarō, *Edo* (Shibundō, 1975; originally published 1966), pp. 79–81. Nomura states that the Kitamura family origins are unclear since the family history was lost in a fire in Edo. This separate history, maintained by relatives in Kanazawa and cited herein, clarifies those origins.

86. *KZ,* 1, ch. 1, doc. 18, p. 6; and *KKSS,* 11, pp. 77–78.

87. *KKSS,* 11, pp. 81–85.

88. *Manji izen osadamegaki,* 2, pp. 212–15.

89. *Keichō nenchū gohatto nukigaki,* p. 1.

90. *MK,* "Hōshun'in-dono Edo yori Kashū e okoshi no koto," pp. 147–48.
91. The description is based on the following documents: *KKS,* 2, "Furoyamachi," p. 15, "Furoya raireki," pp. 15–17, "Kawaramachi," pp. 175–76, "Onigawa kabukiza ato," pp. 270–71, and "Saigawa kawara haiyū tsutaebanashi," pp. 556–57; and *MK,* "Hōshun'in-dono Edo yori Kashū e okoshi no koto," pp. 147–48, and "Kanazawa gojōchū kaji narabi ni Kanazawa shibai no koto," pp. 178–80. Portions of these appear in *KHS,* 2, Genna 6 (1620), pp. 464–67.
92. *MK,* "Ise odori no koto," pp. 180–81; *KKS,* 2, "Ise odori," pp. 365–68; and *Kame no o no ki,* "Shinmeigū," p. 63. Some of these are extracted in *KHS,* 2, Genna 7 (1621), pp. 475–80. There is some possibility that the events described took place in 1602 or 1615, but 1621 is the most likely date.
93. Iwasawa, *Maeda Toshiie,* pp. 312–15.
94. *KHS,* 1, Keichō 7 (1602)/8/14, pp. 861–62; 2, Kan'ei 4 (1627)/9/13, p. 552, Kan'ei 6 (1629)/4/8, p. 589, and Kan'ei 6/10/22, p. 605.
95. Iwasawa, *Maeda Toshiie,* pp. 319–21; Hioki, ed., *Ishikawa kenshi,* 2, p. 412; *KKS,* 3, "Morohashi Gonnoshin den," pp. 176–78, and "Shinji nō kōgyō raireki," pp. 589–91.
96. *KKSS,* 3, p. 143, and 12, pp. 420–21; Akai Tatsurō, ed., *Hokurikudō* (Chikuma Shobō, 1976), 1:77; and *KKS,* 3, "Shinji nō kōgyō raireki," pp. 589–91.

CHAPTER 3

1. For more details on the early seventeenth century, see Ishizaki Naoyoshi, "Kaga hankō no sankin kōtai to Toyama hanryō," *Toyama shidan* 50–51 (August 1971): 42–46.
2. *KHS,* 2, Kan'ei 12 (1635)/11/4, p. 766.
3. Tanaka, *Jōkamachi,* p. 178.
4. For more details on domain finances, see Shimode, *Ishikawa ken no rekishi,* pp. 142–45; and Kuranami, *Kaga: Hyakumangoku,* pp. 101–28.
5. Two additional points should be noted. The rate for villages in Noto was slightly lower than for villages in other parts of the domain. Also, the Chō fief, which comprised fifty-nine villages in Kashima *gun* in Noto, was not brought under direct domain jurisdiction until 1671.
The objectives of the *kaisakuhō* are keenly debated. Most pre-World War II literature, Hioki for example, viewed the reforms in a positive light for stabilizing domain revenues. Shintani was the first to criticize the reforms, arguing that they resulted in a "centralized feudal government." After World War II, Sasaki and Sakai documented the post-reform increase in tax rates and evaluated the reforms in reference to their impact on farming villages. More recently, Kuranami and Shimode have drawn attention back toward the "positive" aspects by arguing that increased centralization of authority in the hands of daimyo government resulted in the end of abuses by local fief holders. For more on this interesting topic, see: Hioki, ed., *Ishikawa kenshi,* 2: 364–65; Kuranami, *Kaga: Hyakumangoku,* pp. 62–89; Kuranami, *Kaga hansei,* pp. 50–75; Nojima Jirō, "Kaga han no tomura seido no seiritsu ni tsuite," *Nihon rekishi* 239 (April 1968): 36–41; Sakai Seiichi, "Kaga han kaisakuhō no ichi kōsatsu—kono hō no mokuteki to sono shikō no kekka," *Nihon rekishi* 180 (May 1963): 39–51; Sasaki Junnosuke, "Kaga hansei seiritsu ni kansuru kōsatsu," *Shakai keizai shigaku* 24:2 (February 1958): 65–87; Ishihara Yosaku, "Kaisakuhō shikōzen no Kaga han no nōso," *Toyama shidan* 43 (March 1969): 16–25; Shintani Kurō, "Kaga han ni okeru shūken-teki hōkensei no kakuritsu," *Shakai keizai shigaku* 6:2 (February 1936):17–43; Shimode, *Ishikawa ken no rekishi,* pp. 133–37; Tanaka Yoshio, "Kaga han kaisakushihō hōkai katei no ichi kōsatsu—toku ni 'hikimen' o tsūjite mitaru," *Hokuriku shigaku* 6 (1957): 33–52; Wakabayashi, *Ishikawa ken,* pp. 123–46; and Wakabayashi, *Maeda Tsunanori,* pp. 15–34.

6. *KHS*, 2, Genna 1 (1615)/3/5, pp. 288–89, and Kan'ei 8 (1631)/3/13, pp. 629–40.
7. *KHS*, 2, Kan'ei 7 (1630)/12/21, pp. 617–18, Kan'ei 7/12/23, pp. 618–19, and Kan'ei 7/12/29, p. 620.
8. *KHS*, 3, Keian 1 (1648), p. 277.
9. Thomas C. Smith has examined the tax rates in Kaga domain from the 1650s to the end of the Tokugawa period. Of the 424 villages studied, taxes decreased in 117 villages (27.5 percent), usually by more than 10 percent. Tax rates were never changed in 64 villages (15 percent). In 233 villages (52.5 percent), rates went up, but only by 5 percent or less. Only in 20 villages (5 percent) did rates increase by more than 5 percent between the 1650s and the end of the Tokugawa period. Thomas C. Smith, "The Land Tax in the Tokugawa Period," in Hall and Jansen, *Studies*, pp. 287–88.
10. A number of rural towns such as Jōhana also experienced rapid population increases at this time. See Sakai Seiichi, "Kaisakuhō to chōnin shihon no shinshutsu: Jōhana no kashikata gyōsha to Gokayama nōmin," *Etchū shidan* 15 (November 1958): 1–7, and 16 (March 1959): 20–26; and his "Kinsei zaigōmachi no kihon-teki seikaku," *Etchū shidan* 17–18 (December 1959): 7–18.
11. *MK*, "Kanazawa-jō saikanan no koto," pp. 196–97, and "Kanazawa kaji ni tsuke roken no koto," pp. 198–99; and *KHS*, 2, Kan'ei 8 (1631)/4/14, pp. 641–46. See also Tanaka Yoshio, "Kanazawa no chōnin kyojū chiiki," *Rekishi techō* 2:5 (May 1974): 18–23.
12. *MK*, "Kanazawa machijū kaji no koto," p. 224; and *KHS*, 2, Kan'ei 12 (1635)/5/9, p. 752.
13. For a description of the course see *KKS*, 1, "Tatsumi suidō," pp. 267–70.
14. The family history itself must be approached with caution, however, since it was submitted to the domain at a time when the Itaya family was requesting an extension of tax exemptions granted to the family earlier. Even if Itaya (whose personal name is also read as Heishirō) was not put to death—and it is difficult to believe that he was since Toshitsune himself supplied the shogunate with almost a meter-by-meter description of the canal's course—the swirl of controversy around Hyōshirō shows that contemporaries thought the canal might have a military significance. For more on Itaya, see *Kokuji shōhi mondō*, p. 64; *MK*, "Kanazawa machijū e suidō tsukuraseraruru koto," pp. 214–15; Nishi Setsuko, "Tatsumi yōsui repōto,' *Rekishi techō* 2:5 (May 1974): 31–34; and *KKSS*, 1, pp. 111–18.
15. For the shogunate's concerns about the canal see *KZ*, 1, ch. 1, doc. 29, p. 11; and the documents and commentary in Hioki, ed., *Ishikawa kenshi*, 2: 368–71.
16. A list of the retainers transferred outside the castle walls is contained in *KKSS*, 1, p. 271; for specific examples see *KS*, "Ōseki gojōnai ni samurai yashiki no koto," pp. 67–68; and *KKS*, 1, "Tsuda Genba," pp. 418–19.
17. *KZ*, 1, ch. 3, doc. 46, p. 105.
18. *KKS*, 1, "Takajōmachi," p. 619; *KHS*, 4, Kanbun 5 (1665)/3/8, pp. 87–88; and *KKSS*, 3, pp. 629–30.
19. *KKSS*, 2, pp. 405–11, contains a convenient list of many of these new samurai wards; see also vol. 3, pp. 608–09, 616–17, and 651. For documents on specific wards see, for example, *OG*, 1, ch. 4, doc. 13, p. 97; *KHS*, 3, Manji 2 (1659)/11/25, pp. 829–33, and Manji 3 (1660)/4/22, p. 872. In *KHS*, v. 4, see Kanbun 7 (1667)/3/24, pp. 172–73, Kanbun 10 (1670)/7/24, pp. 293–94, and Kanbun 10/7/28, pp. 296–97. In addition, see *KKS*, 3, "Okachimachi," pp. 584–85; and *KZ*, 1, ch. 7, doc. 21, p. 271, and 3, ch. 19, doc. 82, p. 745.
20. *KZ*, 1, ch. 1, doc. 39, pp. 17–18; *KHS*, 2, Kan'ei 17 (1640)/11/28, pp. 981–83; and *KKS*, 1, "Tōshōgū shashi," pp. 238–40, and "Ozaki jinja," pp. 386–87.
21. *KHS*, 3, Manji 3 (1660)/1, p. 865.
22. For additional details about the transfer of the commoner wards, see the following: *KKS*, 1, "Kanaya mon," p. 230, "Kanaya demaruguchi," pp. 359–60; 3, "Minamichō,"

pp. 16–17, "Tsutsumichō," pp. 20–21, and "Kanayachō," pp. 700–01; *Kame no o no ki,* "Morimotomachi, Kanayachō, Takamichimachi, Kasugamachi," p. 102; and *KKSS,* 1, pp. 264–65, 649–50, and 4, pp. 1151–52.

23. The first use of such terminology came in 1625. Tanaka, *Kanazawa,* p. 274. During the 1630 to 1670 period, the domain also started to transfer the *monzen-machi* (land that the domain had granted to temples, which the temples then rented to merchants and artisans) to the jurisdiction of the City Magistrates. This process was not finally completed until the nineteenth century. In general, the *monzen-machi* became Ordinary Wards. For additional details, see Tanaka, *Jōkamachi,* pp. 53 and 253–54.

24. For lists, compiled at different times, of the Original Wards and Seven Wards, see *Kanazawa shichū kyūki,* (MS copy, Kanazawa City Library), pp. 85–87; *OG,* 1, ch. 7, doc. 19, pp. 190–92; and *KZ,* 1, ch. 3, doc. 45, pp. 113–17.

25. *KHS,* 5, Genroku 10 (1697), pp. 386–88.

26. *KZ,* 1, ch. 3, doc. 15, pp. 113–17. The domain does not seem to have any incentive to shift the classification of a ward in order to raise taxes since the domain levied a fixed corvée on the Original Wards as a whole. In the second half of the seventeenth century it was set at 102 *kanme,* having been converted into a cash payment. This was then apportioned among the entire number of households, and an individual's rate varied according to the frontage of his house. Consequently, redesignating wards as *honmachi* would not increase domain tax revenues since the existing, set rate would simply be apportioned among more households.

Information about tax rates is very fragmentary. On a per household basis, taxes were probably highest in the Original Wards. In 1659, the 102 *kanme* tax on the Original Wards was apportioned among 2,470 households, for an average of 41.3 *monme* per household. The corvée levy in the Seven Wards came to an average of 2.42 *monme* per household. In addition, each household paid some land tax (*jishigin*), perhaps as much as 200 *mon* of *zeni* per household. According to some accounts, the land tax in the Ordinary Wards in 1659 was 23 *kanme,* which would amount to 2.2 *monme* for each of the 10,600 households. According to other accounts, the tax was 200 *mon* of *zeni* per household. In the 1850s and 1860s, Tanaka reckons that the average levy was only 80 to 90 *mon* per household. At that time, a bowl of noodles cost 18 *mon* and sushi cost 8 *mon* in Edo. For more on taxes, see *KZ,* 1, ch. 5, doc. 18, p. 175; *KKSS,* 11, pp. 116–21; Tanaka, *Jōkamachi,* pp. 51–53; and Shimode, *Ishikawa ken no rekishi,* p. 169.

27. *KS,* "Gofushin kaji tairyaku," p. 73. Tanaka Yoshio treats this subject in detail in his article, "Jōkamachi Kanazawa ni okeru aitaiukechi chiiki no kōzo." A convenient chart listing the percentage of *bushi* living in *chōnin* wards is on p. 140 of his *Kaga han ni okeru toshi no kenkyū.* Some commoner wards remained almost purely *chōnin* wards. Only a few *bushi* lived in Kiguramachi and none lived in Kawaminamichō. Tanaka, *Jōkamachi,* pp. 81–83.

28. For more information on the *aitaiukechi,* see Wakabayashi, *Ishikawa ken,* pp. 157–58; Tanaka Yoshio, "Kinsei jōkamachi hatten no ichi kōsatsu—'Aitaiukechi' kara mita jōkamachi, Kanazawa no baai," *Hokuriku shigaku* 8 (1959): 19–37; Tanaka, "Jōkamachi Kanazawa ni okeru aitaiukechi chiiki no kōzo"; Tanaka, "Kinsei jōkamachi shūhen"; and Tanaka, "Kaga han hiningoya-sei."

29. *KHS,* 3, Manji 2 (1659)/2, p. 795, and Manji 2/2/4, p. 798; Wakabayashi, *Maeda Tsunanori,* pp. 126–29; and Tanaka, "Kinsei jōkamachi hatten."

30. *KHS,* 3, Kanbun 1 (1661)/5/16, pp. 931–32.

31. Tanaka, *Kaga,* p. 110. For additional examples, see *KKSS,* 3, pp. 632–33.

32. *KZ,* 1, ch. 3, doc. 62, pp. 117–18, and ch. 9, doc. 22, pp. 271–72; and *KHS,* 4, Jōkyō 4 (1687)/2/28, pp. 871–74.

33. Tanaka, *Jōkamachi,* pp. 103–06; and Tanaka, *Kaga,* pp. 140–45. These figures are for 1811 but it is likely that the seventeenth-century figures approximated these.

34. *KHS*, 3, Manji 1 (1658)/10/27, pp. 765–69, and Manji 1/intercalary 12/18, pp. 778–79. The Council of Advisers was divided into two sections in 1658. One consisted of Honda Awa no Kami, Chō Kurōzaemon, Yokoyama Saemon, and Obama Kunai. These men met twice monthly and decided overall policies. The second group, composed of Maeda Tsushima no Kami, Okumura Genba, and Tsuda Inaba handled the day-to-day affairs of the realm. Obama and Tsuda were from the *hitomochi* class of retainers, and their appointment to these high-level posts was probably due to the talents of this generation of family heads. From the 1680s the Council would come to consist only of the heads of the Eight Families.

35. Similar changes took place in Edo in the 1630s. See Yoshihara Ken'ichirō, "Edo to machi-bugyō shihai," *Rekishi kōron* 4:7 (July 1978): 60–62.

36. *Kanazawa machijū gohatto no chō* (MS copy, Kanazawa City Library), pp. 10–16; reprinted in *KHS*, 3, Manji 2 (1659)/6/1, pp. 803–06. A copy of the document also appears in Ishii Ryōsuke, ed., *Hanpōshū* (Sōbunsha, 1963), 4, doc. 351, pp. 1023–24. The *Hanpōshū* version, however, is a later eighteenth- or nineteenth-century transcription of the original. Following three of the twenty-two clauses are additions made at the time of transcription which indicate the changes made after 1659. The number of Magistrates, for example, had increased from two to three. For a full translation of the 1659 instructions, see appendix 3.

37. *Keichō nenchū gohatto nukigaki;* p. 1; *Hankoku kanshoku tsūkō*, "Machi-dōshin yonin," pp. 40–41; and *KZ*, 1, ch. 3, doc. 50, pp. 107–08.

38. *OG*, 1, ch. 1, doc. 17, pp. 16–18; and *KZ*, 1, ch. 3, doc. 50, pp. 107–08.

39. Tanaka, *Dentō toshi*, p. 282; and Wakabayashi, *Ishikawa ken*, p. 158.

40. *KKS*, 3, "Machi kaisho ato," pp. 44–45; *Onko shūroku*, 18, "Kanazawa machi kaisho," pp. 1–3; and Tanaka, *Jōkamachi*, p. 233.

41. *KZ*, 1, ch. 1, doc. 3, p. 1.

42. In 1669 the number of City Elders was reduced to ten, and that number was further reduced in the eighteenth century. *Machidoshiyori rekimei narabi ni tsutomekatachō*, pp. 7–58. The name Morimotoya is also sometimes read as Morishitaya.

In 1645 Tsunanori became the fifth daimyo of Kaga domain, and five merchants were named to go to Edo as *chōnin* representatives in order to present gifts (sake, kelp, mackerel, cuttlefish, bonito, *daikon* radishes, and money) and best wishes to the infant daimyo. The five were Kamiya, Asanoya, Kōrinbō, Echizen'ya, and Dōgan'ya, and they were referred to as *machidoshiyori*. It is likely, however, that this was just an honorific title for the journey and not an indication that the men served as urban administrators on a permanent basis. *KZ*, 1, ch. 5, doc. 18, p. 175; and *KHS*, 3, Shōhō 2 (1645)/6/13, pp. 167–69.

43. *KKS*, 3, "Echizen'ya Kiemon den," pp. 52–58; and *KZ*, 1, ch. 3, docs. 85 and 86, pp. 125–26.

44. For additional details, see Tanaka, *Jōkamachi*, pp. 237–39.

45. *Onko shūroku*, 18, pp. 16–38; and *Chōnin shochō (ihon)*, "Nakada Shozaburō," pp. 3–26, and "Hiranoya Hansuke," pp. 103–22. See also *OG*, 2, ch. 14, doc. 75, p. 482; *KZ*, 1, ch. 5, doc. 40, p. 186, and ch. 7, doc. 33, p. 276; and *KHS*, 4, Kanbun 6 (1666), p. 153.

46. *KKSS*, 11, p. 77; and Tanaka, *Jōkamachi*, pp. 249–50.

47. *KZ*, 1, ch. 5, doc. 39, p. 186.

48. *KKSS*, 11, pp. 77–78; and Tanaka, *Jōkamachi*, pp. 251–52. In addition, there was one Representative called *monzen-machi-kimoiri* in each of the Temple Wards (*monzen-machi*) until these wards came under the City Magistrates. The salary and duties of those Representatives were identical to those of other Ward Representatives.

49. *KZ*, 1, ch. 3, doc. 76, p. 120; and *OG*, 1, ch. 7, doc. 1, pp. 177–78. See also Tanaka's discussion of a privately held document in Tanaka, *Kaga*, pp. 329–30.

50. Tanaka, *Kaga*, p. 319.

51. *KKSS*, 11, pp. 79–80.

52. This account is based on *KZ*, 2, ch. 1, doc. 73, pp. 36–37; *KHS*, 3, Manji 3 (1660)/7/10, pp. 889–91; and *KKSS*, 11, pp. 85–86; as well as the information in Tanaka, *Kaga*, pp. 389–95.

53. During the 1650s and 1660s, the domain issued numerous announcements warning people to be careful of fire and outlining procedures to be followed in case a fire did break out. See, for example, *KHS*, 3, Manji 1 (1658)/1/11, pp. 535–36; *OG*, 1, ch. 5, doc. 1, pp. 117–19, and ch. 7, doc. 1, pp. 177–78.

54. Until 1668 or 1669, a man called the *tachiriban* assisted the *teishuban*. *KZ*, 1, ch. 1, doc. 74, p. 37. The documents are not entirely clear, but it is possible that the Ward Patrol (*teishuban*) functioned only in the Original Wards while the equivalent official in the Ordinary Wards was called the *yoban*. See *KZ*, 1, ch. 1, doc. 71, p. 36, and the comments in *KKSS*, 11, pp. 85–86. Also, it may be that the *teishuban* were on duty twenty-four hours a day before the late 1660s and only during the evening hours thereafter, when the post may have become referred to as *itsutokiban*. See the comments in Tanaka, *Kaga*, pp. 389–95; and Wakabayashi, *Ishikawa ken*, p. 159.

55. *KHS*, 3, Manji 3 (1660)/7/10, pp. 889–91.

56. *Kahan kokusho ibun*, 17, pp. 75–84.

57. For further details, see Tanaka, *Kaga*, p. 340.

58. *KKSS*, 11, pp. 81–84.

59. Tanaka, "Kanazawa no chōnin," p. 18; and Tanaka, *Kaga*, pp. 365–66. Here, I have examined several of the ways of dividing the commoner class: by relationship to the daimyo (chartered versus ordinary merchant), by occupation (merchant versus artisan), and by gradations in personal wealth. Recent research on Edo and Osaka has brought to light yet another set of distinctions based on rights to land and property. In Edo, there were landlords (*jinushi*, persons who rented land to others); homeowners (*yamori*, persons who possessed their own land and homes); land renters (*chigarinin*, persons who rented land from others and built their own homes or shops on that land); and shop renters (*tana-garinin*; persons who possessed neither land nor a shop and who rented a shop, but not the land, from others). In Osaka, the division was threefold, with the land renters and shop renters considered together as a single group referred to as *shakuyanin*. All were officially "*chōnin*," but only the landlords and homeowners paid taxes and had the right to hold administrative posts such as Ward Representative or City Elder. In addition, the renters generally were not allowed to participate in the festivals that were organized on a ward basis.

In Kanazawa, it is only at the very end of the seventeenth century that documents begin to mention renters. The exact relationship between these distinctions and an individual's right to hold office and participate in festivals is not clear, but, as noted below, Echizen'ya Kiemon was removed from office when he sold his home.

The entire issue of land rights is very unclear, even in Edo and Osaka, which have been most studied. In theory, of course, the daimyo held superior proprietary rights to all land within his domain, and peasants and townspeople had only the right of usufruct. Yet, some historians have argued that peasant rights to the land came to approximate those of modern-day ownership. In all, much more needs to be done on the specifics of "ownership," who had what rights to land, and how this related to the character of urban administration. For more information, see Yoshihara, "Edo to machi-bugyō shihai," pp. 63–65; Harada Tomohiko, "Bakuhan shakai to mibunsei," *Rekishi kōron* 3:6 (June 1977): 36–45; and Fujimoto Atsushi, "Toshimin no seikatsu to nenchū gyōji," *Rekishi kōron* 4:7 (July 1978): 102–06.

60. In addition, the *bushi* were subject to certain levies, although the method of assessment was somewhat different from the procedures applied to the commoner residents. *Kanazawa shichū kyūki*, pp. 1–8; *Kahan kokusho ibun*, 17, pp. 75–84; *KZ*, 1, ch. 7,

doc. 22, pp. 271–72; and *KHS*, 3, Manji 2 (1659)/11/25, pp. 829–33. See also the comments in Tanaka, "Jōkamachi Kanazawa ni okeru aitaiukechi chiiki no kōzō," pp. 21–23; and Tanaka, *Kaga*, p. 384.

61. The information concerning the functions of the household groups is based on *Manji izen osadamegaki*, 1, pp. 71–82; *KZ*, 2, ch. 10, doc. 57, p. 395; *Hanpōshū*, 4, docs. 4–6 and 23–25, pp. 900–01 and 910–11; Tanaka, *Kaga*, pp. 340–43 and 367–71; and *KKSS*, 11, pp. 84–85.

62. *Kanazawa machijū gohatto no chō*, pp. 10–16 and 21–25; *Kahan kokusho ibun*, 12, pp. 65–80; and *KHS*, 3, Manji 2 (1659)/6/1, pp. 803–06.

63. The 1637 directive is contained in *Manji izen osadamegaki*, 1, pp. 71–82; and is reprinted in *KHS*, 2, Kan'ei 14 (1637)/3/25, pp. 825–28.

The 1642 code appears in *Kahan kokusho ibun*, 17, pp. 75–84; and *KHS*, 3, Kan'ei 19 (1642)/6/1, pp. 35–37. See appendix 2 for a translation of the complete code.

64. The directive can be found in *Kanazawa machijū gohatto no chō*, pp. 10–16; it is reprinted in *KHS*, 3, Manji 2 (1659)/6/1, pp. 803–06. See appendix 3 for a complete translation. For the 1660 code, see *Kanazawa machijū gohatto no chō*, pp. 21–25; reprinted in *KHS*, 3, Manji 3 (1660)/7/10, pp. 889–91. The code is translated in appendix 4.

65. *KHS*, 3, pp. 802–915 passim.

66. The farmers, of course, had to eventually repay the domain. The government further specified that merchants should no longer extend credit terms to those farmers whose debts were assumed by the domain, and that if a merchant did so and the farmer defaulted, the merchant would have to stand the loss.

67. *OG*, 1, ch. 1, doc. 83, pp. 55–56. See also *KHS*, 2, Kan'ei 14 (1637)/4/21, pp. 843–45, and Kan'ei 16 (1639)/5/1, pp. 902–04; 3, Manji 1 (1658)/intercalary 12/8, pp. 776–77; 4, Kanbun 5 (1665)/3/24, pp. 90–92; and Ishikawa-ken Toshokan Kyōkai, ed., *Kyūjōki* (Kanazawa: Ishikawa-ken Toshokan Kyōkai, 1933), pp. 56–57.

68. *Seirinki* (MS copy, Kanazawa City Library), 1, pp. 81–83.

69. *KHS*, 4, Kanbun 3 (1663), p. 43. The procedures for reporting this kind of case can be found in *KHS*, 3, Manji 2 (1659)/5/5, pp. 798–99.

70. *KHS*, 4, Enpō 5 (1667)/4/7, pp. 521–22.

71. *KHS*, 2, Kan'ei 16 (1639)/5/1, pp. 902–04; and *Kahan kokusho ibun*, 17, pp. 75–84. For other early regulations, see *Kahan kokusho ibun*, 18, pp. 150–55; and *KZ*, 2, ch. 9, doc. 11, pp. 343–44.

72. The domain announced the clothing regulations in advance of the enforcement date of 1661/1/1 in order to provide a period of adjustment. The relevant documents are *KHS*, 3, Manji 2 (1659)/1/1, pp. 751–52, Manji 2/1/7, pp. 783–84, Manji 3 (1660)/12/11, pp. 904–907, and Manji 3/12/23, p. 907. Some of these also appear in *KZ*, 2, ch. 13, doc. 11, p. 493; and *OG*, 2, ch. 17, doc. 9, pp. 711–21.

The 1659/1/1 document appears in all three collections. In *KZ* and *OG* it contains eight articles, while only seven appear in *KHS*. The extra article stated that *chōnin* could wear silk (*kinu*) and pongee (*tsumugi*).

73. See, for example, *KHS*, 4, Tenna 3 (1683)/2/29, pp. 701–03, and 6, Kyōhō 14 (1729)/7/27, pp. 673–74.

74. *OG*, 2, ch. 17, doc. 43, p. 767.

75. *OG*, 1, ch. 7, doc. 9, pp. 181–82; and *KHS*, 4, Kanbun 8 (1668)/7/6, pp. 216–19. An earlier document permitted the townspeople only one soup and two vegetables, but allowed three toasts of sake. See *Kahan kokusho ibun*, 17, pp. 84–86.

76. *KHS*, 4, Kanbun 8 (1668)/7/6, pp. 216–19.

77. *KZ*, 1, ch. 5, doc. 16, p. 174; *OG*, 2, ch. 17, doc. 8, pp. 710–11; *Seirinki*, 1, pp. 61–63; *KHS*, 3, Meireki 2 (1656)/10/21, p. 484, and 4, Kanbun 3 (1663)/2/18, p. 5.

78. *KHS*, 4, Kanbun 3 (1663)/12/12, pp. 40–41.

79. See, for example, Ono, *Kinsei jōkamachi*, pp. 155–63; Toyoda, *Nihon no hōken toshi*, pp. 161–75; and Tanaka, "Jōkamachi Kanazawa ni okeru aitaiukechi chiiki no kōzō," pp. 1–25. The structure of rural government was similar to urban government. One common line of interpretation concerning rural government has been to distinguish two discrete levels of administration: the village level (Senior Headman and below), and the domain level imposed upon the village (Rural Magistrate and above). Within this arrangement, the argument was continued, the domain level retained ultimate rights to the exercise of political authority but delegated some responsibilities to the village-level functionaries. (These duties were similar to the functions delegated to urban commoner representatives in Kanazawa.) The delegation of responsibilities to rural residents made the village "autonomous" or "self-governing" units within the framework established by the state. The reason the state delegated some duties was to maintain peace and order in the countryside and to create a means of ensuring that rural residents would obey the laws of the state. For an excellent rendition of this argument in English, see Befu, "Village Autonomy and Articulation with the State," pp. 301–14. For some additional comments comparing rural and urban government, see Henry D. Smith II, "Tokyo as an Idea: An Exploration of Japanese Urban Thought until 1945," *Journal of Japanese Studies* 4:1 (Winter 1978): 50.

80. This is contained in the message discussing general governing procedures issued under the seal of the fourth shogun, Ietsuna, and addressed to Tsunanori. *KHS*, 3, Manji 1 (1658)/intercalary 12/18, pp. 778–79.

81. *KHS*, 4, Kanbun 4 (1664)/6/6, pp. 55–56.

82. *KHS*, 4, Kanbun 4 (1664), pp. 78–79. For more on the mechanisms of conflict resolution and the settlement of crime, see *Kokon osadamegaki* (MS copy, Kanazawa City Library), 2, pp. 3–7, 8–18, and 49–69. See also *KHS*, 3, Manji 2 (1659)/6/1, pp. 800–02 and Manji 3 (1660)/3/7, pp. 891–94; *OG*, 1, ch. 6, docs. 1 and 2, p. 157–59; and *Kyūjōki*, p. 57.

83. Although this incident happened in 1708, it is used here because of the scarcity of examples concerning acts of violence between samurai and *chōnin*. The details—including Kujūrō's confession, testimony of witnesses, the decision, and a report verifying the execution of the judgment—appear in *Kyūjōki*, pp. 63–69.

84. *KHS*, 4, Kanbun 4 (1664)/5/7, pp. 53–54. See also the case of 1663 in which the Office of the Police and Judiciary sentenced to death by suicide an important rear vassal of Honda Awa no Kami who allegedly killed an unidentified woman during a fight at a temple festival. *Kanke kenmonshū* (MS copy, Kanazawa City Library), 2, pp. 104–06.

85. For additional details, see Wakabayashi, *Maeda Tsunanori*, pp. 143–44; Kuranami, *Kaga: Hyakumangoku*, pp. 96–97; Akai, *Hokurikudō*, 1: 85; and *KKSS*, 4, pp. 1020–21, and 5, pp. 2–5. From the 1660s, the relationship became even deeper, with Tsunanori granting permanent stipends to a number of scholars. *KHS*, 4, Enpō 6 (1678), p. 564; Tenna 2 (1682)/7/28, p. 675; Jōkyō 2 (1685)/3/13, pp. 791–96; 5, Genroku 15 (1702)/4/2, p. 571; and 6, Shōtoku 4 (1714)/12/29, pp. 16–17.

For more information on the spread of Neo-Confucianism in Japan, see John W. Hall, "The Confucian Teacher in Tokugawa Japan," in D. S. Nivison and Arthur F. Wright, eds., *Confucianism in Action* (Stanford: Stanford University Press, 1959), pp. 268–301.

86. Each generation a number of daimyo laid claim to the title "model ruler." In some accounts, for instance, Hoshina Masayuki of Aizu and Hosokawa Shigekata of Higo join Tsunanori as the three outstanding rulers of the mid-seventeenth century. Another phrase common at the time was "Kaga one, Tosa two," intended to indicate that these two domains were the best governed in Japan. For more, see Shimode, *Ishikawa ken no rekishi*, p. 156; and Sakai, "Kaga han kaisakuhō," p. 39.

87. *KZ*, 1, ch. 7, docs. 47 and 48, pp. 280–81. For other documents concerning the punishment of sons see *Kokon osadamegaki*, 2, pp. 49–69; and *KHS*, 4, Enpō 8 (1680)/ 11/10, pp. 621–22.

For another case in which the sons were put to death, this time after their father had embezzled public funds equivalent to the price of approximately fifty *koku* of rice, see *KHS*, 4, Jōkyō 4 (1687)/9/27, pp. 915–17.

The domain sometimes reduced the usual sentence when the offenders were young. In 1691, Uchida Sanshirō, age thirteen, and Matsuda Gonbei, aged fourteen (both sons of *ashigaru*) accidentally started a fire while playing. The standard punishment for carelessly starting a fire was crucifixion, but, in this case, the Court pointed out that the offenders were young and asked higher officials if the punishment could be reduced to beheading, a quicker, less painful way of death; and considered more honorable. *KHS*, 5, Genroku 4 (1691)/3/27, pp. 122–23, and Genroku 4/6/26, pp. 140–41.

In general, sons of *chōnin* and peasants were not put to death, although they might be if their father's crime was considered particularly serious. In 1679, the merchant Komeya Rokubei was sentenced to death for making counterfeit coins, and his infant son, less than two months old, was also put to the sword. *KZ*, 1, ch. 7, doc. 49, p. 281.

88. *Kanke kenmonshū*, 7, pp. 115–16. Some details are contained in *KHS*, 4, Kanbun 6 (1666)/4/16, pp. 118–20.

89. *KHS*, 5, Genroku 3 (1690)/7/27, pp. 68–70.

90. *Kyūjōki*, p. 8; and *KHS*, 5, Genroku 3 (1690)/10/18, pp. 87–90.

91. *MK*, "Komatsu machi-dōshin Hirota Gendaiyū no koto," pp. 308–09.

92. *KHS*, 6, Kyōhō 4 (1719)/2/22, pp. 153–55.

93. Tanaka, *Jōkamachi*, p. 61; and Tanaka, *Kanazawa*, pp. 82–83.

94. Tanaka, *Jōkamachi*, p. 71.

95. Most of the men were from Kyoto. Some took up permanent residence in Kanazawa, while others, such as Igawa, stayed in their home cities and worked on Maeda orders. For additional details and information on the dozens of other artisans of high reputation patronized by the Maeda, see Takashashi Isamu, *Kaga no kōgei* (Kanazawa: Hokkoku Shuppansha, 1976), pp. 69–158; Tanaka, *Kanazawa*, pp. 80–89 and 267–68; and Tanaka, *Jōkamachi*, pp. 60–61.

96. The first artisans of this type were known as *saikumono*, but they might not have had their own separate workshop until the 1630s. *Hankoku kanshoku tsūkō*, "Onsaiku-bugyō," pp. 65–66, and "Onsaiku-kogashira," p. 66; *Kokuji shōhi mondō*, pp. 16 and 74; *KKS,*, 1, "Saikusho ato," pp. 274–75; *KKSS*, 3, pp. 712–14, and 12, pp. 411–12; and Akai, *Hokurikudō*, 1, p. 108.

97. *KHS*, 3, Shōhō 2 (1645)/6/13, pp. 167–69.

98. *KHS*, 3, Kanbun 1 (1661)/7/19, pp. 941–43.

99. *Chōnin shochō (ihon)*, 2, "Nakada Buhei," pp. 3–26.

100. *KKS*, 3, "Sangaya Kuhei den," pp. 28–30. This is summarized in Tanaka, *Jōkamachi*, p. 122. Kuhei was the first Sangaya to engage in mercantile activities; his son was named Kurōbei.

101. Tanaka, *Jōkamachi*, pp. 161–62.

102. *KKS*, 2, "Dōjiriya Saburōemon den," pp. 236–39.

103. *KHS*, 2, Keichō 14 (1609), pp. 57–58.

104. For information on pawnshops, see *Kahan kokusho ibun*, 17, pp. 75–84; and *Kanazawa machijū gohatto no chō*, pp. 10–16. For more on peddlers, see *OG*, 1, ch. 6, doc. 1, pp. 157–58.

105. See, for instance, *OG*, 2, ch. 17, doc. 46, p. 768; and *KZ*, 1, ch. 3, doc. 80, pp. 122–24.

106. The situation became more complicated when the pawnshop owner had already sold the goods to another person, but the same principle held: the pawnshop owner bore

ultimate responsibility if he did not demand a guarantor; if there was a guarantor, however, the guarantor was responsible to the victim of the theft. *KHS*, 3, Manji 3 (1660)/7/3, pp. 891–94; and *OG*, 1, ch. 6, docs. 1 and 2, pp. 157–59.

107. In this case, if the original owner wanted the goods back, he had to pay the buyer the price that the buyer had paid, presumably after having collected from the peddler. *KHS*, 3, Manji 3 (1660)/7/3, pp. 891–94; and *OG*, 1, ch. 6, docs. 1 and 2, pp. 157–59.

108. See the commentary and documents in *Kanazawa-shi Ōmichō ichiba-shi*, pp. 19–21; and Tanaka, *Jōkamachi*, pp. 76–77.

109. The regulations even stipulated that shopkeepers or peddlers who bought tea in the Osaka-Kyoto area and retailed it in Kaga, thus avoiding the middlemen, still had to pay the standard commission to the Komatsu wholesalers. *KHS*, 4, Kanbun 3 (1663)/3/1, pp. 8–10.

110. *OG*, 2, ch. 17, doc. 46, p. 768.

111. *KZ*, 1, ch. 3, doc. 25, p. 96.

112. *Kanke kenmonshū*, 3, pp. 16–23; and *KHS*, 4, Enpō 1 (1673), pp. 377–80, and Enpō 2 (1674), pp. 440–43. The harsh punishments stemmed from the fact that the samurai violated a number of laws (entering lotteries with commoners, engaging in business with commoners, and partying with prostitutes) and then, by fleeing, refused to take responsibility for their actions.

The above accounts implicate different samurai. My rendition is based on the information in *Kanke kenmonshū* and the first *KHS* entry. One document, written at a later date, concludes with the reminiscence that "there were other incidents like this in the past. Many songs were written about this episode, and I learned them in my childhood."

113. This directive was signed by the City Magistrates and sent to all Ward Representatives. *KHS*, 4, Enpō 6 (1678)/1/24, p. 534.

114. Shimode, *Ishikawa ken no rekishi*, pp. 142–45; and Kuranami, *Kaga: Hyakumangoku*, pp. 101–08. If the amount spent by the samurai entourage on entertainment, gifts, etc. is taken into account, the total sum expended outside of Kaga domain becomes much larger. The Maeda daimyo's expenses, expressed as a percentage of total domain income, are roughly in line with the figures for Morioka, a domain in northern Japan. See Hanley and Yamamura, *Economic and Demographic Change*, pp. 130–31.

115. The income calculations are based on: *Kokon osadamegaki*, 2, pp. 35–40; *KHS*, 3, Manji 3 (1660)/1/1, pp. 840–62; Manji 3/6/1, pp. 876–82; Kanbun 1 (1661)/6/4, pp. 933–35; 4, Kanbun 4 (1663)/10/6, pp. 72–74; Sakai, "Kaga han kaisakuhō," p. 45; and Tanaka, "Kaga han hiningoya-sei," p. 52.

In Kaga, the official income of the entire samurai class amounted to slightly over 800,000 *koku*, of which the samurai actually received about 320,000 *koku*, minus taxes and the expected gifts and presents.

116. See the sketches in *KKSS*, 2, following pp. 272 and 410.

117. *KHS*, 3, Manji 2 (1659)/1/1, pp. 785–86.

118. *KHS*, 3, Manji 2 (1659)/1/1, pp. 785–86.

119. *KHS*, 3, Manji 2 (1659)/7/9, pp. 819–20.

120. *OG*, 2, ch. 17, doc. 48, p. 768; and *KHS*, 4, Kanbun 3 (1663)/12/12, pp. 40–41.

121. *KHS*, 3, Manji 1 (1658), p. 780.

122. *KHS*, 3, Kanbun 2 (1662)/4/12, pp. 973–94, and 4, Kanbun 4 (1664)/9/30, pp. 70–72.

123. *KHS*, 4, Enpō 3 (1675), p. 487.

124. *OG*, 2, ch. 17, doc. 9, pp. 711–21; and Wakabayashi, *Ishikawa ken*, p. 146. There is a drawing of a residence of a Foot Soldier (*ashigaru*) in Tanaka, *Jōkamachi*, p. 37.

125. *KHS*, 3, Keian 1 (1648)/intercalary 1/11, p. 268–70.

126. Wakabayashi, *Ishikawa ken*, pp. 145–46.

127. *KZ,* 1, ch. 7, doc. 12, pp. 260–62; and *Chōji tsūsai* (MS copy, Kanazawa City Library), 1, pp. 102–04. For salaries paid in other years, see *KHS,* 2, Kan'ei 15 (1638)/2, pp. 859–60, and Kan'ei 16 (1639)/2, pp. 893–95; *Manji izen osadamegaki,* 2, pp. 21–25; and *Tsutsui kyūki* (MS copy, Kanazawa City Library), 3, pp. 200–08.

128. When trying to calculate costs of living Japanese historians also assume a general inflationary spiral that drove the average price of rice to sixty *monme* by the end of the seventeenth century. It should be stressed that these are only very general rule-of-thumb assumptions. In fact the price of rice could vary considerably from the assumed average of fifty *monme* per *koku.* The price in Kanazawa in 1660 was 76 *monme.* After that the price apparently declined dramatically, but then rose again to about sixty-two *monme* in 1670, following a poor harvest. (*KHS,* 3, Manji 3 [1660]/1, p. 865; and *KZ,* 1, ch. 4, doc. 16, p. 138). The documents make clear, however, that these were considered very high price levels, so an average price of fifty *monme* per *koku* in Kanazawa may serve as a useful assumption.

The 1.8 *koku* per year cost of living standard is also a theoretical assumption. It is also further assumed that for families the economies of living together (lower per person housing costs, for example) would pull this figure down so that a family of five (husband, one retired parent, wife, and two children, for instance) might need an income of about six or seven *koku* (300–50 *monme*).

129. Those who went to Edo received an extra five to ten *monme* to cover expenses. See, for example, *Chōji tsūsai,* 1, pp. 102–04.

130. *KHS,* 4, Kanbun 3 (1663)/6/21, p. 27.

131. *KZ,* 1, ch. 5, doc. 4, pp. 169–70; and Shimode, *Ishikawa ken no rekishi,* pp. 173–77.

132. Tanaka, *Jōkamachi,* pp. 145–46. See also the drawing of a wealthy merchant residence on p. 148.

133. Ishii, *Hanpōshū,* 4, doc. 359, p. 1027; and *KHS,* 4, Kanbun 8 (1668)/7/6, pp. 216–19.

134. *OG,* 2, ch. 17, doc. 9, pp. 711–21; and *KHS,* 4, Kanbun 8 (1668)/7/6, pp. 216–19.

135. These are the base wages for carpenters and thatchers employed on domain construction projects. They were meant also to serve as the maximum that private individuals should pay when hiring these artisans, so that the domain could assure its own access to the labor force and hold down its own wage costs. These wages were for a work day that lasted from six A.M. until sunset. Some other workers covered by the wage controls were sawyers, plasterers, tatami makers, and artisans who made *fusuma* (sliding partitions) and *shōji* (paper sliding doors). For each occupational category, the artisans were classified as "superior" (*jō*), "good" (*chū*), and "average" (*ge*) and daily wages in *monme* were stipulated for each category, as follows:

	superior	*good*	*average*
carpenters	1.7	1.4	1.1
sawyers and roof thatchers	1.5	1.3	1.0
plasterers	1.7	1.6	1.5
tatami makers	1.5	1.3	1.0
fusuma and *shōji* makers	1.2	—	—

The domain paid an extra 0.3 *monme* per day in 1659, 1660, and 1661 because, it said, the demand for workers was high. *KZ,* 1, ch. 3, doc. 80, pp. 122–24, and ch. 7, doc. 13, pp. 262–65; and *KHS,* 3, Manji 2 (1659)/8/1, pp. 820–22, and Manji 2/8/7, pp. 822–24.

A couple of additional points should be mentioned. The carpenters' and thatchers' wages were less than those for a number of other artisan occupations. In the late 1650s, for example, stirrup makers received 2–3 *monme* per day (and worked inside; a skilled stirrup maker might earn a thousand *monme* per year); artisans who made Buddhist altars, 3 *monme*; lance makers, 2 *monme;* coopers, 1.5 *monme;* and well diggers, 1.7 *monme. KZ,* 1, ch. 3, doc. 80, pp. 122–24.

    136. *KHS,* 3 Kanbun 2 (1662)/4/1, pp. 970–71. In 1659, when the carpenters and others received a wage increase from the domain, day laborers received 8 *bu* 5 *rin* a day. However, in the early eighteenth century daily wages fell to just 6 *bu* 5 *rin. KZ,* 1, ch. 7, doc. 13, pp. 262–65, and 3, ch. 22, doc. 32, p. 855; and *KHS,* 6, Kyōhō 19 (1734)/ 10/15, pp. 873–74.

    137. Indicative, perhaps, of commoner poverty were the reports of infants, usually girls, abandoned near moats, under the approaches to the bridges, and in people's gardens. These children were abandoned in places where they would be found, and some were three or four years old. Usually a doctor would treat the baby, and if the baby survived, a family generally came forth to adopt him or her. See the numerous reports listed in *KZ,* 2, ch. 10, doc. 51, p. 393, and 3, ch. 20, doc. 8, pp. 757–59.

    138. *KKSS,* 4, pp. 1130–33.

    139. The incident concerning Chaya is described in *KHS,* 2, Kan'ei 8 (1631), pp. 670–72; and *MK,* "Kanazawa yūjo narabi ni shibai sata no koto," pp. 190–92.

    140. This incident took place in the late 1620s and is described in *KKS,* 2, "Kawaramachi furoya tsutaebanashi," pp. 176–77; as well as in the documents cited in n. 139.

    141. *KKSS,* 4, pp. 1105–06; and *Seirinki,* 1, pp. 60–61.

    142. For more information, see Ishikawa-ken Toshokan Kyōkai, ed., *Shibai to Chayamachi* (Kanazawa: Ishikawa-ken Toshokan Kyōkai, 1932), pp. 1–26.

    143. *Kahan kokusho ibun,* 12, 65–80; *Manji izen osadamegaki,* 1, pp. 71–82; *OG,* 1, ch. 1, doc. 83, pp. 55–56; and *KHS,* 2, Kan'ei 16 (1639)/5/1, pp. 902–04. Apparently, there were officially sanctioned "teahouses" that employed prostitutes in Daishōji, the area that became a branch domain in the 1630s. These shops may have drawn some customers from Kanazawa. For details, see Wakabayashi, *Maeda Tsunanori,* p. 77–78.

    144. One of the later pleasure quarters was located on the north bank of the Asano, on the web of streets between the Hokuriku highway and the Kannon shrine and temple complex. The other was behind Shinmei shrine. *Shibai to Chayamachi,* pp. 27–50.

    The suppression of kabuki and prostitution was not unique to Kanazawa, although the Maeda seem to have enforced the laws strictly. Tokugawa Ieyasu expelled kabuki troupes from his headquarters at Suruga as early as 1608, and in 1629 the shogunate banned women performers from the stage in Edo, although it did not enforce that ordinance until the 1640s. Donald H. Shively, *"Bakufu* versus *Kabuki,"* in Hall and Jansen, eds., *Studies,* pp. 234–36. Shively's article is an excellent introduction to the shogunate's reaction to kabuki's supposedly negative effects on public morality. See also Shively's "The Social Environment of Tokugawa Kabuki," in James R. Brandon, William P. Malm, and Donald H. Shively, *Studies in Kabuki: Its Acting, Music, and Historical Context* (Honolulu: University Press of Hawaii, 1978), pp. 1–61.

    145. Wakabayashi, *Maeda Tsunanori,* pp. 74–75.

    146. Shively, *"Bakufu* versus *Kabuki,"* pp. 236–37.

    147. *KHS,* 2, Kan'ei 8 (1631), pp. 670–72.

    148. The following account of the year's festivals is based on *KKSS,* 11, pp. 158–204.

    149. *KZ,* 2, ch. 13, doc. 20, pp. 497–98; and *KKSS,* 11, pp. 138–40.

    150. *KKSS,* 11, p. 144.

    151. *KKSS,* 11, pp. 192–95.

    152. Wakabayashi, *Maeda Tsunanori,* pp. 125–26. The rifle ranges were established in 1663 after the government banned target practice on private residences. *OG,* 2, ch. 17, doc. 24, p. 756.

153. Hunting was prohibited on some days (the anniversary dates of the deaths of all the Maeda daimyo, for instance) and within twelve kilometers of the castle. *KKSS*, 12, pp. 564–66; and *KHS*, 3, Manji 2 (1659)/1/1, pp. 785–86.

154. Due to the expenses involved in the sport, domain laws limited falconry to samurai with official stipends of 3,000 *koku* and above. (In 1743, this was amended to 5,000 *koku* and above). For more information, see *OG*, 2, ch. 17, doc. 88, p. 787; *KZ*, 2, ch. 11, doc. 16, p. 419, and 3, ch. 19, doc. 49, p. 723; Ishikawa-ken Toshokan Kyōkai, ed., *Kaga han shoki no samurai-chō* (Kanazawa: Ishikawa-ken Toshokan Kyōkai, 1942), pp. 12–13; and *KHS*, 2, Keichō 11 (1606)/4/26, p. 4; 3, Manji 1 (1658)/8/10, pp. 550–51; 4, Kanbun 4 (1664)/6/21, pp. 57–58, and Enpō 4 (1676)/8/10, p. 500.

CHAPTER 4

1. The Hayashi school of Chu Hsi Neo-Confucianism was not unchallenged. Nakae Tōju (1608–48), for instance, expounded a rival school of Confucian thought known as *yōmei* (derived from the teachings of Wang Yang-ming). In an over-simplified fashion, it might be said that the Hayashi family argued that through study anyone could learn to understand the Confucian relationships and obligations, and thereby become a moral man. Nakae's teachings were more subjective. He believed that moral sense did not have to be taught. Rather, it existed within each person, and intuitive action based on that sense led to moral conduct. A second early critic of the Hayashi family was Yamazaki Ansai (1618–82), although his attacks mostly chided the Hayashi family for not putting their professed beliefs into practice. Kumazawa Banzan (1619–91) was another proponent of the *yōmei* school of thought. An adviser to the Ikeda daimyo of Okayama domain, Kumazawa attacked the shogunate's policies in his writings and, for this, was severely criticized by the Hayashi family.

2. For more on the *ton'ya* in Kyoto and Osaka, see Crawcour, "Changes in Japanese Commerce in the Tokugawa Period," pp. 197–99; and Hauser, *Economic Institutional Change*, pp. 16–23. Hauser makes the additional point that the early *ton'ya* in Osaka were often receiving agents (*niuke ton'ya*) who handled a variety of goods produced in a single geographic area, while the later *ton'ya* usually specialized in particular commodities.

3. See, for instance, *OG*, 1, ch. 11, doc. 5, pp. 255–56; and *KHS*, 3, Kanbun 1 (1661)/8/8, p. 945, and 4, Kanbun 12 (1672)/9, p. 360.

4. Quoted in Tanaka, *Kaga*, p. 277.

5. *KHS*, 5, Genroku 10 (1697), pp. 386–88, and Hōei 7 (1710)/6/21, pp. 894–95.

6. *OG*, 2, ch. 14, doc. 59, p. 478.

7. For example, in 1687 the government incorporated 190 households into the city. Wards added later included Ishiura-shinmachi in 1696, Matsumotochō in 1725, and Hirookamachi in 1727. *KHS*, 4, Jōkyō 4 (1687)/2/28, pp. 871–74; and *KKSS*, 1, p. 275, and 3, pp. 609, 612–13, and 780. For other examples, see Tanaka Yoshio, "Genroku-ki ni okeru jōkamachi chiiki no kakudai to jōkamachi shōnin," *Kanazawa Keizai Daigaku ronshū* 13:3 (March 1980): 105–09.

8. *KHS*, 4, Kanbun 9 (1669)/5/25, p. 249, and Tenna 4 (1684)/2/24, pp. 744–45; and *KK*, 2, pp. 22–23 and 108–09.

9. *KHS*, 4, Tenna 3, (1683)/intercalary 5/28, pp. 721–22.

10. *KZ*, 1, ch. 3, doc. 55, pp. 109–10.

11. *KK*, 2, p. 162.

12. *KZ*, 1, ch. 3, doc. 57, p. 110.

13. *KHS*, 5, Genroku 13 (1700), p. 515. For more on the development of local towns throughout Japan in the nineteenth century, see Thomas C. Smith, "Pre-modern Economic Growth: Japan and the West," *Past and Present* 43 (1973): 127–60.

14. *KHS*, 4, Jōkyō 3 (1686)/11/23, pp. 852–54. For additional details, see Kuranami, *Kaga hansei*, pp. 143–144.

15. Tanaka, *Jōkamachi*, p. 236.

16. *KZ*, 1, ch. 7, doc. 24, pp. 272–74; and *KHS*, 4, Enpō 6 (1678)/8/29, pp. 553–55.

17. *KZ*, 1, ch. 2, doc. 33, pp. 59–60.

18. The following is based on *KKSS*, 5, pp. 4–5; *KZ*, 3, ch. 21, doc. 14, pp. 798–99; and *KHS*, 4, Enpō 6 (1678), p. 564, Tenna 2 (1682)/7/28, p. 675, Tenna 3 (1683)/7/22, pp. 724–25, Jōkyō 2 (1685)/3/13, pp. 791–96, Jōkyō 2/10/22, p. 817; 5, Genroku 15 (1702)/4/2, p. 571; and 6, Shōtoku 4 (1714)/12/29, pp. 16–17. For secondary accounts, see Kuranami, *Kaga: Hyakumangoku*, p. 96; and Wakabayashi, *Maeda Tsunanori*, pp. 142–45.

19. Based on *KHS*, 4, Kanbun 3 (1663)/6/12, pp. 26–27, and Kanbun 9 (1669)/10/12, pp. 265–66.

20. *Seirinki*, 1, pp. 92–93; and *KHS*, 4, Kanbun 10 (1670)/6/22, pp. 283–90, and Kanbun 10/8/10, pp. 298–99. One document, written at a later date, gives 1669 as the year of establishment: *Kokuji shōhi mondō*, p. 69.

21. *KZ*, 1, ch. 2, doc. 67, p. 73; and *KHS*, 5, Hōei 4 (1707)/3/29, pp. 745–46; and 6, Kyōhō 2 (1717)/2, p. 81, and Kyōhō 18 (1733)/7/4, pp. 827–30.

22. *KHS*, 6, Kyōhō 18 (1733)/7/4, pp. 827–30.

23. See, for example, the two petitions in *Hanpōshū*, 4, docs. 35 and 36, pp. 915–16.

24. Hioki, ed., *Ishikawa kenshi*, 2: 652.

25. Wakabayashi, *Maeda Tsunanori*, p. 95.

26. *KHS*, 4, Kanbun 10 (1670)/6/22, pp. 284–90, and Enpō 6 (1678)/8, pp. 555–57; *KK*, 1, p. 264; and Hioki, ed., *Ishikawa kenshi*, 2: 651. One document states that the rice allowance was five *gō* per day for adult males. This ration may have been given to those who worked on craft production. *KHS*, 4, Enpō 6 (1678)./8, pp. 555–57.

27. *KHS*, 6, Kyōhō 18 (1733)/7/4, pp. 827–30. This document lists the population of the Poorhouses on the first day of 1699 at 4,525 persons. It then states that 3,685 persons died or were released during the year and that the same number were admitted, for a resident population of 4,525 on the last day of the year. It would seem likely that some of the "newly admitted" early in the year were among the categories "released" or "died" later in the year. If so, 3,685 would be only the net total of new admittees for the year, and the actual turnover rate would have been higher.

It is unclear how many of the 3,685 died. The only other figures available are for the period 1709/7/16 through 1709/7/25. During that ten-day period twelve of 2,210 residents were discharged from the Poorhouses and an additional ten persons died. If these same rates prevailed for an entire year, then twenty percent of the original residents would have been released and another sixteen percent would have died. The death rate (about 1,629 per 10,000 on an annual basis) seems rather high. Whether this was due to inadequate treatment in the Poorhouses or to the fact that many of the admittees were already ill and starving when they entered is not clear. *Shūri kenmonroku* (MS copy, Kanazawa City Library), 2, pp. 55–56.

28. *KK*, 2, p. 148.

29. *Kashū kōrikata kyūki* (MS copy, Kanazawa City Library), 6, pp. 89–93; and *KKS*, 2, "Hiningoya raireki," pp. 58–62.

30. Kuranami, *Kaga: Hyakumangoku*, pp. 90–91. Some modern historians have continued the praise; see Wakabayashi, *Maeda Tsunanori*, pp. 93–95. Tanaka, however, in his "Kaga han hiningoya-sei" criticizes the domain for not being generous enough.

31. In the middle of the eighteenth century there were about one thousand *tōnai* families resident in Kaga domain, and many lived near Kanazawa. Information about the *tōnai* is drawn from Ishikawa-ken Toshokan Kyōkai, ed., *Iburaku ikkan*, (Kanazawa:

Ishikawa-ken Toshokan Kyōkai, 1932), "Tōnaigashira ni kyūrei nado aitazunesōrō ik-ken," pp. 1–4, "Tōnaigashira San'emon Ninzō nado ryōgin no bu," pp. 12–18, and "Tōnai narabi ni monoyoshi nado no gi, tōnaigashira Ninzō San'emon yori shirabedashisōrō kakitsuke," pp. 18–20; *KKS*, 2, "Ninzō San'emon raireki," pp. 578–87; *KZ*, 1, ch. 2, doc. 40, pp. 61–62; *KHS*, 5, Genroku 6 (1693)/5/13, pp. 224–26; and *KK*, 1, pp. 204 and 298.

32. *Iburaku ikkan*, "Tōnaigashira ni kyūrei," pp. 1–4, and "Tōnai narabi ni monoyoshi nado no gi," pp. 18–20; *KZ*, 3, ch. 23, doc. 26, pp. 910–12, and doc. 28, pp. 912–14; *OG*, 1, ch. 7, doc. 20, pp. 192–93; and *KKS*, 3, "Asano hininmachi," p. 557. In other domains, the term *hinin* usually referred to outcasts in general. In Kaga, its use was more limited and the term was applied to those who made a living by begging.

33. *KZ*, 3, ch. 23, doc. 27, p. 912; and *KHS*, 5, Genroku 4 (1691)/2/14, p. 109. The documents read as if the beggars requested licensing. However, the domain itself may have decided on such a procedure before the above documents were written. A year earlier, in 1690, a massive fire swept through Kanazawa, destroying over 6,000 houses. There were many complaints of beggars looting in the aftermath of the fire. Licensing thus served both to protect the interests of established beggars and to give the domain a way of policing this outcast group. For instance, officials instructed the Beggars' Headman to report any beggar who was a kleptomaniac and to assemble all beggars after a major fire.

34. Information about the *monoyoshi* comes from *KKS*, 2, "Monoyoshimachi," p. 590, and "Monoyoshi no raireki," pp. 591–92; *KZ*, 1, ch. 2, doc. 40, pp. 61–62; and Wakabayashi, *Ishikawa ken*, pp. 161–62.

35. The *monoyoshi* went to samurai households on such auspicious occasions as New Year's, the Festival in Honor of Ancestors, the Five Festivals (1/1, 3/3, 5/5, 7/7, and 9/9), the succession to family headship, adoption, birth of a male child, an audience with the daimyo, construction of a new house, and wedding ceremonies. For *chōnin*, the occasions included New Year's, the Five Festivals, buying or selling a house, adoption, Buddhist memorial services, and the birth of a male child. A complete list can be found in *Iburaku ikkan*, "Tōnai, hiningashira, monoyoshi iwai moraiukesōrō kajō ikken," pp. 20–21.

36. Another outcast group was the *maimai*, dancers and entertainers. Very little is known of this group except that Toshinaga and Toshitsune granted them stipends and occasionally invited them to the castle to perform. Tsunanori later withdrew the stipends, and they became beggars. See *KKSS*, 12, pp. 451–53.

37. In addition, the status of outcasts in the medieval period generally was not heredi-tary, and in many instances outcasts did not live in defined, geographically segregated areas. For more, see Harada Tomohiko, "Bakuhan shakai to mibunsei," pp. 36–45. For information on outcasts in Edo, Osaka, and Kyoto, see Yamada Mitsuji, "Toshi buraku no jōkyō," *Rekishi kōron* 3:6 (June 1977): 56–62; and the essays in Buraku-mondai Kenkyūjō, ed., *Buraku-shi no kenkyū: zenkindaihen* (Buraku-mondai Kenkyūjō Shuppanbu, 1978). Tanaka Yoshio presents a slightly different interpretation of the outcast experience in Kanazawa, arguing that discrimination began only during the Genroku period. See his "Kaga han 'tōnai' no kenkyū, Edo jidai senminkō josetsu," *Ishikawa rekishi kenkyū* 2 (1961): 50–80; and "Edo jidai hisabetsu burakumin no chii—toku ni Kaga han 'tōnai' no tochi shoyū o chūshin ni shite," *Shizen to shakai* 23 (1969): 8–12.

38. *KHS*, 4, Kanbun 3 (1663)/3/6, pp. 10–12. The tea wholesalers lived in Komatsu. Some tea was grown in Kaga domain, but by law this too was supposed to pass from producer to the Kamatsu wholesalers to the peddlers and, finally, to the retailers.

39. *KZ*, 2, ch. 11, doc. 1, pp. 408–09. For more on the relationship between these merchants and economic development in general, see my "Jōkamachi no toshika ni okeru daimyō to chōnin—jūnanaseki no Kanazawa," *Hokuriku shigaku* 29 (December 1980): 27–41.

40. *KK*, 2, pp. 39–40. This includes both the petition to the domain requesting

authorization of monopoly rights (dated 1683/7/24) and the domain's approval (1683/8/2). For more on paper manufacturing in the eighteenth and early nineteenth centuries, see Takada Naganori, "Kaga han no kōzo shihō ni tsuite," *Hokuriku shigaku* 18 (1970): 14–28.

41. *Okabe-shi goyōdome* (MS copy, Kanazawa City Library), 2, pp. 64–67; *KK,* 1, p. 325; and *KHS,* 4, Tenna 3 (1683)/8/4, pp. 725–27.

42. *KK,* 2, pp. 42–43. Nothing was said about the association in Komatsu that imported cotton from Osaka, and presumably those merchants were allowed to continue operations.

43. *KK,* 2, p. 42.

44. Two different authorizations were granted. Itoya Matabei and Aburaya Magobei received permission to lend sumac plants and money to farmers. When the seeds were sold after harvesting the farmers and the two merchants split the profits 80/20. *KK,* 2, pp. 34–35.

A separate license authorized Sumedaniya Tazaemon of Minamichō, Kinuya Yoemon of Katamachi, and Miyajimaya Magozaemon of Imamachi to buy directly from producers and people who collected seeds from plants growing in the wild.

Some printed documents list the recipients as Kinuya, Miyajimaya, and a Michidaniya Tazaemon. This Michidaniya was presumably the same person as Sumedaniya. *Okabe-shi goyōdome,* 2, pp. 40–41; *KHS,* 4, Tenna 3 (1683)/6/8, p. 722; and *KK,* 2, p. 34.

45. *KK,* 2, pp. 31–32.

46. *KKSS,* 12, p. 279.

47. Information on the rice brokers is from: *Chōji tsūsai,* 1, pp. 144–45; *KK,* 2, pp. 38–39; *KZ,* 2, ch. 10, doc. 70, p. 402; and *KHS,* 5, Genroku 2 (1689)/1/28, p. 1, and 6, Kyōhō 6 (1721)/6/28, p. 240. For a secondary account, see Tanaka, *Jōkamachi,* pp. 86–89 and 257–58.

48. For a specific example concerning two new fish wholesalers, see *KHS,* 3, Shōhō 4 (1647)/3/13, pp. 235–36.

49. In 1657, for instance, the annual fee charged the tea wholesalers was forty *mai* of silver; in 1647, the fish wholesalers paid seventy *mai;* and in the 1650s the merchants who imported processed cotton paid a tax equivalent to about five percent of the value of the imports. *KHS,* 3, Meireki 3 (1657)/4/5, pp. 515–16; 4, Shōhō 4 (1647)/8/1, pp. 260–62; and *KZ,* 2, ch. 11, doc. 1, pp. 408–09.

50. *KK,* 1, p. 325.

51. *KZ,* 1, ch. 3, doc. 31, p. 98.

52. *KHS,* 3, Keian 4 (1651)/3/26, p. 334.

53. Tanaka, *Jōkamachi,* pp. 134–35.

54. *KZ,* 1, ch. 5, doc. 52, pp. 193–94.

55. *KKS,* 3, "Kaji yashiki," pp. 285–87; and *KHS,* 6, Kyōhō 1 (1716)/4/14, pp. 47–48.

56. *Zoku zentoku zakki,* 10, pp. 151–52; *KKS,* 2, "Hinin Kiyomitsu den," pp. 63–66, "Katana kaji Kiyomitsuya ato," p. 73, and "Kaji Yukimitsu Kiyomitsu den," pp. 403–05; *KZ,* 1, ch. 2, doc. 14, pp. 46–47, and ch. 5, doc. 51, pp. 191–93; and *KHS,* 4, Enpō 6 (1678)/8, pp. 555–57.

57. In 1818 the domain recognized the following twelve families: Kanaya Hikoshirō, Kataoka (Echizen'ya) Magobei, Asanoya Jirōbei, Hiranoya Hansuke, Kamiya Shozaburō, Nakaya Hikoemon, Kōrinbō Heisuke, Motoyoshiya Sōemon, Morimotoya Hachizaemon, Miyatakeya Junzō, Kameda (Miyatakeya) Yosuke, and Kashiya Kichizō. The following year, six more families were added: Musashi Kiichirō, Kiguraya Chōemon, Masuda Kurōbei, Nagase Seitarō, Nakayama Kasue, and Kitamura Hikoemon. Tanaka, *Jōkamachi,* pp. 166–67. For a list of the thirty families that had received *goyō* charters in the 1583 to 1600 period, see Tanaka, *Dentō toshi, pp. 36–37.*

58. *KKS*, 3, "Echizen'ya Kiemon kyūtei," p. 52, and "Echizen'ya Kiemon den," pp. 52–58; *KZ*, 1, ch. 3, doc. 85, pp. 125–26; and *KHS*, 2, Keichō 12 (1607)/2/15, pp. 23–24.

59. *KKS*, 3, "Tōfuya Taemon kyūtei," p. 578, and "Tōfuya Taemon den," pp. 578–79; and *KZ*, 1, ch. 3, doc. 30, pp. 97–98, and ch. 7, doc. 45, p. 279.

60. *KZ*, 1, ch. 3, doc. 84, p. 125, and 3, ch. 20, doc. 5, pp. 753–55.

61. The crime was not specified. *KKS*, 3, "Takeya Nihei kyūtei," pp. 398–99; and *KZ*, 1, ch. 3, doc. 86, p. 126.

62. *KKS*, 3, "Nakaya Hikoemon den," pp. 19–20; and *Machidoshiyori reikimei narabi ni tsutomekatachō*, pp. 7–86.

63. *KKS*, 2, "Kameda Iemon den," pp. 243–44.

64. *KZ*, 1, ch. 2, doc. 80, p. 78.

65. *KZ*, 1, ch. 13, doc. 43, pp. 278–79. Apparently the three merchants were not successful, for, about twenty-five years later, farmers who lived on the northern fringe of Kanazawa sent in a petition which stated that three *chōnin* had earlier failed in the *onsen* business at Tatsunokuchi and requested permission to open a new *onsen* there. *KHS*, 6, Kyōhō 16 (1731)/10/2, pp. 760–71.

Three hotels are in business today at Tatsunokuchi. The largest publishes a brochure which claims that, according to local legend, the *onsen* first opened in the Kan'ei period (1624–44). Although the owner admits that he has no written evidence of this, there is a document dated 1701 (carried in *KHS*, 5, Hōei 3 [1701]/1/16, pp. 710–12) which states that an *onsen* had existed at Tatsunokuchi earlier. The efforts of the three *chōnin*, then, may have been the second ill-fated attempt to establish a business at Tatsunokuchi.

66. *Kame no o no ki*, "Nō yakusha Takeda Gonbei," p. 28; *KZ*, 1, ch. 5, docs. 46 and 47, pp. 188–89; and *KHS*, 2, Kan'ei 5 (1628)/2/10, pp. 566–67.

67. *KKSS*, 12, p. 400.

68. *Kame no o no ki*, "Nō yakusha Morohashi Gonnoshin," p. 57; *KZ*, 1, ch. 4, doc. 26, p. 146; *KKSS*, 12, pp. 404–06; and *KKS*, 3, "Morohashi Gonnoshin den," pp. 176–78.

69. See, for example, *KHS*, 5, Genroku 3 (1690)/10/10, pp. 86–87; 6, Shōtoku 4 (1714)/2/29, p. 3, and Genbun 1 (1736)/5/9, p. 936.

70. *KHS*, 4, Jōkyō 4 (1687)/11/9, pp. 922–24; 5, Genroku 5 (1692)/1/2, p. 155, and Genroku 5/9/14, pp. 196–98.

71. *Seirinki*, 1, pp. 75–78; and *KHS*, 6, Kyōhō 10 (1725)/9/28, pp. 535–36.

72. See, for example, *Seirinki*, 1, pp. 151–63; *KHS*, 4, Kanbun 3 (1663)/7, p. 28; 5, Genroku 4 (1691)/6/12, p. 138; Genroku 12 (1699)/11/26, pp. 466–67; Hōei 7 (1710)/4/4, pp. 885–86; and Hōei 7/11/13, p. 901.

By this time the Maeda-Tokugawa consanguinity had become rather complicated. Tsunanori's grandmother (Tentokuin) had been the daughter of the second shogun (Hidetada); his mother was an adopted daughter of the third shogun (Iemitsu) (she was adopted from the Tokugawa line at Mito, a younger brother of Hidetada); and his wife was the daughter of Hoshina Masayuki, daimyo of Aizu and the younger brother of Iemitsu.

73. *KHS*, 5, Genroku 3 (1690)/4/26, pp. 50–51; Genroku 3/5/10, p. 52; Genroku 3/5/13, pp. 52–53, and Genroku 3/11/13, pp. 92–93.

74. Tanaka, *Kanazawa*, p. 89; and *KHS*, 4, Kanbun 10 (1670)/7/11, p. 292.

75. *KZ*, 1, ch. 3, doc. 60, p. 111, and ch. 5, doc. 38, pp. 184–86; and *KKSS*, 3, p. 798, and 12, pp. 523–26.

76. Wakabayashi, *Maeda Tsunanori*, pp. 144–55.

77. *KKSS*, 12, p. 422.

78. See, for example, *Seirinki*, 1, pp. 75–78.

79. Hioki, ed., *Ishikawa kenshi*, 2: 414–15.

80. *KHS*, 4, Kanbun 12 (1672)/4/16, p. 350, and Kanbun 12/intercalary 6, pp. 353–54. The quotation is cited in Tanaka, *Kanazawa*, p. 73. Tanaka claims that there was

a spread of cultural norms from daimyo to retainers to *chōnin* and that even merchants held weekly tea ceremonies for their shop clerks. Tanaka, *Kanazawa*, pp. 78–80.

81. See, for example, *Seirinki*, 4, pp. 1–22. In this instance farmers reported that Motohō Kishiemon, whose theoretical income was 2,000 *koku*, was hunting on one of the daimyo's preserves. Kishiemon was placed under house arrest.

82. *KKSS*, 12, p. 570.

83. This activity had a long history and Toshiie had occasionally been the guest of Toyotomi Hideyoshi. *KHS*, 1, Keichō 9 (1598)/3/15, pp. 566–67.

84. *Kame no o no ki*, "Ōhi Hasubatake," p. 124.

85. *KHS*, 6, Kyōhō 12 (1727)/10/11, p. 594.

86. *KKSS*, 11, p. 25.

87. *KHS*, 6, Kyōhō 14 (1729)/8, pp. 680–82.

88. *KHS*, 4, Tenna 1 (1681)/5/26, p. 643. The priest was also accused of eating meat. The document is the priest's execution order. It does not name the woman or any punishment she might have received. The site of the execution—in front of the priest's temple rather than the execution grounds—shows the domain's particular abhorrence for this kind of crime.

89. *OG*, 2, ch. 17, doc. 48, p. 768; and *KHS*, 4, Kanbun 3 (1663)/10/30, p. 36, and Kanbun 3/12/12, pp. 40–41.

90. *KHS*, 4, Kanbun 3 (1663)/11/4, p. 37.

91. *KK*, 1, pp. 298–99.

92. *KHS*, 5, Genroku 10 (1697)/2/4, pp. 380–82; *KKS*, 2, "Furoya raireki," pp. 15–17; and *KKSS*, 12, pp. 317–20.

93. *Seirinki*, 3, pp. 40–73.

94. *KHS*, 5, Shōtoku 2 (1712)/6/18, pp. 944–45.

95. *KHS*, 5, Shōtoku 2 (1712)/7/30, p. 950.

96. There are also a number of documents that state that kabuki and houses of prostitution died out quickly after the 1630s; see, for example, the excerpts and commentary in *KKSS*, 12, pp. 498–522.

97. *KKSS*, 12, pp. 430–31.

98. See, for example, *KHS*, 4, Tenna 3 (1683)/2/29, pp. 701–03, and 6, Kyōhō 14 (1729)/7/27, pp. 673–74.

99. Some historians have even asserted that noh and the other arts associated with the samurai set the tone for all cultural life in Kanazawa in the late seventeenth and early eighteenth centuries. Kuranami claims that the "culture of Kaga was the daimyo culture that centered around Tsunanori," and "*chōnin* culture played merely a supporting role; the main role always belonged to the *bushi* and *bushi* culture." Kuranami, *Kaga: Hyakumangoku*, p. 94. See also Shimode, *Ishikawa ken no rekishi*, pp. 154–66; and Tanaka, *Kanazawa*, pp. 79–80.

100. Ishikawa-ken Toshokan Kyōkai, ed., *Nezame no hotaru* (Kanazawa: Ishikawa-ken Toshokan Kyōkai, 1931), pp. 1 and 6–8, contains some reports of prostitution and kabuki in outlying rural villages.

101. Akai, *Hokurikudō*, 1: 73; Tanaka, *Jōkamachi*, pp. 54–56; and *KKSS*, 12, pp. 500–01.

102. *KKSS*, 12, pp. 535–38.

103. *KKSS*, 12, pp. 542–61.

104. See, for example, *KZ*, 1, ch. 1, doc. 84, p. 39; *KHS*, 4, Kanbun 11 (1671)/10/10, pp. 334–35, Enpō 4 (1676)/3/30, p. 494, Enpō 8 (1680)/11/6, pp. 619–20, and 5, Genroku 16 (1703)/1/17, p. 620.

105. *KZ*, 1, ch. 8, doc. 37, p. 327.

106. *KZ*, 1, ch. 1, docs. 82 and 84, p. 39; and *KHS*, 4, Enpō 4 (1676)/3/30, p. 494, and Enpō 8 (1680)/12/11, p. 627.

107. *KKS*, 2, "Saigawa sangyo," pp. 252–55. However, Tsunanori banned fishing on the section of the Sai River visible from the castle at times when he was resident in Kanazawa. Given the frequency with which these orders were reissued, however, it does not appear that they were very closely observed. See, for example, *KZ*, 1, ch. 2, doc. 15, p. 48, and 3, ch. 21, doc. 44, p. 824; *KHS*, 4, Kanbun 5 (1665)/5/27, pp. 95–96; and *KKSS*, 1, p. 103.

108. It is not clear why sightings were reported. *KZ*, 1, ch. 2, doc. 28, pp. 56–57; and *KHS*, 5, Genroku 9 (1696)/8/22, p. 366.

CONCLUSION

1. For an excellent review of recent Japanese scholarship on "people's history" (*min-shūshi*), see Carol Gluck, "The People in History: Recent Trends in Japanese Historiography," *Journal of Asian Studies* 38:1 (November 1978): 25–50.

2. Massie, *Peter the Great*, pp. 361–62.

3. Bernard, *The Emerging City*, pp. 17 and 91.

GLOSSARY

aitaiukechi 相対請地 Land whose usage was decided privately, through negotiations between individuals

bakufu 幕府 The Tokugawa shogunate or government.

bushi 武士 Armed fighter; members of the warrior status group; also called samurai

chōnin 町人 Members of the merchant and artisan status groups who resided in cities.

daimyō 大名 Territorial lord; ruler of a domain during the Tokugawa period.

ginza 銀座 Office of Currency Control; staffed by merchants after 1620; oversaw domain minting activities and inspected coins.

goyō shokunin 御用職人 Artisans who were employed by the daimyo.

goyō shōnin 御用商人 Merchants who possessed charters that allowed them to purvey goods to the daimyo.

gun 郡 District or county.

han 藩 Domain of a daimyo.

Hokuriku region 北陸地方 The area corresponding to the present-day Fukui, Ishikawa, Toyama, and Niigata prefectures.

kanme 貫目 Unit of currency in silver and a measure of weight; equal to 1,000 *monme*.

Kantō region 関東地方 The eight provinces surrounding Edo.

kashindan 家臣団 Band of warrior retainers.

kenchi 検地 Cadastral survey.

koku 石 Measure of capacity equal to 180 liters or 4.96 bushels.

kōri-bugyō 郡奉行 Rural Magistrate; post staffed by samurai; administered rural areas.

kujiba 公事場 Office of Police and the Judiciary; investigated crimes, apprehended and punished criminals; post staffed by samurai.

machi 町 Ward; an administrative unit within a city. Also pronounced *chō*.

machi-bugyō 町奉行 City Magistrate; post staffed by samurai; charged with the administration of urban areas.

machi-dōshin 町同心 Constables; assisted the City Magistrates; post staffed by samurai.

machidoshiyori 町年寄 City Elder; post staffed by merchants and artisans; assisted the City Magistrates.

machi-kimoiri 町肝煎 Ward Representative; assisted the City Elders; post staffed by merchants and artisans.

mai 枚 Unit of currency in silver; equal to 43 *monme*.

monme 文目, 匁 Unit of currency in silver and a measure of weight; 1.325 oz. or 3.76 grams.

nakagai 仲買 Intermediary merchant or consignment agents.

samurai 侍 Generally used to mean any warrior, the term is sometimes restricted to those middle- and upper-level warriors who had the privilege of personally attending their lord.

shōgun 将軍 Head of the Tokugawa house and chief official in the *bakufu*.

ton'ya 問屋 Individual merchants or merchant houses who worked as wholesalers and as receiving and shipping agents.

BIBLIOGRAPHY

1. UNPUBLISHED SOURCES

Chōji tsūsai 庁事通載 [A record of government affairs]. MS copy, Kanazawa City Library. Vols. 1 and 3.

Chōnin shochō (ihon) 町人緒帳(異本) [Lineages of townspeople (Additional family histories)]. MS copy, Kanazawa City Library. 3 vols.

Chōnin yuishochō 町人由緒帳 [Lineages of townspeople]. MS copy, Kanazawa City Library. 3 vols.

Enpō ezu 延宝絵図 [The Enpō period (1673–1681) map]. Ishikawa Prefectural Library.

Kahan kokusho ibun 加藩国初遺文 [Literary remains of early Kaga domain]. MS copy, Kanazawa City Library. Vols. 12, 17, and 18.

Kanazawa machijū gohatto no chō 金沢町中御法度之帳 [City ordinances of Kanazawa]. MS copy, Kanazawa City Library.

Kanazawa shichū kyūki 金沢市中旧記 [Old diaries of the city of Kanazawa]. MS copy, Kanazawa City Library.

Kanbun ezu 寛文絵図 [The Kanbun period (1661–1673) map]. Ishikawa Prefectural Library.

Kanke kenmonshū 菅家見聞集 [The Kanke records]. MS copy, Kanazawa City Library. Vols. 2, 3, and 7.

Kashū kōrikata kyūki 加州郡方旧記 [The old rural diaries of Kaga]. MS copy, Kanazawa City Library. Vol. 6.

Keichō nenchū gohatto nukigaki 慶長年中御法度抜書 [An ordinance from the Keichō period]. MS copy, Kanazawa City Library.

Kokon osadamegaki 古今御定書 [Ordinances from all the ages]. MS copy, Kanazawa City Library. Vol. 2.

Machidoshiyori rekimei narabi ni tsutomekatachō 町年寄歴名並勤方帳 [A list of City Elders and their duties]. MS copy, Kanazawa City Library.

Manji izen osadamegaki 万治以前御定書 [Ordinances issued through the Manji period]. MS copy, Kanazawa City Library. 2 vols.

Okabe-shi goyōdome 岡部氏御用留 [The public service records of the Okabe family]. Vols. 2 and 3.

Onko shūroku 温故集録 [Records of the past] MS copy, Kanazawa City Library. Vols. 6 and 18.

Seirinki 政隣記 [Government records]. MS copy, Kanazawa City Library.

Shōunkō saishū ihen 松雲公採集遺編 [Some records of Maeda Tsunanori]. MS copy, Kanazawa City Library. Vol. 141.

Shūri kenmonroku 袖裏見聞録 [Observations on a sleeve lining]. MS copy,

Kanazawa City Library. Vol. 2.

Shūri zakki 袖裏雑記 [Notes on a sleeve lining]. MS copy, Kanazawa City Library. Vol. 1.

Tsutsui kyūki 筒井旧記 [The Tsutsui diaries]. MS copy, Kanazawa City Library. Vol. 3.

Zoku zentoku zakki 続漸得雑記 [A second series of miscellanea]. MS copy, Kanazawa City Library. Vols. 10 and 40.

2. PUBLISHED SOURCES

Hioki Ken 日置謙, ed. *Kaga han shiryō* 加賀藩史料 [Documents of Kaga domain]. Ishiguro Bunkichi, 1929–33. Vols. 1–6.

Ishii Ryōsuke 石井良助, ed. *Hanpōshū* 藩法集 [A collection of domain laws]. Sōbunsha, 1963. Vol. 4.

Ishikawa-ken Toshokan Kyōkai 石川県図書館協会, ed. *Hankoku kanshoku tsūkō* 藩国官職通考 [A general description of domain offices and their functions]. Kanazawa: Ishikawa-ken Toshokan Kyōkai, 1932.

———. *Iburaku ikkan* 異部落一巻 [Outcast communities]. Kanazawa: Ishikawa-ken Toshokan Kyōkai, 1932.

———. *Kaga han shoki no samurai-chō* 加賀藩初期の侍帳 [The early samurai rosters of Kaga domain]. Kanazawa: Ishikawa-ken Toshokan Kyōkai, 1942.

———. *Kaisakusho kyūki* 改作所旧記 [The records of the office of rural reform]. Kanazawa: Ishikawa-ken Toshokan Kyōkai, 1939; reprinted 1970. 3 vols.

———. *Kame no o no ki* 亀の尾の記 [The tail of the tortoise]. Kanazawa: Ishikawa-ken Toshokan Kyōkai, 1932.

———. *Kinjō shinpiroku* 金城深秘録 [The secrets of Kanazawa castle]. Kanazawa: Ishikawa-ken Toshokan Kyōkai, 1937.

———. *Kokuji shōhi mondō* 国事昌披問答 [Questions and answers about affairs of the realm]. Kanazawa: Ishikawa-ken Toshokan Kyōkai, 1970.

———. *Kokuji zasshō* 国事雑抄 [A miscellany of domain affairs]. Kanazawa: Ishikawa-ken Toshokan Kyōkai, 1931–33. 3 vols.

———. *Kyūjōki* 旧条記 [Old court records]. Kanazawa: Ishikawa-ken Toshokan Kyōkai, 1933.

———. *Mitsubo kikigaki* 三壺聞書 [The jottings of Mitsubo]. Kanazawa: Ishikawa-ken Toshokan Kyōkai, 1931.

———. *Nezame no hotaru* 寝覚の蛍 [The awakening firefly]. Kanazawa: Ishikawa-ken Toshokan Kyōkai, 1931.

———. *Shibai to Chayamachi* 芝居と茶屋町 [Theaters and the Ward of Teahouses]. Kanazawa: Ishikawa-ken Toshokan Kyōkai, 1932.

Kanazawa Bunka Kyōkai 金沢文化協会, ed. *Kaga han osadamegaki* 加賀藩御定書 [Ordinances of Kaga domain]. Kanazawa: Kanazawa Bunka Kyōkai, 1936. 2 vols.

Kinai Bin 喜内敏, comp. *Kanazawa jōkaku shiryō* 金沢城郭史料 [Documents concerning Kanazawa castle]. Kanazawa: Ishikawa Kenritsu Toshokan Kyōkai, 1976.

Morita Heiji 森田平次, comp. (Edited and revised by Hioki Ken 日置謙.)

Kanazawa kosekishi 金沢古蹟志 [Old places in Kanazawa]. Rekishi Tosho-kan, 1976. 3 vols.

3. LOCAL HISTORIES WITH DOCUMENTS AND COMMENTARY

Hioki Ken 日置謙, ed. *Ishikawa kenshi* 石川県史 [A history of Ishikawa prefecture]. Kanazawa, 1928. Vol. 2.

Kanazawa-shi Ōmichō Ichiba-shi Hensan Iinkai 金沢市近江町市場史編さん委員会, ed. *Kanazawa-shi Ōmichō ichiba-shi* 金沢市近江町市場史 [A history of the market at Ōmi Ward in Kanazawa]. Kanazawa: Hokkoku Shuppan-sha, 1980.

Wada Bunjirō 和田文次郎, ed. *Kōhon Kanazawa shishi* 稿本金沢市史 [A manu-script history of Kanazawa]. Kanazawa: Kanazawa Shiyakusho, 1916–33. Vols. 1–5, 11, and 12.

4. SECONDARY SOURCES, JAPANESE

Akai Tatsurō 赤井達郎. "Hokkokuji to kinsei kaiga" 北国路と近世絵画 [The Northern Highway and sketches from the early modern period]. In Akai, ed., *Hokurikudō* 1 : 147–54.

———, ed. *Hokurikudō* 北陸道 [The Hokuriku road]. Chikuma Shobō, 1976. Vol. 1.

Aono Shunsui 青野春水. "Jōkamachi no kensetsu: Fukuyama no baai" 城下町の建設：福山の場合 [The construction of a castle town: Fukuyama]. In Ōishi, ed., *Edo to chihō bunka*, pp. 289–312.

Buraku-mondai Kenkyūjo 部落問題研究所, ed. *Buraku-shi no kenkyū: zenkin-daihen* 部落史の研究：前近代篇 [Research on the history of outcast com-munities: the premodern period]. Buraku-mondai Kenkyūjo Shuppanbu, 1978.

Fujimoto Atsushi 藤本篤. "Toshimin no seikatsu to nenchū gyōji" 都市民の生活と年中行事 [The life and yearly festivals of townspeople]. *Rekishi kōron* 4 : 7 (July 1978): 102–09.

Hara Hidesaburō 原秀三郎 et al., eds. *Taikei: Nihon kokkashi* 大系：日本国家史 [A systematic history of the Japanese state]. Tōkyō Daigaku Shup-pankai, 1975. Vol. 3.

Harada Tomohiko 原田伴彦. "Bakuhan shakai to mibunsei" 幕藩社会と身分制 [Early modern society and the status system]. *Rekishi kōron* 3 : 6 (June 1977): 36–45.

———. *Nihon hōken toshi kenkyū* 日本封建都市研究 [Research concerning feudal cities in Japan]. Tōkyō Daigaku Shuppankai, 1973; originally pub-lished 1957.

Hirotani Kijūrō 広谷喜十郎. "Kōchi ni okeru jōkamachi-teki keizaiken no tenkai katei" 高知における城下町的経済圏の展開過程 [The evolution of a castle town type of economic sphere in Kōchi]. *Rekishi techō* 6 : 3 (March 1978): 24–29.

Hotta Shigeo 堀田成雄. "Nōshū Ninomiya eki ni okeru shukunuke ni tsuite—

Kaga han kinsei shukuekisei no ichi kōsatsu" 能州ニノ宮駅における宿抜
について―加賀藩近世宿駅制の一考察 [The system of post towns in
Kaga domain during the early modern period—affairs in the post town of
Ninomiya on the Noto peninsula]. *Hokuriku shigaku* 13–14 (1965): 23–34.

Inoue Toshio 井上鋭夫. *Ikkō-ikki no kenkyū* 一向一揆の研究 [Research on the
Ikkō-ikki]. Yoshikawa Kōbunkan, 1968.

Ishihara Yosaku 石原与作. "Kaisakuhō shikōzen no Kaga han no nōso"
改作法施行前の加賀藩の納租 [The system of rural taxation in Kaga
domain before the implementation of the *kaisakuhō* rural reforms]. *Toyama·
shidan* 43 (March 1969): 16–25.

Ishizaki Naoyoshi 石崎直義. "Kaga hankō no sankin kōtai to Toyama
hanryō" 加賀藩侯の参勤交代と富山藩領 [Participation of the daimyo of
Kaga domain in the system of alternate residence and Toyama domain].
Toyama shidan 50–51 (August 1971): 42–46.

Iwasawa Yoshihiko 岩沢愿彦. *Maeda Toshiie* 前田利家 [Maeda Toshiie].
Yoshikawa Kōbunkan, 1969.

Kameda Yasunori 亀田康範. "Kaga han no baishin—hitomochi Aoyama
kashindan no kōzō" 加賀藩の陪臣―人持青山家臣団の構造 [Rear
vassals in Kaga domain—the case of the Aoyama rear vassals]. *Hokuriku
shigaku* 18 (1970): 29–45.

Kanazawa Daigaku Kanazawa-jō Gakujutsu Chōsa Iinkai, "Kanazawa-jō"
Henshūiin 金沢大学金沢城学術調査委員会「金沢城」編集委員, ed. *Kana-
zawa-jō* 金沢城 [Kanazawa castle]. Kanazawa: Kanazawa Daigaku Seikatsu
Kyōdōkumiai Shuppan, 1968.

Kitanishi Hiroshi 北西弘. "Ikkō-ikki to Kanazawa Gobō" 一向一揆と金沢
御坊 [Kanazawa Gobō and the *Ikkō-ikki*]. *Rekishi techō* 2:5 (May 1974):
52–55.

Kuranami Seiji 蔵並省自. *Kaga hansei kaikakushi no kenkyū* 加賀藩政改革史の
研究 [Research on the history of political reforms in Kaga domain]. Sekai
Shoin, 1973.

―――. *Kaga: Hyakumangoku* 加賀百万石 [Kaga: the one million *koku* do-
main]. Hachiyo Shuppan, 1974.

McClain, James L. "Jōkamachi toshika ni okeru daimyō to chōnin—jūnana-
seiki no Kanazawa" 城下町都市化における大名と町人――七世紀の
金沢 [Daimyo, merchants, and the urbanization of castle towns—Kanazawa
in the seventeenth century]. *Hokuriku shigaku* 29 (December 1980): 27–41.

Matsumoto Jirō 松本二郎. "Hagi-jō no kōzō—chikujōji o chūshin ni" 萩城
の構造―築城時を中心に [The structure of Hagi castle—the period of
castle construction]. *Rekishi techō* 5:8 (August 1977): 26–30.

Matsumoto Shirō 松本四郎. "Toshi to kokka shihai" 都市と国家支配 [Cities
and the authority of the state]. In Hara et al., eds., *Taikei: Nihon kokkashi*,
3:223–60.

Morisue Yoshiaki 森末義彰, Hōgetsu Keigo 宝月圭吾, and Kimura Motoi
木村礎, eds. *Taikei: Nihonshi sōsho 16: seikatsushi II* 体系日本史叢書16：
生活史II [Series on Japanese history (vol. 16): life and livelihood (no. II)]
Yamakawa Shuppansha, 1977; originally published 1965.

Murai Masuo 村井益男. "Hōkensei no kakuritsu to toshi no sugata   封建制の

確立と都市の姿 [The establishment of the feudal system and urban forms.]. In Morisue, Hōgetsu, and Kimura, eds., *Taikei: Nihonshi sōsho 16: seikatsu II*, pp. 117–53.

Nakabayasi Tamotsu 中林保. "Kinsei no jōkamachi Tottori" 近世の城下町鳥取 [Tottori as an early modern castle town]. *Rekishi techō* 5:9 (September 1977): 21–28.

Nakabe Yoshiko 中部よし子. *Jōkamachi* 城下町 [Castle towns]. Yanagihara Shoten, 1978.

Nakai Nobuhiko 中井信彦. *Chōnin* 町人 [Townspeople]. Shōgakkan, 1975. (Vol. 21 in the series *Nihon no rekishi* 日本の歴史).

Nishi Setsuko 西節子. "Tatsumi yōsui repōto" 辰巳用水レポート [A report on the Tatsumi canal]. *Rekishi techō* 2:5 (May 1974): 31–34.

Nishiyama Matsunosuke 西山松之助. *Edokko* 江戸っ子 [Commoners of Edo]. Yoshikawa Kōbunkan, 1980.

Nojima Jirō 野島二郎. "Kaga han no tomura seido no seiritsu ni tsuite" 加賀藩の十村制度の成立について [The establishment of the system of senior village headmen in Kaga domain]. *Nihon rekishi* 239 (April 1968): 36–41.

Nomura Kentarō 野村兼太郎. *Edo* 江戸 [Edo]. Shibundō, 1975; originally published 1966.

Ōishi Shinzaburō 大石慎三郎, ed. *Edo to chihō bunka* 江戸と地方文化 [Edo and regional culture]. Bun'ichi Sōgō Shuppan, 1977.

Ono Hitoshi 小野均. *Kinsei jōkamachi no kenkyū* 近世城下町の研究 [Early modern castle towns]. Shibundō, 1928.

Sakai Seiichi 坂井誠一 "Kaga han kaisakuhō no ichi kōsatsu—kono hō no mokuteki to sono shikō no kekka" 加賀藩改作法の一考察—この法の目的とその施行の結果 [The *kaisakuhō* rural reforms in Kaga domain: their purpose and consequences]. *Nihon rekishi* 180 (May 1963): 39–51.

————. "Kaisakuhō to chōnin shihon no shinshutsu: Jōhana no kashikata gyōsha to Gokayama nōmin" 改作法と町人資本の進出—城端の貸方業者と五ケ山農民 [The *kaisakuhō* rural reforms and the advance of merchant capital: the credit financiers of Jōhana and the peasants of Gokayama]. *Etchū shidan* 15 (November 1958): 1–7 and 16 (March 1959): 20–26.

————. "Kinsei zaigōmachi no kihon-teki seikaku" 近世在郷町の基本的性格 [The basic characteristics of local towns in the early modern period]. *Etchū shidan* 17–18 (December 1959): 7–18.

Sakata Yoshio 坂田吉雄. *Chōnin* 町人 [Townspeople]. Shimizu Kōbundō Shobō, 1968.

Sasaki Junnosuke 佐々木潤之介. "Kaga hansei seiritsu ni kansuru kōsatsu" 加賀藩制成立に関する考察 [The emergence of Kaga domain]. *Shakai keizai shigaku* 24:2 (February 1958): 65–87.

Shimode Sekiyo 下出積与. *Ishikawa ken no rekishi* 石川県の歴史 [A history of Ishikawa prefecture]. Yamakawa Shuppan, 1975. (Vol. 17 of the series *Kenshi shiriizu* 県史シリーズ, issued under the general editorship of Kodama Kōta 兒玉幸多.)

Shintani Kurō 新谷九郎. "Kaga han ni okeru shūken-teki hōkensei no kakuritsu" 加賀藩に於ける集権的封建制の確立 [The establishment of centralized feudalism in Kaga domain]. *Shakai keizai shigaku* 6:2 (February 1936): 17–43.

Takada Naganori 高田長紀. "Kaga han no kōzo shihō ni tsuite" 加賀藩の楮仕法について [Ordinances concerning paper mulberry production in Kaga domain]. *Hokuriku shigaku* 18 (1970): 14–28.

Takahashi Isamu 高橋勇. *Kaga no kōgei* 加賀の工芸 [The Arts and Crafts of Kaga]. Kanazawa: Hokkoku Shuppansha, 1976.

Tanaka Yoshio 田中喜男. "Edo jidai hisabetsu burakumin no chii—toku ni Kaga han 'tōnai' no tochi shoyū o chūshin ni shite" 江戸時代被差別部落民の地位—特に加賀藩「藤内」の土地所有を中心にして [The position of outcasts in the Edo period—with special reference to land-holding by the "tōnai" of Kaga domain]. *Shizen to shakai* 23 (1969): 8–12.

———. "Genroku-ki ni okeru jōkamachi chiiki no kakudai to jōkamachi shōnin" 元禄期における城下町地域の拡大と城下町商人 [The geographical expansion of the castle town and castle town merchants in the Genroku period]. *Kanazawa Keizai Daigaku ronshū* 13:3 (1980): 105–22.

———. *Jōkamachi Kanazawa* 城下町金沢 [The castle town of Kanazawa]. Nihon Shoin, 1966.

———. "Jōkamachi Kanazawa ni okeru aitaiukechi chiiki no kōzō" 城下町金沢における相対請地々域の構造 [The structure of *aitaiukechi* lands in the castle town of Kanazawa]. *Hokuriku shigaku* 11–12 (1963): 1–25.

———. "Kaga han hiningoya-sei seiritsu no jijō ni tsuite" 加賀藩非人小屋制成立の事情について [Conditions surrounding the establishment of the system of poorhouses in Kaga domain]. *Nihon rekishi* 183 (August 1963): 45–67.

———. "Kaga han kaisakushihō hōkai katei no ichi kōsatsu—toku ni 'hikimen' o tsūjite mitaru" 加賀藩改作仕法崩壊過程の一考察—特に「引免」を通じてみたる [The breakdown of the *kaisakuhō* rural reforms in Kaga domain—with particular reference to the system of "discounting the official tax rate"]. *Hokuriku shigaku* 6 (1957): 33–52.

———. *Kaga han ni okeru toshi no kenkyū* 加賀藩における都市の研究 [Research on cities in Kaga domain]. Bun'ichi Sōgō Shuppan, 1978.

———. "Kaga han 'tōnai' no kenkyū, Edo jidai senminkō josetsu" 加賀藩「藤内」の研究—江戸時代賤民考序説 [Research concerning the 'tōnai' of Kaga domain—an introduction to studies on outcasts of the Edo period]. *Ishikawa rekishi kenkyū* 2 (1961): 50–80.

———. *Kaga hyakumangoku* 加賀百万石 [The one million *koku* domain of Kaga] Kyōikusha, 1980.

———. "Kaga hyakumangoku no jōkamachi o kochizu ni saguru" 加賀百万石の城下町を古地図に探る [Exploring the castle town of the one million *koku* Kaga domain in old maps]. In *Kanazawa-Nagoya*, pp. 26–29. Edited by Yamori Kazuhiko.

———. "Kanazawa no chōnin kyoju chiiki" 金沢の町人居住地域 [The residential land of townspeople in Kanazawa]. *Rekishi techō* 2:5 (May 1974): 18–23.

———. *Kanazawa: Saihakken* 金沢再発見 [Kanazawa: A rediscovery]. Nihon Shobō, 1970.

————. "Kinsei jōkamachi hatten no ichi kōsatsu—'aitaiukechi' kara mita jōkamachi, Kanazawa no baai" 近世城下町発展の一考察—「相対請地」からみた城下町, 金沢の場合 [The development of an early modern castle town—the case of Kanazawa and *aitaiukechi* land]. *Hokuriku shigaku* 8 (1959): 19–37.

————. "Kinsei jōkamachi shūhen ni okeru shokugyō kōsei no ichi jirei—Kanazawa hokubu aitaiukechi chiiki o chūshin ni shite" 近世城下町周辺における職業構成の一事例—金沢北部相対請地々域を中心にして [The distribution of occupations in the vicinity of a castle town—*aitaiukechi* and on the northern edge of Kanazawa]. *Shizen to shakai* 29–30 (1963): 38–42.

————. *Waga machi no rekishi Kanazawa* わが町の歴史金沢 [The history of our city Kanazawa]. Bun'ichi Sōgō Shuppan, 1979.

Tanaka Yoshio 田中喜男, Shimamura Noboru 島村昇, and Yamagishi Masao 山岸政雄. *Dentō toshi no kūkan ron: Kanazawa* 伝統都市の空間論：金沢 [Urban space in traditional cities: Kanazawa]. Kōjunsha, 1977.

Toda Shōzō 戸田正三, ed. *Ishikawa ken no kinsei shiryō* 石川県の近世史料 [Documents of the early modern period in Ishikawa prefecture]. Kanazawa: Kanazawa Daigaku Kaga Han Shomin Shiryō Chōsa Iinkai, 1961.

Tokuda Kōjun 徳田浩淳. "Utsunomiya-jō to jōkamachi puran no kōsatsu" 宇都宮城と城下町プランの考察 [Utsunomiya castle and the urban plan of the castle town]. *Rekishi techō* 6:4 (April 1978): 36–42.

Toyoda Takeshi 豊田武. *Nihon no hōken toshi* 日本の封建都市 [Japanese feudal cities]. Iwanami Shoten, 1976; originally published, 1952.

Urada Masayoshi 浦田正吉. "Shoki Maeda kashindan no jikata chigyō ni tsuite no ichi kōsatsu" 初期前田家臣団の地方知行についての一考察 [The direct fiefs held by Maeda vassals in the early period]. *Hokuriku shigaku* 17 (1969): 1–24.

Wakabayashi Kisaburō 若林喜三郎. *Ishikawa ken no rekishi* 石川県の歴史 [A history of Ishikawa Prefecture]. Kanazawa: Hokkoku Shoseki, 1972.

————. *Maeda Tsunanori* 前田綱紀 [Maeda Tsunanori]. Yoshikawa Kōbunkan, 1972.

Yamada Mitsuji 山田光二. "Toshi buraku no jōkyō" 都市部落の情況 [Urban outcast communities]. *Rekishi kōron* 3:6 (June 1977): 56–62.

Yamori Kazuhiko 矢守一彦. *Toshizu no rekishi* 都市図の歴史 [A history of city maps]. Kōdansha, 1974.

————, ed. *Kanazawa-Nagoya* 金沢—名古屋 [Kanazawa and Nagoya]. Kōdansha, 1977. (Vol. 12 in the series *Nihon no kochizu* 日本の古地図.)

Yoshihara Ken'ichirō 吉原健一郎. "Edo to machi-bugyō shihai" 江戸と町奉行支配 [Edo and the authority of the City Magistrates]. *Rekishi kōron* 4:7 (July 1978): 60–65.

5. SECONDARY SOURCES, ENGLISH

Befu, Harumi. "Village Autonomy and Articulation with the State." In Hall and Jansen, ed., *Studies*, pp. 301–14.

Bernard, Leon. *The Emerging City: Paris in the Age of Louis XIV*. Durham: Duke

University Press, 1970.

Blanning, T. C. W. *Reform and Revolution in Mainz 1743–1803*. Cambridge: Cambridge University Press, 1974.

Brandon, James R., William P. Malm, and Donald H. Shively, *Studies in Kabuki: Its Acting, Music, and Historical Context*. Honolulu: University Press of Hawaii, 1978.

Butler, John. "A Bicentennial Harvest." *Journal of Urban History* 4:4 (August 1978): 485–97.

Crawcour, E. Sidney. "Changes in Japanese Commerce in the Tokugawa Period." In Hall and Jansen, *Studies*, pp. 189–202.

Davis, David L. "*Ikki* in Late Medieval Japan." In Hall and Mass, eds., *Medieval Japan*, pp. 224–47.

Friedrich, Carl J. *The Age of Baroque*. New York: Harper & Brothers, 1952.

Galantay, Ervin Y. *New Towns: Antiquity to the Present*. New York: George Braziller, 1975.

Gluck, Carol. "The People in History: Recent Trends in Japanese Historiography." *Journal of Asian Studies* 38:1 (November 1978): 25–50.

Hall, John W. "Castle Towns and Japan's Early Modern Urbanization." In Hall and Jansen, eds., *Studies*, pp. 169–81.

————. "The Confucian Teacher in Tokugawa Japan." In Nivison and Wright, eds., *Confucianism in Action*, pp. 268–301.

————. "Foundations of the Modern Japanese Daimyo." In Hall and Jansen, eds., *Studies*, pp. 65–77.

————. "The Ikeda House and Its Retainers in Bizen." In Hall and Jansen, eds., *Studies*, pp. 79–88.

Hall, John W., and Marius B. Jansen, eds. *Studies in the Institutional History of Early Modern Japan*. Princeton: Princeton University Press, 1968.

Hall, John W., and Jeffrey P. Mass, eds. *Medieval Japan: Essays in Institutional History*. New Haven: Yale University Press, 1974.

Hall, John W., Nagahara Keiji, and Kozo Yamamura, eds. *Japan before Tokugawa*. Princeton: Princeton University Press, 1981.

Hanley, Susan B., and Kozo Yamamura. *Economic and Demographic Change in Preindustrial Japan, 1600–1868*. Princeton: Princeton University Press, 1977.

Hauser, William B. *Economic Institutional Change in Tokugawa Japan*. Cambridge: Cambridge University Press, 1974.

————. "Osaka: A Commercial City in Tokugawa Japan." *Urbanism Past & Present* 5 (Winter 1977–78): 23–36.

Jansen, Marius B. "Tosa in the Seventeenth Century: The Establishment of Yamauchi Rule." In Hall and Jansen, eds., *Studies*, pp. 115–30.

Kaplow, Jeffrey. *The Names of Kings: The Parisian Laboring Poor in the Eighteenth Century*. New York: Basic Books, 1972.

McClain, James L. "Castle Towns and Daimyo Authority: Kanazawa in the Years 1583–1630." *Journal of Japanese Studies* 6:2 (Summer 1980): 267–99.

Massie, Robert K. *Peter the Great*. New York: Alfred A. Knopf, 1980.

Mumford, Lewis. *The City in History*. New York: Harcourt, Brace & Company, 1961.

Nivison, D. S., and Arthur F. Wright, eds. *Confucianism in Action*. Stanford:

Stanford University Press, 1959.

Oliva, L. Jay. *Russia in the Era of Peter the Great.* Englewood Cliffs, N. J.: Prentice-Hall, 1969.

Pinkney, David H. *Napoleon III and the Rebuilding of Paris.* Princeton: Princeton University Press, 1958.

Pounds, N. J. G. *An Historical Geography of Europe 1500–1840.* Cambridge: Cambridge University Press, 1979.

Putnam, Peter Brock. *Peter, the Revolutionary Tsar.* New York: Harper & Row, 1973.

Ranum, Orest. *Paris in the Age of Absolutism.* New York: John Wiley & Sons, 1968.

Rozman, Gilbert. "Edo's Importance in the Changing Tokugawa Society." *Journal of Japanese Studies* 1: 1 (Autumn 1974): 91–112.

———. *Urban Networks in Ch'ing China and Tokugawa Japan.* Princeton: Princeton University Press, 1973.

Saalman, Howard. *Haussman: Paris Transformed.* New York: George Braziller, 1971.

Sakai, Robert. "The Consolidation of Power in Satsuma-han." In Hall and Jansen, eds., *Studies*, pp. 131–39.

Sasaki Gin'ya with William B. Hauser. "Sengoku Daimyo Rule and Commerce." In Hall, Nagahara, and Yamamura, eds., *Japan before Tokugawa*, pp. 125–48.

Shively, Donald H. "*Bakufu* versus *Kabuki*." In Hall and Jansen, eds., *Studies*, pp. 231–61.

———. "The Social Environment of Tokugawa Kabuki." In Brandon, Malm, and Shively, *Studies in Kabuki,* pp. 1–161.

Smith, Henry D., II. "Tokyo as an Idea: An Exploration of Japanese Urban Thought until 1945." *Journal of Japanese Studies* 4:1 (Winter 1978): 45–80.

Smith, Thomas C. "The Land Tax in the Tokugawa Period." In Hall and Jansen, eds., *Studies*, pp. 283–99.

———. "Pre-modern Economic Growth: Japan and the West." *Past and Present* 43 (1973): 127–60.

Tilly, Charles, ed. *An Urban World.* Boston: Little, Brown & Company, 1974.

———. *The Formation of Nation States in Europe.* Princeton: Princeton University Press, 1975.

Ugawa Kaoru. "Social Structure and Land Use in Japan: The Case of Yonezawa." *Rikkyō keizaigaku kenkyū* 30 : 2 (September 1976): 107–28.

Varley, H. Paul. *Japanese Culture.* Charles E. Tuttle, 1973.

Wakita Osamu with James L. McClain. "The Commercial and Urban Policies of Oda Nobunaga and Toyotomi Hideyoshi." In Hall, Nagahara, and Yamamura, eds., *Japan before Tokugawa*, pp. 224–47.

Williams, Alan. "The Police and the Administration of Eighteenth Century Paris." *Journal of Urban History* 4:2 (February 1978): 157–82.

Willis, F. Roy. *Western Civilization: An Urban Perspective.* Lexington, Mass.: D. C. Heath & Company, 1973. Vol. 1.

INDEX

Adachi, Rokuhyōe, 23
Akechi, Mitsuhide, 16, 18, 19
Artisans' Workshop, 102
Asanoya family, 87, 110
Ashikaga, Yoshiaki, 16

Bathhouses, 64, 113, 115, 143, 150
Bodin, Jean, 4

Cadastral surveys, 20, 21, 28–29
Chartered merchants (*goyō shōnin*), 29–30, 40–41, 48–54, 70, 78–80, 81, 87–88, 102–03, 114, 121, 136–38, 151
Chō family, 35, 76, 80–81, 109, 148
City Elders (*machidoshiyori*), 49, 50, 51, 54, 61, 87–88, 95, 96, 98, 102, 127, 136, 151, 163
City Magistrates (*machi-bugyō*), 41, 49, 57, 59, 61, 84, 85–86, 91, 95, 99, 100, 126, 127, 128, 135, 136, 137, 138, 144, 159, 161–63
Comédie Française, 6
Commanders, 94
Constables (*machi-dōshin*), 61, 86, 88, 116, 126
Construction Office (*sakujisho*), 35
Council of Advisers (*yoriaishū*), 85–86, 95, 99, 126, 157

Dōjiriya family, 43, 103, 137, 138

Echizen'ya Kiemon family, 87–88, 137
Echizen'ya Magobei family, 39–40, 50, 61, 70–71, 87, 102, 110
Edo, 11, 68, 70, 75, 85, 99, 103, 106, 110, 114, 119, 122–23, 132, 139
Eight Families (*hakka*), 80, 83, 94, 107, 126, 157
Eta, 45. *See also* Outcasts

Ginza. See Office of Currency Control
Goyō shōnin. See Chartered merchants
Group Headmen (*kumiaigashira*), 89–90, 95, 96, 128, 151, 160
Group of Ten Households (*jūningumi*), 62, 88–89, 90–91, 92, 96, 98, 127, 160, 161, 164
Gyokusen'in, Lady, 50, 63–64

Hakka. See Eight Families
Hashiba Hideyoshi, 18
Hiranoya family, 39–40, 50, 54, 61, 87
Hōenji, 37–38, 50, 149
Hōjō family, 20, 21–22
Honda Awa no Kami family, 35, 91, 96, 106–07, 108, 112
Honda Masanobu, 35
Honmachi. See Original Wards
Hoshun'in, Lady, 52, 63–64
Hoshun'in Temple, 26

Igarashi, Dōhō, 101
Ikkō federation, 16–18, 32, 78
Imaeda family, 16, 21, 23, 37, 74
Imagawa Yoshimoto, 16, 21, 23
Inspectors (*yokome-kimoiri*), 88, 112
Ishida Mitsunari, 22, 25–26
Ishiyama Honganji, 16, 17–18

Jishimachi. See Ordinary Wards
Jūningumi. See Group of Ten Households
Junior Assistants (*machi-gedai*), 61, 86

Kabuki, 63–65, 112, 113, 114, 123, 144–45, 150
Kabukimono, 59, 60, 67, 94, 159–60
Kamiya family, 51–52, 54, 61, 70–71, 87, 88, 100, 102, 103, 137, 138
Kanaya family, 45, 49–50, 70–71, 87, 102

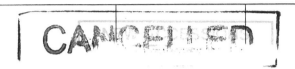